GLOBAL DEVELOPMENT
THE HUMAN FACTOR WAY

GLOBAL DEVELOPMENT THE HUMAN FACTOR WAY

Senyo B-S. K. Adjibolosoo

TO: Hadley Mitchell

It is always true that the Truth of God always stands. And when we create the environment and opportunity for others to grow in the qualities of Christ so they too can develop and maximize their human potentials, we are true leaders. May He lead us to be the leaders he desires us to be. Blessings on you and may he use you

PRAEGER

Westport, Connecticut
London

mightily. from Senyo adjibolosoo
BBKSJhml.
2007-09-30

Library of Congress Cataloging-in-Publication Data

Adjibolosoo, Senyo B-S. K.
    Global development the human factor way / Senyo B-S. K.
Adjibolosoo.
        p.   cm.
    Includes bibliographical references and index.
    ISBN 0–275–95966–X (alk. paper)
    1. Economic development.   2. Scarcity.   3. Natural resources.
4. Resource allocation.   5. Comparative economics.   I. Title.
HD75.A33   1998
338.9—dc21   97–18062

British Library Cataloguing in Publication Data is available.

Library of Congress Catalog Card Number: 97–18062
ISBN: 0–275–95966–X

First published in 1998

Praeger Publishers, 88 Post Road West, Westport, CT 06881
An imprint of Greenwood Publishing Group, Inc.

Printed in the United States of America

The paper used in this book complies with the
Permanent Paper Standard issued by the National
Information Standards Organization (Z39.48–1984).

10   9   8   7   6   5   4   3   2   1

This book is dedicated to Adzo Blemewu Adjibolosoo, Dofui Blemewu Adjibolosoo, and all people who are concerned about the future state of all humanity and are willing to explore all available avenues in order to find workable solutions to problems that not only militate against global development, but also pose significant threats to the very survival of humanity and planet earth.

deep down the alleys of our souls
exists not only a state of desperation
but also a zone beyond panic
as we are driven by drunken desires
on the highways of emotions
where we ditch our lean days
in the valleys of idleness
there the swords of unbelief
tear the seedlings of our thoughts
and force us to loiter
on the planes of uncertainties
in the prisons of the mind

—Senyo Adjibolosoo

CONTENTS

FIGURES AND TABLES

PREFACE

One of the greatest problems that has continuously faced humanity throughout the centuries is the scarcity of resources. As such, most human efforts in all previous and currently existing civilizations have been directed at finding solutions to the problem of scarcity. Yet, regardless of all these efforts, humanity does not seem to be anywhere closer to conquering or subduing this primary economizing problem. This is so because, while human needs (i.e., the ends) are unlimited, the resources (i.e., the means) required to fulfill them are very limited. However, even in the presence of continuing failure to overcome this problem, humanity has not given up its search for permanent solutions. Men and women still continue to look for procedures with which to overcome the pertinent limitations placed by scarcity on human progress, development, well-being, and happiness. At this point in human history, the ongoing search for solutions has culminated in the invention or innovation of technologies and advanced electronic tools and gadgets that are aimed at gaining mastery over the environment and therefore exercising adequate command over scarcity.

Indeed, the battle against scarcity and its attendant problems continues unabated, regardless of the tremendous advances made in modern science, technology, management science, production theory, legal systems, and so on. Men and women throughout the centuries have always sought and still continue to look for a good social order and a workable political economy in which liberty, justice, and equity would prevail for all people. To facilitate the process for the achievement of these objectives, many scholars from all fields of academic study have come out with hypotheses, theories, principles, and laws regarding the development and establishment of a good social order and a workable political economy.

The pursuit of research and development and technological advancement has brought many changes to human life, work, and play in many countries, especially the developed nations. Not only have the developed nations been successful in feeding a large percentage of their populations, they have also improved living standards and enhanced longevity. Average labor productivity has also improved dramatically in the developed and newly industrializing countries. These great achievements have, however, not been very successful in fostering the highly desired social order and the efficient political economy that would arrest the scarcity problem and then promote continuing liberty, justice, and equity for all humanity. Instead, what we see today across the whole world are societies that have been torn apart for diverse reasons—excessive criminal activities, injustice, various forms of discrimination, abject poverty, famine, urban sprawl, territorial incursions or wars, unemployment, inflation, system and institutional failures, and so on.

Today, human efforts are continuously being directed toward the development and improvement in technology, systems, and institutions. That is, the bulk of resources made available for education and training programs are devoted to systems enhancement and developments in technology and law enforcement. As far as total human development is concerned, the emphasis is narrowly placed on human-capital acquisition alone. The primary objective of schooling and training programs is to produce scholars who can think and build better, smarter, and more powerful machines for human use. Human quality engineering and improvement are not necessarily important concerns. Yet, since technology, institutions, systems, and the like are inanimate, they cannot run optimally without having people who have acquired the necessary human factor (HF)—*a spectrum of personality characteristics and other dimensions of human performance that enable social, economic, and political institutions to function and remain functional over time* (Adjibolosoo 1995a, 33).

It seems to me, therefore, that though continuing progress in the political economy of nations requires improvements in the interactive performance of people on one hand and the efficient functioning of social, economic, political, and educational (SEPE) institutions on the other, almost every society is continuously paying less and less attention to the development of the relevant HF. Countries are always trying in a frenzy to design and create powerful, computer-operated machines and also seek to enhance the performance of SEPE institutions without paying keen attention to HF development. Yet to be successful, every human endeavor requires people who possess the necessary HF, without which plans, policies, programs, and projects will fail.

In view of these observations, the objective of this book is threefold. First, in Part I, the book discusses the concept of scarcity and its significance to the evolution of the existing social order and political economy of nations. Second, in Part II, using historical evidence, the book presents detailed discussions and analyses on various human inventions and innovations whose primary objective is to assist men and women to successfully deal with the scarcity problem. The ineffectiveness of humanity's social engineering process is also presented and discussed in Part II. Both the positive and negative impacts of these developments are highlighted and critically evaluated. Third, in Part III, it is argued that the primary reason why SEPE institutions and technology are failing to successfully deal with scarcity and its related problems in all countries is human factor decay and under-development in society. The role of the HF in the development of the desired social order and efficient political economy is highlighted and critically examined. In this section, the book proposes relevant procedures for the achievement of total HF development. It is argued that any successes attained in this regard will lead to the globally sustainable human-centered development of a social order and political economy that will promote long-lasting liberty, justice, and equity for all humanity.

This book is aimed at explaining how all humanity can attain a workable social order and efficient political economy within which every human being will experience the desired good life, filled with true liberty, justice, and social equity. It is written for scholars and students of every discipline, and also many nongovernment organizations, government policy planners, development program directors, international organizations, research institutes, and college and university libraries. Its multidisciplinary approach will make it palatable to scholars of every discipline and persuasion. Above all, it will be of tremendous value to those who plan education, training, mentoring, and other related human-resource development programs. It is a must-read for everyone who is concerned about the future of planet earth and is interested in doing something today to help sustain its survival tomorrow.

ACKNOWLEDGMENTS

It is always a great pleasure when a difficult task is completed. Yet, since no human being is an island, we all receive help from different people at different points in time when we work on different projects. I am no exception. Many people have contributed in different ways to make this book a reality. As is always the case, this work would not have been completed without the unflinching support of my wife, Sabina Adjibolosoo, and our daughters, Selassie and Selorm. May I take this opportunity to express my sincerest appreciation to them for their ongoing support and encouragement.

I also want to thank my colleagues, Mr. John de Wolf and Ms. Mary Portulance, for their ongoing friendship, encouragement, and support. To Dr. Francis Adu-Febiri and Dr. Harold Harder, may I say thank you very much for reading through several chapters and providing me with your insights and suggestions for revision. In addition to these people, my gratitude would be incomplete if I failed to give my deep appreciation to Dr. Benjamin Ofori-Amoah, Dr. Abour Cherif, Dr. Mahamudu Bawumia, Mr. Salomon Agbenya, Dr. Joseph Mensah, and Dr. Alam Matiul for their support and encouragement.

My appreciation also goes to the students at Trinity Western University who took several courses in which human factor related principles were taught and discussed. Their insights, questions, and discussions have been very useful to me in writing this book. Indeed, Mrs. Brenda Sawatzky, our faculty secretary, deserves a very big thank you for being there to provide me with secretarial assistance, especially in the preparation of the various figures. Finally, I am extremely thankful to Ms. Cynthia Harris, my acquisitions editor, and the Greenwood Press for their help and support while preparing the manuscript for publication.

PART ONE

GENERAL INTRODUCTION

_____

CHAPTER ONE

SCARCITY
The Central Focus of All
Human Action and Endeavor

When it comes to the critical issue of discussing the origin of this universe (i.e., humanity, the species, the galaxy, the water bodies, other living and non-living things, etc.), human beings have never agreed on what the true answer to this question is. This is the case because there is no human being alive today who was also there at the beginning, and could tell us exactly about what he or she saw happen. Yet the growing desire to unravel the mystery regarding the birth of the universe has led many scholars to formulate theories to provide meaningful clues that may help us gain some intelligent insights into how it all happened. The debate, though, is far from being over. In many circles today, the contention among scholars regarding how the universe came into existence continues to gain momentum. It is, however, interesting to note that the groups involved in this age-old debate can be partitioned neatly into two camps—Evolutionists and Creationists. While those who believe in the doctrine of evolution argue that the universe came into being through some unengineered phenomenon (i.e., the big bang), Creationists argue that since the universe is neatly ordered it could not possibly have evolved by itself. It has been divinely ordained. As such, they argue that it is created by God. To the Creationists, without God's own divine plan this universe would not have come into being. The Evolutionists disagree with this view. In what follows, I present in a nutshell the core perspectives of each group and then discuss how each group of scholars has come to explain the origins of both living and non-living things, how scarcity sneaked into this beautiful universe, and its significance to all human action and endeavor.

According to the big bang theory, the universe came into being many billions of years ago from an enormous explosion of matter. In the process of the fast expansion that ensued, the existing elements became formed into the planets from the dust produced by the big bang. This phenomenon is also the origin of the solar system. As such, many scientists believe that the earth developed through an evolutionary process, beginning from the inception of the big bang to what it is today. Their theories discuss the evolution of the galaxy, the earth, and then the appearance of plant and animal lives.

In 1796, Laplace suggested that the rotation of great gaseous clouds contracted. As the process contrived, rings of gas were thrown off to become the planets, each with its own satellites (the Nebular Hypothesis). This view was disputed by J. C. Maxwell in 1859. He maintained that the earth could not have been formed from gaseous rings. By the 1900s, Chamberlin and Moulton's hypothesis about the formation of the earth replaced that of Laplace. They argued that through a gravitational pull, a star that came very close to the sun took huge masses of matter from it. These later were condensed into the planets (the Chamberlin–Moulton Hypothesis). This view was disputed by Henry Morris, Layman Spitzer, Jr., and several others. It finally collapsed and was replaced by Fred Hoyle's hypothesis that the sun had a sister sun which later exploded to form the planets. This hypothesis did not stand the criticisms of Russel and Spitzer. As noted by Ward (1965, 15), "At the present several scientists are working on the theory that the entire solar system formed from a giant cloud of gas and dust within the galaxy. Most of the gas formed the sun while eddies formed the planets."

Creationists, taking their knowledge from the Holy Bible, maintain that the universe has been created and is also continuously sustained by God (Genesis 1:1–2:24). The biblical account notes the following:

In the beginning when God created the heavens and the earth, the earth was a formless void and darkness covered the face of the deep, while a wind from God swept over the face of the earth. Then God said, "Let there be light," and there was light. And God saw that the light was good; and God separated the light from the darkness. God called the light Day, and the darkness he called Night. And there was evening and there was morning, the first day. And God said, "Let there be a dome in the midst of the waters, and let it separate the waters from the waters." So God made the dome and separated the waters that were under the dome from the waters that were above the dome. And it was so. God called the dome sky. And there was evening and there was morning, and the second day. . . . Then God said, "Let us make humankind in our image, according to our likeness; and let them have dominion over the fish of the sea, and over the birds of the air, and over the cattle, and over all the wild animals of the earth, and over every creeping thing that creeps upon the earth." So God created humankind in his image, in the image of God he created them; male and female he created them. (Genesis 1:1–27)

Creationists, in view of this biblical account, argue that this universe did not come into existence by chance. The Creator, *Yahweh*, made it. As such, it is not only ordered, but also continually declares his greatness, authority, and power (Psalm 19:1–6).

Yahweh invested a significant power in men and women and also gave them the authority to rule and have dominion over every creature in the universe (Genesis 1:26–28). *Yahweh* imbued all humanity with the ability to subdue the whole universe. Men and women were not only furnished with significant resources to use for food, but also charged by God to not abuse the universe and its contents, but rather care for them.[1] However, regardless of how reasonably convincing the creation account is, Evolutionists do not buy into it.

In recent years, this debate has escalated. Neither side has yet claimed victory nor is ready to concede defeat. Thus, it seems to me that as long as this universe remains and follows its established course as evidenced in sunrise and sunset, no human beings will resolve this puzzle successfully through intellectual and/or academic debates. Yet, regardless of this failure to arrive at a globally accepted view about the true origin of the universe, scholars of all persuasions and/or camps do accept some specific conclusions. Thurman (1978, 97), for example, observed the following:

Despite their obvious differences, creationists and evolutionists do agree on many things. For example, they both agree that (1) the universe, life and basic forms came into existence in the past; (2) these origins were one-time events, not repeatable by us, nor were they observed by any human witness; and (3) we do not have and probably never will obtain direct knowledge of how these origins occurred, regardless of how many ways we demonstrate that they could have occurred.

Indeed, this conclusion in itself not only clouds the picture regarding what the social, economic, political, and educational (SEPE) life is all about, but also fails to answer many pertinent questions. For example, regardless of the beauty of this universe and its many contents, how did it happen that men and women had to be faced with the severe scarcity problem? That is, how did the basic economizing problem, scarcity, enter into the lives of men and women all over the world? Are there any viable explanations? If there are any, what are they? What role does scarcity play in human behavior and action?

In what follows, I present several discussions regarding the various views about the origins of scarcity, the central economizing problem. It is hoped that this discussion will help shed further illumination on the sources of the plight of all humanity and the corresponding behavior and action of men and women. In this chapter, I also analyze in detail what ancient civilizations sought for as they pursued their SEPE life. The views of many philosophers, political scientists, social thinkers, psychologists, sociologists, economists, and many others regarding how humanity could attain the most effective and workable social order are presented and discussed in Chapters 2 through 6. Specifically, in Chapter 2 the primary ideas on which the concepts regarding the evolution of the social order and the political economy of development are based are discussed. In Chapters 7 through 11, I also discuss the human plight, the failure of SEPE institutions, and the relevant concepts and critical principles that must underlie every social, economic, political, and educational activities if people desire to attain the best outcomes for every person in every society.

SCARCITY: VARYING VIEWS ABOUT ITS ORIGIN

It never ceases to amaze me that in this beautiful world of ours most people cannot just very easily acquire any items and resources they desire and also determine how they plan to use them.[2] It seems to be the case that while human needs, desires, and wants are numerous, the means to satisfying every one of them are extremely limited. As such, all through the centuries, men and women have always thought about creative ways of putting the few resources they possess to their best uses. While most people have come to accept scarcity as a human reality, they hardly ever spend any significant amount of time thinking about how all humanity came into face-to-face confrontation with this basic economizing problem. Though it can be argued that the origins of scarcity could be numerous, some of the more prominent sources and/or explanations for its existence include human selfishness and greed, rapid population growth rates, human exploitation in its many forms, drought and famine, and the fall of Adam and Eve in the Garden of Eden. The remainder of this chapter focuses on providing explanations for the origins of scarcity and how its presence affects and/or directs the SEPE life.

Human Selfishness and Greed

Using the Greek comprehension and conceptualization of what wealth and poverty are perceived to be, scarcity could be viewed as a result of greed and excessively compulsive human desire for personal wealth acquisition. As such, while some people amass wealth for themselves and live in total affluence, others are left disadvantaged and live in abject poverty. To these poor people, scarcity is real because they are usually unable to either meet or satisfy their desire for every basic necessity of life. In a similar way, because of overemphasis on personal selfishness and greed, rich people also face scarcity problems because regardless of the magnitude of the amount of affluence they have already amassed and could also boast of, their ongoing greed denies them the ability of human satiation. More (of money or wealth) is always preferred to less. To most human beings, since their marginal utility for money is forever increasing, the more money they acquire, the better they think they will be. Thus, they crave more of it. As such, the quantity of money one possesses is at each point in time never enough. The affluent are always longing for more financial resources and are never satisfied. The acquired wealth of these individuals is never sufficient to help them obtain everything they desire in order to enjoy the "good life."

Rapid Population Growth Rates

Rapid population growth has always been viewed by many economists and students of population theory as one of the key sources of human poverty, as is evidenced by the ongoing scarcity problem in all societies, especially in the developing countries. That is, as many more people are born, it becomes more and more difficult to feed all mouths. Thus, people in many developing countries are not able to produce sufficient food to feed themselves. Even in the case of the developed countries, there is a countless number of people who are unable to obtain their own basic necessities of life. As the universe advances in age, it is becoming increasingly difficult to satisfy all human needs and longings. In some cases, human beings create artificial shortages in order to make monetary gains at the expense of others.[3]

Exploitation in Its Many Forms: The Marxian View

Thinking in terms of the distribution of natural resources, while certain areas have been well-endowed with huge stocks of land and other natural resources, others have not. For example, the continent of Africa has been a significant repository for various forms of minerals such as gold, diamonds, manganese, and iron, and other forms of resources such as marine and wild life, plants, and many others. Yet during the era of colonization and its accompanying slave trade, Africans lost full control over their own resources to European colonizers. Since colonization of many parts of Africa placed the various resources under colonial authority, a great deal of these natural resources were harnessed and transported to Europe for the use of European merchants and manufacturers. This overharvesting of these resources to be used elsewhere heightened the scarcity problems in Africa. These observations, from the Marxian perspective, is exploitation of one individual or country by another.

Drought and Famine

For generations, drought and famine have created problems for all humanity living in the four corners of the earth. There have been severe droughts and famines in Africa, Asia, Europe, and Latin America. Since at the dawn of civilization men and women depended mostly on mother nature to provide them with the required amount of water for agricultural purposes through rainfall, people usually had little or no crops when the rains failed to come as expected. The lack of enough rainfall usually led to continuing droughts and famines. The drying up of rivers, lakes, and streams led to the closure of irrigation channels. Thus, since people could not find water for the seeds sown and the crops planted, they failed to make sufficient harvest to last them until the next planting season. In this way, all areas hit by drought suffer severe consequences from the ensuing famine and hunger. The scarcity of sustenance created usually leads to significant loss of lives, animals, and vegetation.

In some cases, famine comes as a result of disease epidemics that destroy both plant and animal lives. In a similar way, the arrival of pests like locusts, grasshoppers, and many others usually create severe food shortages because these insects destroy most of the crops. In addition to these, bush fires also create problems at certain times of the year—especially during the dry seasons. The process of desertification steals arable land gradually away from agriculturalists by rendering their cultivable lands extremely barren. As is often the case, barrenness increases food scarcity.

The Fall of Adam and Eve

From the perspective of the Creationists, the origin of scarcity is the fall of humanity from grace (divinely provided abundance) to grass (humanly selected abject poverty) in the Garden of Eden. This was the time, according to the Holy Bible, when Adam and Eve disobeyed God, pushed aside God's perfect blueprint and plan for their lives, and selected their own path of life and work. In God's plan for humanity, everything else was provided by divine providence (Genesis 2:9, 16; Matthew 6:25–34; Luke 12:22–34). Unfortunately, according to the biblical account, the choice Adam and Eve made brought them into an immediate confrontation with the problem of scarcity. Their choice led to huge opportunity costs in that they lost the wonderful provisions made for them by God and instead engaged themselves in a life of toil, pain, suffering, and affliction.

Even though the magnitude of the opportunity costs incurred through the exercise of human free will was high, God did not dispossess humanity completely of the gift of talents, abilities, other human potentials, and the knowledge that Adam and Eve were furnished with from the beginning of their earthly lives. In a similar way, although the ability to live forever was terminated completely, the power to invent and also innovate remained to be used by men and women throughout the centuries (Genesis 2:19–20). Humanity, however, chose its own work life. According to Lowry (1987, 45), God has to come in from time to time to assist humanity to cope with the excessively difficult path of life it has chosen. This is the case because humanity does not possess the required capability to both care for itself and also deal successfully with the scarcity problem it unleashed on itself at the fall in the Garden of Eden.

The Views of Classical and Modern Economists

In general, the classical and modern economists maintain that scarcity is a result of the fact that, while human needs are numerous (i.e., unlimited), the available resources to be used to satisfy these needs are extremely limited. Thus, human needs will always continue to exceed the existing means for satisfying them.

In view of the discussion so far, the critical question that arises is what role the presence of scarcity in this world plays in all human actions and endeavors. That is, what is the significance of scarcity to the SEPE life?

THE SIGNIFICANCE OF SCARCITY TO THE SEPE LIFE

Regardless of which of these views one holds, two things are obvious from the reality of scarcity. Scarcity, in reality, is a two-edged sword. First, it militates against human progress in the sense that it hinders the full enjoyment of human life and the achievement of long-lasting human fulfillment in this physical world through the lacks and shortages it creates. In cases where certain societies are afraid of not having enough sustenance, water, land, and many other types of resources for the desired good life, nations usually go to war and kill each other to secure permanent property rights over these resources. As such, it can therefore be argued that the basis of the economizing problem, scarcity, encourages wars and/or unhealthy competition among nations. In the same way, scarcity can be viewed as a significant factor in hate crimes, various forms of personal and business rivalries, sabbotage, personal relationships (i.e., acquaintances, marriages, friendships, etc.), competition for job opportunities and employment, and so on.

Second, the presence of scarcity in human life has led to the development of a good work ethic among people who have come to believe that they could deal successfully with it. It has led people along paths where they were able to discover various techniques, systems, institutions, and all other forms of methodologies for dealing with this difficult problem. In terms of institutions, scarcity can be credited for its role in the evolution of legal systems, the rule of law, rules and regulations, property rights, and many others. It has also encouraged continuing teamwork between business partners, employees, groups of individuals, and even nations. This teamwork has also facilitated an ongoing search for both effectiveness and efficiency in human performance. Men and women, in their search for permanent solutions to the scarcity problem, have engaged themselves in joint programs that have led to expansions in agricultural activities and productivity (i.e., new seeds of plants and breeds of animals, new technologies and procedures for more effective cultivation and rearing of animals, etc.) and ongoing investments in the creation of productive capital. The presence of scarcity has, indeed, forced and continues to force men and women to devise creatively ingeneous procedures and techniques for dealing with it and its accompanying problems. Indeed, the ongoing striving of men and women to overcome the basic economizing problem has led to the development of various options for dealing with scarcity. In traditional economic analysis, there are three main options for dealing with the problem of scarcity.

Economists often argue that societies confronted with the scarcity problem can deal with it by (1) expanding their existing capacity to produce, (2) improving the use of all available resources, and (3) lowering human expectations. In the case of option number 2, each society must pursue the attainment of allocative efficiency, distributional equity, and aggregate efficiency (see details in Tinari, 1986; see also Figure 1.1). It is the continuing pursuit of various activities and programs by men and women to contain the scarcity problem that has birthed different forms of human actions and endeavors (see details in Chapters 2 through 7). Indeed, every civilization has a vision, a plan, and a mission. In the absence of any of this trio, a civilization will lose the primary reasons for its existence and may begin to decline thereafter, having lost its focus or reason for existence.

In the last few decades, men and women all over the world have begun to realize that if human restraint is not exercised in the use of available natural resources,

Figure 1.1
Options for Dealing with Scarcity

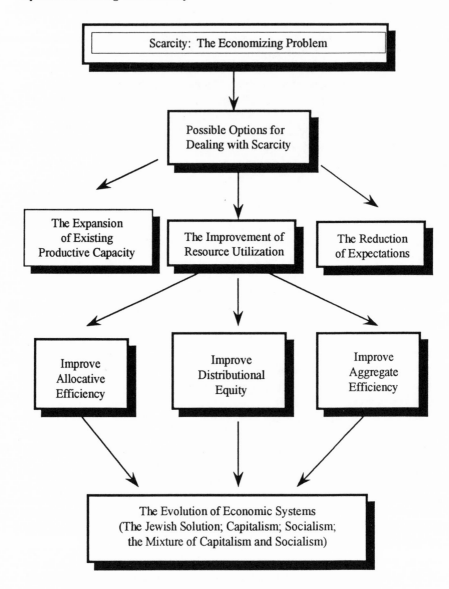

Source: Adapted from F. D. Tinari, 1986, 2.

the existing stock of resources may become depleted. Thus, the reality of scarcity is currently forcing humanity to observe and express detailed concerns for the environment. People are becoming more and more aware of the air quality in the environment around them. These concerns have also promoted the development and use of recycling technology and programs to help preserve nonrenewable resources and improve the quality of the environment.

By so doing, humanity has developed various forms of procedures, institutions, and advanced technology that have become extremely useful in helping men and women to explore the physical world further. It can also be argued that the existence of scarcity has provided all humanity with the necessary incentives to subdue nature and turn it to human advantage (see details in Chapters 5 through 7). In what follows, a brief analysis is presented regarding scarcity and the diurnal drama of all humanity.

Scarcity and the Diurnal Drama of All Humanity

When one wakes up every morning, gets ready with either a great deal of anxiety or excitement, and leaves home for work, school, office, shopping mall, or the like, one goes about one's daily life in order to acquire relevant resources to be used to contain the scarcity problem. People work and also engage themselves in all kinds of SEPE activities because they have come to believe that there are no better alternatives for dealing successfully with the problem of scarcity. In this world it has become an accepted fact that everyone has to work to provide sufficient sustenance for himself and immediate family. Most people are extremely eager to provide services to others in many different ways to simultaneously increase their personal wealth, joy, and satisfaction and that of those whom they serve. To most people, the real purpose of the SEPE life of all humanity is to deal successfully with the scarcity problem in order to enjoy the good life. As people live, move, and exist, they engage themselves in SEPE activities that are aimed at providing sufficient sustenance for themselves. In the final analysis, most people continue to engage in the SEPE life and do not cease to look for the true meaning of life on planet earth. Regardless of whether people are successful in their SEPE activities, their daily rat race of looking for resource abundance from the four corners of the earth continues in perpetuity.

This rat race is so fast that most people are always on the move in order to survive in the cogs of the social, economic, political, and educational wheels. It is for this reason (i.e., the speed of it all) that most people seem to be locked up within themselves, usually either premeditatively unmindful of or forgetfully disregarding the presence of others as they move around to undertake their social, economic, political, and educational activities. Today, for example, in elevators, trains, buses, subways, skytrains, shopping malls, grocery stores, school campuses, public parks, and a lot of other places where people often find themselves and see and meet others, there is little interaction among them. In such places, it usually seems as if everyone has an unwritten but glaringly displayed notice on his or her forehead, usually sensed by others through individual radiations and/or vibrations, indicating to all others around them that they desire to be left alone to successfully accomplish their daily tasks and responsibilities. They are usually possessed and controlled by thoughts of how to make enough money or other resources to overcome the scarcity problem they face.

Those who feel that they might either be disturbed or distracted away from their objectives by others anyway, regardless of the strength of the physically invisible signs they exhibit through the contortions of their facial muscles, do not only guard against such disturbances with a "walkman" or "walkwoman" glued to the cochlea of their ears, but also strap their eyes with heavily darkened sunglasses to warn others that they neither want to hear nor see nor smell nor feel what happens to others around them. Those who cannot afford these portable cassette or compact disk players usually read newspapers, novels, and other types of reading materials. In addition, since they are determined to be artificially mute and have little or no desire to interact with others, their mouths are full of assorted brands of all sorts of bubblegum that are chewed mercilessly to death moment by moment like cows chewing their cud. They just do not want to be involved in the lives of others. They are also blind and deaf on purpose. If their peace is disturbed, they fear that they may not make enough financial resources to care for themselves. As such, they desire to be left alone and undisturbed. The magnitude of the seriousness, advertised to everyone else but themselves, makes the hearts of onlookers scamper into places of safety as squirrels would do when frightened. Everyone must work and deal successfully with his or her scarcity problems.

Indeed, all the toils and struggles of men and women are aimed at conquering scarcity, the basic economizing problem. While the individual aims at maximizing personal self-satisfaction, the corporation focuses on the discovery and utilization of techniques that promote the most efficient use of resources in order to maximize its business profits. Thus, in relation to physical human needs, these are the ultimate goals of all social, economic, political, and educational activities in which men and women engage themselves (see Figure 1.2).

These observations bring many questions to mind. These include the following: Why is there this lack of concern for the plight of others around us? Is it true that the SEPE life is solely concerned about the manner in which men and women make choices by employing their scarce resources in their best alternative uses? If this is so, why is it that while some economic agents receive the maximum returns for the use of their resources, others lose what they have in the same process of change? What are the constituents of maximum human satisfaction? Must the social, economic, political, and educational activities of all humanity be geared solely for the attainment of tangible goods and services for the individual to the total detriment and/or neglect of those intangible ones that are also equally invaluable?

The dilemma postulated by these questions continues to force avid social thinkers to go on searching for the true meaning, goals, and proper conduct of the SEPE life and all business activities engaged in by every human being. In other words,

Figure 1.2
Human Life and Economic/Business Activity

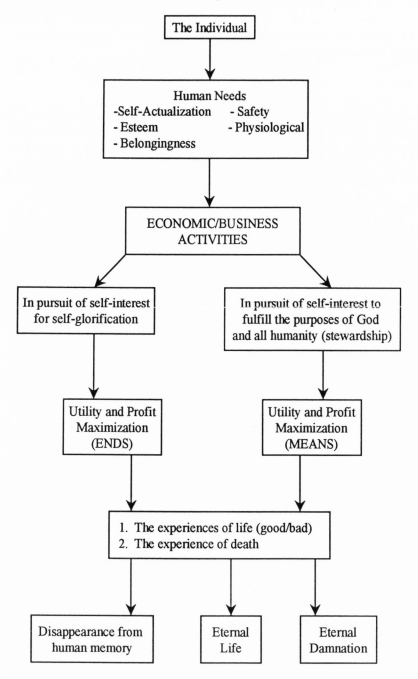

if one wants to comprehend the meaning of and the basis for the SEPE life and activity, one needs to decipher the hidden (usually unrecognized by modern social, economic, and political analysis) primary universal principles that underlie every economic activity. This issue is discussed in detail in Chapter 10. Indeed, the ongoing human striving for food, shelter, clothing, and belongingness has led to the birthing of the dawn of different civilizations.

All Civilizations Evolve around Scarcity

A civilization is nothing more than a culture that has been brought into being by its developers to a level that is advanced enough to accomplish certain complicated tasks in the areas of the SEPE life of a people. Jones noted that "a civilization is a culture which has attained a degree of complexity usually characterized by urban life" (1960, 10). In most cases, people who settle together in specific geographical areas do not only cultivate crops and domesticate animals but also live by rules and regulations. Jones noted that between 3000 and 1500 B.C. three different civilizations—the Egyptian, Mesopotamian, and that of the Indies Valley—flourished (see details in Chapter 2). These civilizations grew in river valleys and depended heavily on agriculture. They experienced strong and capable governments, whose leadership was either ascribed with or perceived as possessing strong divine powers (as in Babylonia), or even equated to the gods or viewed to be their representatives on earth (as in Egypt). In these civilizations, men and women alike engaged themselves in farming, hunting, commerce, industry, metallurgy, architecture, and many other forms of art and craft. Literature, science, music, theology, folklore, military strategy, and many other academic disciplines were also developed and used.

In such civilizations, people developed varying types of architecture, art, craft, political organizations, and methods of economic production, exchange, distribution, and consumption. Workable forms of legal systems and institutional structures were developed to help facilitate everyday economic and business activities. These aspects of a civilization include the social, economic, political, cultural, intellectual, educational, and technological inventions and innovations and many others. They are usually built on critical ideologies and/or philosophical foundations which also facilitate the development of relevant programs for conquering the highly formidable scarcity problem. When these aspects of a civilization turn out to be effective and efficient, society is able to achieve higher productivity goals and development. Any successes achieved in this regard usually increase the potency of a people's civilization in dealing with their nagging problems and hindrances to progress. As is usually the case, it is the ongoing desire to overcome the problem of scarcity that leads each civilization to continue searching for efficient and effective procedures for enhancing human performance and happiness.

In subsequent chapters of this book, the attempt is made to present in a step-by-step fashion the various ways whereby people of all cultures have tried throughout the centuries to overcome scarcity and its attendant problems. A detailed analysis of the ongoing human struggle to conquer scarcity is described and made explicitly clear.

CONCLUSION

The race to subdue the problem of scarcity began many many centuries ago when men and women began to look for ways to cater for themselves. As noted, the search for a life of plenty and continuing survival of the human race and other species led to the creation and evolution of techniques, systems, methods, institutions, and many other ways to help all humanity to achieve sustenance and permanent shelter.

Since the physical and mental capabilities of humanity have not been significantly altered throughout the centuries, men and women have always tried to discover the most efficient and effective ways of accomplishing tasks similar to those in which previous generations engaged and exercised themselves (Jones, 1960, 1). This is one major way through which most civilizations deal with the basic scarcity problem. Thus, the various aspects of civilizations mentioned in this chapter are the results of human attempts to contain the scarcity problem by gaining access to the critical knowledge, understanding, and wisdom required to subdue and rule over nature. In Chapters 2 through 6, a detailed presentation is made regarding the earlier beginnings of the ideolgy of political economy of development. While Chapter 7 focuses on the various factors that are forging the evolution of the global village, Chapter 8 discusses the human plight and predicament. Chapters 9, 10, and 11 discuss the role of the human quality in the failure of SEPE institutions and global development.

NOTES

1. See details in Genesis 1:28–31. Biblical quotations throughout are from the New Revised Standard Version.

2. The view presented here is based on the assumption that people will be honest and resist the nagging temptation of duping or usurping from others what belongs to them. That is, people will not be taken undue advantage of.

3. For example, in the business world, some merchants may create artificial shortages to increase prices and then earn excessively high economic profits.

PART TWO

HUMAN RESPONSES AND PREDICAMENTS

DEALING WITH SCARCITY

The Evolution of Ideologies of Social Order and Political Economy of Development

It is clear from Chapter 1 that all humanity has been affected by the problem of scarcity. Throughout the centuries, it has become obvious that men and women prefer pleasure and the good life to pain and suffering. Thus, since scarcity, the economizing problem, has always served as a serious hindrance to the achievement of the desired goals of all humanity, men and women have always sought for ways and means through which to deal successfully with the scarcity problem. The desire to conquer and subdue scarcity has led humanity to develop and evolve ideas, theories, principles, and procedures that could be used to accomplish their intended objectives. The human search for solutions for scarcity has come a long way through many centuries of hard work and search. In what follows I discuss the beginnings of the ideology of social order and political economy of development. The views of certain prominent scholars are presented and analyzed. Thus, the principal objective of this chapter is to highlight how, right from the dawn of civilization to today, men and women have worked relentlessly to develop and use relevant ideologies, theories, and principles and their accompanying methodologies and institutions to help them successfully deal with scarcity.

To deal with their daily problems in relation to the basic necessities of life, men and women began to develop ideologies, theories, and principles to help them. In what follows I present a historical overview of how people of ancient civilizations went about trying to develop and bring lasting progress into their societies. One thing that must be clear to us today is that when these people were faced with the problem of scarcity, which threatened to deny them the ability and the chance to develop and maintain excellent social order and workable political economy, they tried their best to come out with suggested solutions. These ideas were the off-spring of thoughtful people who were concerned essentially about the scarcity problem and its attendant difficulties in their own societies. Their thoughts served as the foundations of pre-Adamite ideologies of social order and political economy of development.

THE BEGINNINGS OF THE STRUGGLE TO CONQUER SCARCITY

In the beginning of humanity, nomadic people wandered from one area to an-other, attempting to flee from areas of less food and severe famine to places where they could fend for themselves easily. To them, scarcity was like a wild and vi-cious animal that stalked them continuously. They were aware that if they allowed this animal of lack to catch up with them, their lives and dreams of attaining the pleasures of the good life could be shattered forever. Thus, since people desired to achieve and enjoy the good life, they searched for new locations where they could hide away successfully from that which stalked their very life—the prob-lem of scarcity. In the areas of their new residence, they pursued vocations in the hunting of animals and the gathering of wild roots, fruits, berries, and other food. Most of their days were filled with continuing foraging, with the hope of gaining both personal and group liberty from the cruel chains of scarcity. This desire was an excessive force that led men and women to continue their search for freedom from the limitations placed on them by nature. These searches and developments led to the evolution of the great civilizations of the past (e.g., ancient Israel, Assyria, Babylon, China, Egypt, Greece, India, and Rome).[1]

The Ancient Jews

The Bible presents a vivid and extended account of how Abraham and his descen-dants coped with the scarcity problem. These people (i.e., the Jews) developed pro-cedures and activities to help facilitate their effort and programs to survive even in the face of severe scarcity. The Bible provides detailed accounts regarding how Abraham overcame scarcity successfully by exercising his faith in and obedience to the God of his forefathers (Genesis 12:1–4). By exercising his faith in and obe-dience to God, *Yahweh* blessed him both exceedingly and abundantly with a herd of cattle and other material goods (Genesis 24:35). While Jacob and Joseph dealt with the scarcity problem by appealing to their God-given wisdom (Genesis 30:32–34; 47:13–26), Moses depended on his faith in God to lead Israel out of Egypt and also provided them with the abundance of sustenance in the wilderness (Exodus 16:4–15; 17:1–7; Numbers 11:31–35). Lowry (1987, 46) observed that "Joseph emerges [in the courts of Egypt] as the consultant administrator without peer [Genesis 47:13–26]. He manipulated the tools of macroeconomic policy to deal with the onset of scarcity on a grand scale, and much to the profit of his ruler."

Moses's books of Leviticus and Deuteronomy present detailed evidence to show how God promised to help the descendants of Abraham to overcome the scarcity problem by blessing them with abundance if they obeyed His laws. For example, Moses made the following proclamations to the people of Israel:

If you will only obey the LORD your God, by diligently observing all his commandments that I am commanding you today, the LORD your God will set you high above all the nations of the earth; all these blessings shall come upon you and overtake you, if you obey the LORD your God. Blessed shall you be in the city, and blessed shall you be in the field. Blessed shall be the fruit of your womb, the fruit of your ground, and the fruit of your livestock, both the increase of your cattle and the issue of your flock. Blessed shall be your basket and your kneading bowl. Blessed shall you be when you come in and blessed shall you be when you go out. (Deuteronomy 28:1–14)

On another occasion, Moses charged the Jews as follows:

Therefore keep the commandments of the LORD your God, by walking in his ways and by fearing him. For the LORD your God is bringing you into a good land, a land with flowing streams, with springs and underground waters welling in the valleys and hills, a land of wheat and barley, of vines and fig trees and pomegranates, a land of olive trees and honey, a land where you may eat bread without scarcity, where you will lack nothing, a land whose stones are iron and from whose hills you may mine copper. You shall eat your fill and bless the LORD your God for the good land that he has given you. Take care that you do not forget the LORD your God, by failing to keep his commandments, his ordinances, and his statutes, which I am commanding you today. (Deuteronomy 8:6–11)

Moses also discussed the severity of the curses and human suffering that would ensue when the people pursued a path of complete disobedience to the laws of God (Leviticus 26:3–5; Deuteronomy 28:11–26; 28:15–68). Other types of solutions to the scarcity problem that the people of *Yahweh* believed in and used included the use of welfare programs to help the poor and disadvantaged (Exodus 21:1–27; Leviticus 25:35–37); mediation (Isaiah 60:1–7); the apocalyptic solution (see details in the book of Daniel); and seeking the Kingdom of God as proclaimed by Jesus Christ (see the gospels according to Matthew, Mark, Luke, and John). The apostle Paul, in his epistles to all Christian communities of his time, argued and maintained that hard work (i.e., the Protestant work ethic) was necessary for dealing with the scarcity problem (I Thessalonians 4:10–12; II Thessalonians 3:11–12; Ephesians 4:28).[2]

The Jews, like pilgrims who had no permanent homes, also traveled from one place to another, either looking for sustenance or as slaves themselves. This wandering way of life has also been the plight of people in many other societies, including those discussed earlier. Over time, men and women began to realize that they could stay in one location and improve their livelihood. This realization led many people to begin to pursue an ongoing vocation in the domestication (i.e., primitive science of breeding) and/or cultivation of plants and animals for daily sustenance. Both agriculture and animal husbandry began to bloom and blossom. It did not take too long for men and women to perceive that if they continued to put many more acres of land under continuing cultivation, they would be in the position to feed themselves on an ongoing basis. Thus, people began to think and believe that they could overcome the critical economizing problem of scarcity. They worked harder each time, growing crops, hunting animals, fishing, and developing storage facilities to help them stockpile and preserve any excess supply of commodities they acquired during excellent harvest seasons.

The Greeks and the Ideology of Social Order and Political Economy of Development

One of the greatest philosophers among the Greeks was Socrates. Socrates devoted his whole life to the pursuit of knowledge, understanding, and wisdom. To him, virtue was knowledge. The Athenians once charged Socrates as not only being impious, but also for speaking against the gods and corrupting the Athenian youth. For this reason, he was to be tried and, if found guilty, killed by drinking hemlock (Lavine 1989, 13–19). Fearing that Socrates might bring about counterrevolution through his views and the teachings he had been giving to the Athenian youth, the leadership of the day decided to do away with him. In his own defense, Socrates clearly outlined his own philosophy of life and what constituted it. He spelled out clearly that (1) the only true wisdom is one's ability to recognize that he or she knows nothing; (2) the highest good in one's life is to pursue wisdom and truth, and, above all, caring for and developing one's soul; (3) each individual is not only unique, but also a gift to all humanity from the gods, so if society destroys such a person it can never have a perfect replacement; and (4) virtue is knowledge. That is, to Socrates, to know is to do (see details in Lavine 1989, 16). He was subsequently tried, found guilty, and killed.

Indeed, as noted by Lavine (1989, 17–18), the death of Socrates was not only an indictment of personal freedom, but also an indication of the supremacy of state powers over individual rights, liberty, and freedom. As such, Plato's observation of the great injustice exhibited by the Athenian democratic leadership of the time led him to lose interest in Athenian democracy. Plato, a student and admirer of Socrates and his wisdom, was extremely appalled by the immorality and wickedness of Athenian leadership. Plato did not believe that individual freedom should be destroyed through oppressive state power. Knowing that he shared the views of his teacher, Socrates, and that the Athenian leadership might come ruthlessly after his own life, he left Athens. He later developed his concept of the philosopher king: the philosopher who becomes king, or the king that studies and becomes a philosopher. Plato developed his philosophical ideas regarding an ideal society and government in his book, the *Republic*. Plato developed the concepts of justice in relation to a society that is just and good. To him, only the philosopher king would be the best person to lead government and rule society because such a person would possess the required knowledge about what constitutes true justice in society. Without the philosopher king, Plato did not think that society could be properly organized and administered to achieve its desired objectives of the SEPE life. To help deal effectively with this phenomenon, Plato devoted the rest of his life to the preparation of that philosopher who would have the capability to become the philosopher king and then help men and women to live the good life by overcoming scarcity, human injustice, and oppression.

Indeed, Plato's world almost came crashing down when the Athenian leadership killed Socrates. To him, since true justice, fairness, and freedom were denied Socrates, the existing Athenian democracy was not capable of providing a just and fair leadership. He never again believed in the Athenian democracy. Plato, therefore, engaged himself in a lifelong crusade to find and comprehend what the concepts of justice and state were. In the process, he asked questions about human nature, the good life, reality, the physical world, virtue, good conduct, and many other issues (see Lavine 1989, 23).

In his allegory of the cave, Plato did his best to portray several problems facing his society and the critical conditions in which the Athenians found themselves. His allegory, in general, talked about the ongoing decay and ignorance in Athenian society. He viewed the men and women of his society as being asleep and ruled by people who were ignorant and lacked virtue and moral sense. The allegory illustrated the ongoing corruption, intellectual decadence, and moral confusion in Athenian society of the time. Plato, by using the allegory of the cave, tried to send out the message that a society that has fallen into such a state of decay needed a savior or a group of people to redeem it from its final intellectual and moral nadir. It was necessary for such a society to be brought out of its own chains of self-love to the paradise of eternal truth and good life. Again, his concept of the philosopher king still comes out clearly in the allegory of the cave. He seems to be suggesting that only the philosopher king would provide the necessary environment within which society can be rescued from self-destruction. Lavine (1989, 30), in his attempt to put meaning to the allegory of the cave, noted the following:

For us, as for Plato, the allegory of the cave is an allegory of despair and hope. Like Plato, we live in a time of loss of meaning and commitment, of crumbling standards of truth and morality, of corruption in political life and decline in personal integrity. This is our despair. But there is a hope that we share with Plato's allegory, the hope of ascending to the truth and values which are the best we can know as guides to the good life. For us, as for the prisoner freed from his chains, the first step is to recognize current illusions for what they are, the current flickering shadows on the wall of our cave.

The concepts of specialization, division of labor, efficiency, hard work, and the like were developed and used by the Greeks and other civilizations of the ancient time period.

SOME PRACTICAL PROGRAMS TO DEAL WITH SCARCITY

The increasing levels of business and economic activities led men and women to begin to look for greater organization and order in society regarding every activity people engaged themselves in. These desires and/or expectations led to the evolution of local governments, social and religious institutions, social rituals, moral codes, ethical principles, social ethos, legal systems, and magic or sorcery to tame nature. These developments led to the ongoing evolution of permanently established communities of people who decided to live together in one location to support each other in fighting the ongoing war against the critical problem of scarcity. The social, economic, and political organizations and educational systems that evolved were charged with the duty of making sure that everyone lived and worked by established rules and regulations. New technologies and procedures of production, exchange, distribution, and consumption were fashioned and continuously developed.

Swamps were drained to reclaim land for agricultural purposes. The increasing role of land in human activities forced people to realize that there was the need to develop procedures for the attainment of continuing order, fairness, equality, and freedom to pursue business and economic activities as desired. To accomplish these desires, tribal and/or lineage leaders finally turned themselves into administrators, lawyers, adjudicators, counselors, and so on (Jones 1960, 20). Over time, it became obvious that it was critical to develop principles of private property ownership to (1) guide the establishment of procedures for the acquisition of individual property ownership; (2) protect personal property rights; and (3) maintain order, rules, and regulations in society. Jones (1960, 21) noted the following:

The new life brought new concepts of the gods. The old hunting gods became the gods of the farmer; they were invested with new powers and functions. Sometimes new gods were created. In order to exercise the proper supernatural controls, man surrounded every simple technological act with ritual and ceremony. The planting of crops was accompanied by rites which often involved human sacrifice; the ceremonies of the harvest, however, were more cheerful and free of tension. Nevertheless, the gods demanded attention; they must be continually propitiated and made happy with gifts. It was also possible to bind mysterious powers to do one's bidding if the proper magic spells were recited and magical acts performed. In every community there were certain men who appeared to have potent spells at their command. These were the medicine men, or witch doctors, and they were to become the first professional men of history.

New tools were invented and developed for the expansion of agricultural production. With this expansion came the desire to trade with others who also produced desirable commodities. This ongoing exchange also led to more production. The growing volume of trade facilitated the development of both land and water transportation routes. Successes achieved in these activities facilitated the mass movement of goods and services from one area of abundance to another being faced with severe scarcity problems. The birth of transportation systems also led to the promotion of voyages of discovery, which reached their peak between the thirteenth and sixteenth centuries. These expeditions were used to look for other sources of resources and inputs to be used to facilitate domestic production.

People who lived in areas of lack and could not fend adequately for themselves sometimes migrated to other places where they could engage themselves in more gainful economic activities. As such, migration from one area to another also provided people with another opportunity through which they could deal with their ongoing scarcity problems.

Because of the recalcitrant nature of the scarcity problem, all human endeavors have always persisted. In the Paleolithic (Old Stone) Age, men and women fashioned flint or obsidian and used these as tools for hunting and weapons for defending themselves and protecting their property against enemies. In the Neolithic (New Stone) Age, new techniques were evolved for the creation of tools from harder rocks and stones. These implements were also used to acquire sustenance through the hunting of animals and the gathering of edible plant species. In the Bronze Age, better and more powerful tools were made from bronze (an alloy of tin and copper). The Iron Age replaced the Bronze Age. This was the era when people developed their tools from iron. Indeed, throughout the various time periods (i.e., the Age of Primitive Culture or Paleolithic age [up to about 6000 B.C.]; the Age of Agriculture or Neolithic era [up to about 3000 B.C.]; and the Age of Civilization and the appearance of cities [starting around 3000 B.C.]), men and women were continuously confronted with the scarcity problem. Indeed, most of their activities and tools were aimed at finding good solutions to the scarcity problem.

Forms of elementary specialization and division of labor were practiced. Jones (1960, 39) observed further that "civilizations are built upon foundations provided by past cultures. . . . We have borrowed from our ancestors and from peoples not related to us. . . . None of our great inventions or discoveries of the twentieth century could have been made without the support of the knowledge accumulated by our predecessors."

Further developments in agriculture also led to land reclamation, soil fertilization through manure, rapid population growth, specialization, division of labor, improved communal life, complex social organizations, and the evolution of governments, religion, and so on (Jones 1960, 21–23). Indeed, people began to develop procedures for storing any accruing marketable surpluses. They learned to preserve farm produce, game, and fish through the methods of drying, frying, salting, and many others. The technology of electrical refrigeration was not available to these people until recently. Though their technology was very simple compared to what pertains today, people who developed and lived in earlier civilizations (i.e., Egyptian, Babylonian, Greek, Roman, Chinese, etc.) were trailblazers of workable procedures, systems, techniques, and methodologies used to deal with the scarcity problems of their time. Most of their basic procedures formed the primary foundations of modern technological development and advancement.

The desire and commitment to evolve a workable social order and a viable political economy to deal successfully with the scarcity problem led to the evolution of varying ideologies, theories, principles, and the like. From these flowed plans, policies, programs, and projects aimed at dealing successfully with scarcity. The evolving ideologies, theories, and principles were not due to mere intellectual curiosity, but were followed with practical efforts and activities to accomplish the intended tasks of dealing with scarcity.

As noted, men and women devised many different types of programs that were aimed at solving the scarcity problem. Thus, to arrive at continuing abundance of resources for satisfying their daily needs, people cultivated plants and domesticated animals. Sometimes, they engaged in wars of conquest. In cases where they were successful in their military incursions, they seized land and water bodies from other people. They did not only employ these lands to increase their agricultural productivity, but also used the people they captured in wars as slaves to cultivate the land and do the menial jobs. Existing historical records and stylized data reveal that very many different forms of slavery were practiced in ancient Egypt, Babylon, Mesopotamia, Greece, Rome, China, and other ancient kingdoms. The people who developed extensive capabilities were able to travel far and wide to other lands to trade with them. Feudalism and its accompanying manorial systems were used extensively as means of increasing human productivity. Landlords placed their lands at the disposal of individual tenants who wanted to use them to grow crops and rear animals. Sharecropping procedures were developed and contracts drawn to help determine how the harvest was to be distributed between landlords and the peasants who cultivated the land.

The ongoing race to contain scarcity and its accompanying difficulties led to the development of many ideologies, theories, and principles which were employed to explain how men and women should go about dealing successfully with the problem. The human desire to attain permanent freedom from its servitude to nature and then master scarcity is always gathering momentum from one generation to another. As such, every new generation not only employs the ideas and techniques used by previous generations, but also evolves its own methods for dealing with the never-ending problem of scarcity.

PRE-ADAMITE IDEOLOGIES OF SOCIAL ORDER
AND POLITICAL ECONOMY OF DEVELOPMENT

In ancient Greece, economics related to activities that were undertaken to help maintain the social order in society. Indeed, the Greeks believed that a good social order bred the desired society in which men and women were not isolated. In most cases, however, these pursuits were neither accomplished in isolation nor with the ultimate motive of personal aggrandizement at the expense of the rest of society. In regard to Athens, for example, Lavine (1989, 10–11) observed the following:

The Golden Age of Athens, the Age of Pericles, which lasted from 445 to 431 B.C., has come to symbolize perfection in human civilized life.... The Athenian state had a constitution and a supreme court, which incorporated a jury system of six thousand jurors, divided into panels, and for the basis of Athenian democracy, and in political life through direct democratic debate and voting. There was freedom of speech and humane treatment of aliens and slaves. In the Age of Pericles there was full employment and great national prosperity through trade and domestic industry. The city government was viewed as a model of justice for the known world and Athenians had feelings of intense pride and loyalty for the city itself.

Durant (1939, 285–286) observed further:

The Athenian government used a system of economic individualism and socialistic regulation to achieve an increased wealth for the Athenians. In cooperation with all Athenians, the government was able to protect and maintain free trade, private property and the opportunity to make profits since these were considered to be necessary requirements for human liberty and strong incentives for industry, commerce and prosperity. The carefully articulated balancing of the pursuit of individual Self-Interest and government, social and economic policy led to increased income for an increasing number of households in Athens.

In light of these observations, it can hardly be denied that in ancient and medieval times economic activity was aimed at the continuing confrontation with the scarcity problem to benefit everyone in society. Social thinkers of all persuasions focused on justice, fairness, equity, and integrity in all business ventures, economic activities, and other human dealings.

In their economic setting, there existed strong interdependencies and people knew that they had to act in ways that were beneficial not only to themselves, but also to the whole community. To them, proper economics referred to good household management. Goudzwaard (1979) noted that the Greeks used two words to describe human economic activity. These words are *oikonomia* and *chrematistike* (or *chrematistics*). In his own words, *oikonomia* "designated the behavior of the steward whose task it was to manage the estate entrusted to him in such a way that it would continue to bear fruit and thus provide a living for everyone who lived and worked on it. Central to this concept, therefore, was the maintenance of productive possessions on behalf of everyone involved."

Thus, it is obviously clear that one of the Greek conceptions of economics and economic activity not only refers to good and efficient management, but also management with a human face. They were concerned about the welfare of people in their society. Their economic thinking was intricately intertwined with the conduct of economic activity and the sharing of its rewards (Soule 1963). They maintained that economic activities and management practices take the community's interests into account. The writings of Socrates, Plato, Aristotle, and Xenophon (just to name a few) are all indicative of the fact that, to the Greeks, the principles of a good social order and efficient political economy combined and used legal precepts, religious dogma, moral codes, and other related disciplines to achieve intended purposes.

The other word used to illustrate the Greek conceptualization of economic activity (which most patriotic Greeks abhorred and shunned) was *chrematistike*. This word connotes the notion of the passionate chasing after riches and material

wealth for oneself (even up to the point of attaining these self-enrichment prospects at the expense or to the detriment of fellow human beings) (Goudzwaard
1979, 211). Economic pursuit from this perspective was not edifying to the
Greeks. Since no human being is an island, the ancient Greeks felt that
chrematistike economic ventures could be detrimental to the whole society in the
long term. Given that the likelihood of an individual Greek pursuing self-enrichment at the expense of the whole Greek society was existent, people often raised
questions about and exhaustively discussed what must constitute true or just
wealth in Greek society.

Saint Thomas Aquinas and Scholasticism

Between the thirteenth and the sixteenth centuries, scholasticism emerged. A
large number of these writers were monks and religious priests who wrote and
discussed issues relating to the conduct of economic activities in their societies.[3]
These scholars were not necessarily interested in how much economic activity
occurred in medieval society. Instead, they discussed and analyzed moral and ethical foundations of the various exchanges and transactions that occurred in the free
market economy. Landreth (1976, 14–19) noted that "the scholastic writers were
educated monks who tried to lay down moral and religious guidelines for use in
secular activities. The perspective of the scholastics was not so much to analyze
what little economic activity was taking place, but to prescribe rules of economic
conduct compatible with religious dogma."

Among this group of scholars, the most influential individual was Saint Thomas Aquinas. As a highly learned theologian, he developed a thesis on economic
activity which was a synthesis of biblical principles, Greek philosophy, and Roman law. His major themes and principles revolved around God and creation, man
and his nature, and Christ and the sacraments. His expositions on these issues were
incisively deep, thorough, and expansive. He wrote on value, price, money, and
interest (usury). In his major work, the *Summa Theologica*, he discussed the issue
of justice as it relates to interest taking and money. Aquinas believed that every
economic activity must be conducted in such a way that it provided resources for
a personally vibrant spiritual life. Gordon (1975, 157) noted that, to Aquinas,
"economic reasoning is integrated with moral philosophy and the establishment
of legal precepts. Moral philosophy is seen as a discipline which deals with actions of men as individuals, their conduct as members of households, and their
behavior as citizens. . . . Economic analysis undertaken for the sake of determining appropriate standards in dealings between citizens. Above all, it is an aspect
of the enquiry into justice."

From his conceptualizations, formulations, and writings, it is clear that since he
was an avid scholar of the Bible, Greek philosophy, and Roman law, his views about
economics and economic activity were no different from the biblical and Greek conceptions of what constitutes acceptable economic behavior. It is therefore evidently

clear that before Adam Smith the ideology of the political economy of development in relation to economic activities was not only based on moral, legal, ethical, and religious principles, but also considered an option for dealing effectively with the scarcity problem.[4] This observation led Gray (1959, 46) to conclude that "if one word were sought to cover all phases of medieval economic teaching, it would probably be found in the idea of justice. . . . We are brothers and should behave as brothers [and sisters], respecting each other's rights and position in life. Each should receive that to which he [or she] is entitled. Justice, as the medievalists understand it, should be done. No one, under any circumstances, should take advantage of his [or her] neighbor. This is the sum and substance of medieval economic teaching."

As is obvious from the writings of Saint Thomas Aquinas, economic analysis at this point in time concentrated on the person as (1) a unique individual, (2) a member of a household, and (3) a citizen of a state or nation. Thus, even though individual freedom and self-interest were protected, maintained, and fought for, people were also expected to go about their daily economic activities and ventures within the confines of moral, ethical, legal, and religious stipulations of society. To Saint Thomas Aquinas, social institutions that are not in agreement with the laws of God and have, therefore, become unjust have to be altered to meet the needs of people.[5] Where possible, rulers who have become godless must either be warned to change or face the consequences of being deposed. By subscribing to this view, Aquinas justified rebellion in certain circumstances (see details in Becker and Barnes 1952, 248). Aquinas noted that every society is filled with various kinds of human inequalities. He argued that some of these inequalities are results of differences in human capacities. He, therefore, did not see anything wrong with such inequalities, believing they could have been willed by God.[6] To him, in most cases, the differences in human capacities usually serve as the basis for division of labor.

Economic activity, though a means of providing for oneself and one's immediate family and other dependents was not to be deliberately pursued to the detriment of the interests of the rest of society. Every person was expected to respect the rights and property of all others. Thus, self-interest, individual sympathy, self-love, and fellow-feeling were meshed in order to attain the best for the whole society.

In summary, the economic thinking of the ancient civilizations provided people with sufficient guidance regarding how they must behave and act in relation to economic and business activities. Some of their major conceptualizations and their underlying themes of thoughts and principles in relation to what constitutes a good social order and effective political economy of development include the following:

1. The supremacy of God and his relationship with nature and all humanity.

2. Agriculture is the mother of all business and economic activities and also the primary foundation of human livelihood.

3. Economic and business practices and/or activities were aimed at prudent (i.e., effective and efficient) household management. In addition, economic and business activities were to be carried out in a manner commensurate with the moral, ethical, religious, and legal precepts of society. In carrying out these activities, everyone was expected to be their neighbor's keeper.

4. Production and exchange were encouraged and promoted. Indeed, both specialization and division of labor were known to increase input efficiency and productivity.

5. It is critical to maintain an appropriate social order and effective political economy. These will foster continuing justice, liberty, equity, and fairness in society. That is, everybody must receive what is due to him or her.

6. The development and use of tools of social control were necessary for keeping order and developing a viably productive political economy of development.

7. Obedience to secular, rational, and legal contracts was emphasized as *sine qua non* to the development of a peaceful social order and a progressive political economy of development.

8. People's moral lives and the physical universe were believed to be highly interrelated. Thus, any violation of existing moral principles usually brought disaster to the violator and probably to the whole society at large. To avoid calamity, people were usually admonished and encouraged to live in harmony, union, accord, or agreement with moral principles and the physical universe. In light of this view, men and women were to "follow the sacred ways in order to maintain both social solidarity and cosmic harmony. When the times are out of joint it is because men [and women] have failed to keep them right" (Becker and Barnes 1952, 46–47).

9. Overemphasis on personal search for and/or acquisition of wealth could ruin the social order and the political economy of development. Thus, while certain types of employment and/or activities are viewed as being noble, others are treated as being ignoble.

These ancient ideas of social order and political economy of development were discussed, analyzed, and extended further by many other scholars. The key and more relevant ideas and principles developed by a few of these scholars are presented in Table 2.1 and discussed briefly in the following sections.

John Locke

One of the greatest writers on classical democratic liberalism was John Locke (see Table 2.1). He believed in and argued strongly in favor of a minimal state. In Locke's view, the responsibility of the government included the continuing protection and preservation of life, liberty, and property.[7] Indeed, Locke cogently argued that the boundary of the state's authority is the dimension of the natural rights of men and women. Locke extensively discusses the concept of the social contract. He believed in it and defended it. In a nutshell, some of the obvious principles discussed by Locke on the social contract and democratic liberalism include the following:[8]

1. The chief and immediate cause of man's leaving the state of nature was the increase of property and the desire to use and preserve it in safety.

2. The social contract is the agent for initiating civil society. Locke maintained that the social contract lies at the basis of all civil societies (see his two treatises of government [Locke, 1690]).

3. The uncertainties and inconveniences of the pre-political state rendered the institution of civil society imperative (see also the views of Rousseau).

4. Locke held the view that the natural state of nature is characterized by liberty and not war, equality, and independence.

5. Man is endowed with a nature which compels him to seek society, and to enjoy and perpetuate it.

6. According to Locke, the primary (first) society is between man and wife, the second society is between parents and children, and the third society is between master and servants.

7. To him, these societies are not political. To be viewed as political societies, Locke argued that a union into one body, a common law, and an authority to decide controversies and punish offenders must exist. These are the three Lockean canons that distinguish civil societies from all others.

8. In Locke's view, an absolute monarchy is not a type of civil society, since the monarchy controls all powers and there exist no other avenues for subjects to seek redress (appeal).

9. The consent of people must form the basis of civil societies. Locke writes, "That which begins and actually constitutes any political society is nothing but the consent of any number of free men [or women] capable of a majority, to write and incorporate into such a society. And this is that and that only which did or could give beginning to any lawful government in the world."

10. The reason why free men and women would yield to political control is primarily for the preservation and protection of property, and its enjoyment and continuing ownership. Locke writes, "The great and chief end, therefore, of men [and women] uniting into commonwealths, and putting themselves under government, is the preservation of their property; to which in the state of nature there are many things wasting." This view forms the economic basis of the state.

11. While, to Rousseau, civil society rests on private ownership of land, to Locke, its foundation is the invention of money.

12. In Locke's view, men and women sacrifice two major powers through the decision to become members of civil society. These are the rights to engage in everything possible to preserve themselves and the authority to engage in punitive measures against those who violate the laws of nature on which their liberty, equality, and independence depend.

13. By surrendering all these privileges that could be enjoyed in the state of nature, men and women have agreed to live by the stipulations of civil law and also to work hand in hand with the state to punish those who fail to uphold and live by civil law. Indeed, majority rule is key and supreme.

Table 2.1
Political Ideologies and Philosophies

Years	Scholar	Area of Ideological Concern
1632–1704	John Locke	Property and the dissolution of government
1712–1778	J. J. Rousseau	Social contract; inequality and personality
1723–1790	Adam Smith	Laissez-faire system and wealth creation
1729–1797	Edmund Burke	Social change and the French Revolution
1737–1809	Thomas Paine	The rights of men and women
1751–1836	James Madison	Political theory and strong central government
1756–1836	William Godwin	Property ownership
1771–1858	Robert Owen	On government and human welfare
1806–1873	John Stuart Mill	Liberty
1818–1883	Karl Marx	Capitalist development; human struggles
1840–1921	Peter Kropotkin	Law and authority
1856–1939	Sigmund Freud	Civilization and its discontents
1859–1952	John Dewey	Educational problems in society
1870–1924	Vladimir. I. Lenin	Imperialism, the highest state of capitalism
1875–1965	Albert Schweitzer	Ethics and developing the human potential
1879–1940	Leon Trotsky	The theory of permanent revolution
1879–1963	Sir William H. Beveridge	The welfare state and its policies
1883–1946	John Maynard Keynes	Unemployment, money, wages, and interest; government involvement in the economy
1883–1945	Benito Mussolini	The political and social doctrine of fascism
1889–1954	Adolf Hitler	The twenty-five points
1894–1963	Aldous Huxley	Morality
1905–1982	Ayn Rand	Rational self-interest and *laissez-faire* economics
1906–	Hannah Arendt	The final solution, killing
1912–	Milton Friedman	Monetarism and *laissez-faire* capitalism
1913–	Gro Harlem Brundtland	Proposal for institutional and legal change
1914–	Stuart Hampshire	Justice and the dispossessed
1919–	Pierre Elliott Trudeau	Nationalism and confederation
1938–	Robert Nozick	Distributive justice

Sources: McCullough 1995; Ingersoll and Matthews 1991

14. Locke argued that the primary act of every political society is the establishment of supreme authority—the legislative.

15. Locke maintained that when rulers violate the stipulations of the contract establishing the government it is a social obligation and a moral and legal right to engage in a revolution to dethrone the government. That is, since it is government's duty to entrench and protect the natural rights of men and women (i.e., life, liberty, and property), when these are being destroyed by the government, its fundamental purpose for existence ceases to prevail.

Thus, Locke's views and propositions focused on the development of a social order and political economy that promotes and fosters freedom, liberty, equity, and justice. To him, therefore, the development of a society that will help men and women to deal successfully with the scarcity problem and then enjoy the good life was a *sine qua non* to human progress. In such a society, effective and efficient means of social control must be developed, promoted, and perpetrated.

David Hume

David Hume, like John Locke, also discussed certain aspects of the concept of social contract.[9] Hume argued the following:

That the Deity is the ultimate author of all government, will never be denied by any, who admit a general providence, and allow, that all events in the universe are conducted by an uniform plan, and directed to wise purposes. As it is impossible for the human race to subsist, at least in any comfortable or secure state, without the protection of government, this institution must certainly have been intended by that beneficent Being, who means the good of all his creatures: and as it has universally, in fact, taken place, in all countries, and all ages, we may conclude, with still greater certainty, that it was intended by that omniscient Being who can never be deceived by any event or operation. (quoted in Stewart 1986, 32)

According to Hume, therefore, since people are the origin of power, nothing else can take that power away from them.[10] They themselves, for the sake of peace, protection, and order in society, may voluntarily give up their power and be ruled by the sovereign through rules and regulations. Hume pointed out that the people in government are nothing more than first among equals. As such, when a people surrender their natural power and/or rights, they do so on predetermined principles that must not be violated by the sovereign. In general, Hume's ideas, principles, and theories regarding the original contract and the source of power are summarized as follows:[11]

1. To Hume, the sex instinct is the primary cause of society. It causes spontaneous association between male and female. This association leads to the establishment of the family.

2. The family is kept together through sympathy and later influenced by custom and habit. As the family increases in size, it is held together through mutual aid.

3. The gravity of people's selfishness minimizes the strength and/or power of these forces in upholding the family, security, property, and so on. As such, it is critical to establish the government to have the job done.

4. In Hume's view, the desire to preserve property is the origin of civil society. To him, this contract is a tacit or informal agreement and evolves gradually by itself.

5. Hume attacked the theory of the social contract and argued that force rather than contract was the basic factor in the formation of civil society and government. He argued that most civil societies and governments of his time were mostly based on force and usurpation.

6. Hume believed further that though the basis of civil government is force, people's moral obligation to pay allegiance to it is a result of their belief that society could not exist without government.

7. Hume rejected the social contract view that there existed a pre-social state of nature. People must be viewed as social from the beginning. Laws of nature were invented "from a sense of utility and the force of necessity" (Becker and Barnes 1952, 398).

8. The whole notion of the state of nature paints a picture of a time period filled with wars, violence, and injustice.

9. People are obliged to maintain society. It is, therefore, critical that a political society is established for the achievement of this goal (safe, peaceable, and profitable life). Hence the objective of government is to administer justice. So it is for every other department.

10. Although obedience is the social cement for the administration and maintenance of justice in civil society, weak human nature might be more interested in present enjoyment to the detriment of a good future. In view of this, the mere perception of the beauty of justice may not lead men and women to pursue it. As a result, it is important to establish the government to enforce the principle of obedience.

11. Those who gain power and authority to rule and lead the government need to have certain critical human qualities, such as bravery, integrity, and prudence—highly admired human characteristics.

12. Government probably had an accidental beginning and leadership might have been discovered through warfare. To Hume, through a careful combination of "force and consent" a leader could establish his authority.

13. Hume argued that "habit soon consolidates what other principles of human nature had imperfectly founded; and men, once accustomed to obedience, never think of departing from that path, in which they and their ancestors have constantly trod, and to which they are confined by so many urgent and visible motives."

14. Hume believed that "the general obligation which binds us to government, is the interest and necessities of society; and this obligation is very strong."

15. Hume maintained that the greatest value of society is embedded in mutual aid, division of labor, higher production, and availability of commodities. These are possible as a result of fixed social relations.

16. The fundamental principles of justice, according to Hume, appear in the family and are usually extended and deepened as society grows.

17. Hume also discussed the doctrine of sympathy.

Like Locke, Hume's views regarding the social contract revealed his comprehension about how men and women could construct a just social order and an efficient and effective political economy. The ideas of these scholars and many others have exerted a significant impact on how men and women continued to evolve techniques to deal with the pertinent scarcity problems they faced (see detailed listing in Table 2.1).

Other Scholars

Other scholars who discussed the issue of the power of the sovereign state include Jean-Jacques Rousseau. Adam Smith, Thomas Paine, John Stuart Mill, and many others (see relevant summaries in Table 2.1). To Rousseau, the key role of the political state is being a legislator, who may know and legislate what the people desire, but must necessarily serve as a servant to the people. The state is not to make itself the people's master and lord it over them. In general, the state must use the power and authority vested in it by the people to both promote equality before the law and guarantee people's freedom. As is discussed in detail in Chapter 3, Adam Smith maintained that the government should get off people's backs and give them the chance and freedom to pursue their own self-interest. To Adam Smith, the invisible hand of the free market rather than progress-inhibiting visible hands of government must be allowed to lead and direct people to promote their own self-interests. By so doing, according to Smith, the people will both deliberately enhance their own interests and at the same time unconsciously promote the interests of society. The resulting outcome will be social, economic, and political progress in society. In the views of Thomas Paine, no government should be allowed to use its power to invade the natural rights of people (see Table 2.1). To Paine, since the national constitution is the act of the people, it therefore predates the government of the day. John Stuart Mill sketches the details of the classical liberal view of liberty (see Table 2.1). To Mill, people may interfere with the rights of others in situations and/or circumstances where these people pose threats to themselves or the rights of others. No one has the right to infringe upon the rights and privileges of other citizens. Everyone must have his or her freedom to enjoy his or her natural rights and privileges. In general, most scholars of classical democratic liberalism maintained that individual rights must be placed over that of the state. That is, they all argued that individual rights must be emphasized, and those of the government must either be marginalized or totally curtailed.

To discuss this issue further, Chapters 3 and 4 present detailed discussions and analyses on some of the main ideologies, theories, principles, and the corresponding activities they birthed as measures for arresting the scarcity problem in human civilizations. In these chapters, detailed discussions and analyses are presented on some of the key ideologies and techniques developed and used by modern men and women to deal with the pervasive scarcity problem.

CONCLUSION

This chapter has presented a detailed discussion on scarcity and its role in social, economic, and political analysis, and theorizing and policy formulation as men and women strive to develop a just, fair, and free workable social order and political economy of development. The discussions revealed that men and women throughout the centuries have done their best to evolve relevant ideas, principles, and theories on which they could build effective and efficient social order and political economy. In Chapters 3 and 4, the two major economic systems—capitalism and socialism—will be discussed.

NOTES

1. Due to the lack of space, two of these civilizations are briefly reviewed. Interested scholars should refer to relevant historical records.

2. For detailed discussions on each of these solutions, see Lowry (1987, 45–58).

3. Other Scholastic writers include Augustine of Hippo (A.D. 354–430), Lactantius (A.D. 250–325), Tertullian (A.D. 160–223), St. Jerome (A.D. 342–420), and Clement of Alexandria (A.D. 150–215).

4. Adam Smith is the man credited with the title of father and founder of modern economics. His pioneering works laid down a solid foundation for subsequent work on what has become known as the laissez-faire or free enterprise economic system.

5. Aquinas's social theories are evident in his doctrine of the Four-Fold law. These are (1) Eternal Law (God's own will and purpose for the universe); (2) Natural Law (the progressive expression of the eternal law in reason); (3) Human Law (the application of natural law to human needs as the basis of the human social order, which it derives its authority from its conformity to natural law); and (4) Divine Law (supplementing human reason and human law in regard to people's eternal destiny and salvation as revealed in the holy scriptures).

6. It must be pointed out that while it is sensible to argue that differences in human capacities may form the basis of division of labor, it is not correct to maintain that there is nothing wrong with the organization of society either into classes or professions on the basis of physical human characteristics and other such differentiations.

7. See detailed discussions on the social and political thoughts of John Locke in Becker and Barnes (1952).

8. These points are developed from the authors listed in note 7.

9. See detailed discussions on the social and political thoughts of David Hume in Becker and Barnes (1952).

10. Note, however, that Creationists argue from the biblical perspective that all power belongs to God (Psalm 62:11; Isaiah 40:26; Matthew 28:18–20; Romans 13:1) and that it is God who promotes and demotes people (Psalm 75:6–7; Matthew 9:8).

11. The points listed here are developed from the work of the authors cited in notes 7 and 8.

_____

CHAPTER THREE

CONQUERING SCARCITY
THE CAPITALIST WAY
Models and Theories of Economic
Growth and Development

For many decades, economists have been trying to understand and unravel the various factors that influence and promote economic growth. As such, many models and theories have been developed to explain this process. Economic growth has been defined, in simplified terms, as increases in output and national income over a period of time (Adelman 1961; Maddison 1964; Hamberg 1971; Zuvekas 1979; Guha 1981; Hahn 1995; etc.). Arndt (1978, 1) observed that economists view economic growth theory as relating to models aimed at providing explanations for the process of economic growth.

Many different models have been developed to explain how economic growth occurs. The models usually focus on different variables that are deemed critical to promoting and/or propelling economic growth. A great deal of empirical evidence has been gathered in an effort to determine which variables affect growth. In what follows, I present a review of economic growth theories and models.

The remainder of this chapter is presented as follows: While the most immediate section focuses on the historical review of the various models and theories of economic growth modeling, the succeeding section deals with policy recommendations and conclusions arrived at based on the orthodox economic growth model. These theories and models are taken to task in Chapter 4 by Karl Marx and his followers.

HISTORICAL REVIEW OF MODELS OF ECONOMIC GROWTH

Models, and the theories used to generate them, reflect the set of assumptions underlying them. The variations in the assumptions correspond to the variations in the shape the theory takes. Hahn (1995, 85) noted that most growth models depend on varying assumptions. Most of these models assume that factors such as physical and financial capital stock, human capital, research and development (R&D), labor force, and many others are the central factors that drive the economic growth of nations. The problem lies in deciding which theory and which particular set of factors is right. All of them make compelling yet conflicting arguments as to which factors determine economic growth. What is common to these models, however, is their focus on the determination of steady-state equilibrium growth rates. To evaluate how economies grow, special high-powered mathematical formulations have been developed to help explain the growth process of output and income. As such, growth theory is not only mainly concerned with empiricism, the development and defense of laudable mathematical functional depictions of growth processes of all forms that can be proven or falsified, but is also an energy-intensive and resource-consuming exercise in discovering the nature and causes of the growth of the gross domestic product (GDP). The developers of these models hope that their theories and models about economic growth will possess greater explanatory powers than other rival models developed by other economists of varying persuasions. Obviously, few people build theories with the aim of having them falsified in the long run.

MERCANTILISM AND ECONOMIC GROWTH

Mercantilist writers have a great well of knowledge about economic growth theory and information regarding the critical factors that, in their opinion, cause economic growth. Mercantilism as an economic doctrine contends that the critical variables in economic progress include the central role of gold accumulation, external trade, and industrial activities, along with government intervention, critical and specific policy formulation, and the subordination of individual interests to collective national interests (Spengler 1960, 4). The Mercantilists, according to Spengler (1960, 26), "assigned primary importance to labor, secondary importance to land, and tertiary importance to capital." As such, their theory of economic growth maintains that growth in production is mainly possible through increases in the labor force. In their view, therefore, GDP can be raised in volume through the increased use of the available labor force (especially the unemployed and the underemployed). Second, they argued that in areas where labor shortages existed, the shortfalls could be corrected by importing labor from other areas (both from inside or outside the country). Immigration was deemed to be one of the primary means whereby this objective could be fulfilled. As observed by Spengler (1960, 28–29), Mercantilists believed that immigrants often brought capital, new industries, better methods, and preferred value attitudes with them. Thus, their coming was encouraged, except when ecclesiastical or shortsighted balance-of-trade considerations stood in the way. Skilled minorities were particularly welcome, and the establishment of recruiting agencies was advocated and implemented. Emigration, on the other hand, was usually opposed, except in cases where it was perceived to be beneficial to the national economy in the long run.

Some other issues Mercantilist writers regarded as relevant to the economic growth process include the maintenance of favorable balance of payments, scientific development and innovation, technical education, government intervention, the acquisition of colonies, and many others (Spengler 1960, 18–54). Mercantilist views on economic growth are, therefore, extremely diverse and illuminating.[1]

PHYSIOCRATIC PERSPECTIVES ON ECONOMIC GROWTH

The birth of physiocracy could be said to have been in 1756, when Quesnays's first essay on economics was published in the *Grande Encyclopedie* (Oser and Brue 1988, 33). The Physiocrats rejected the idea of too many government regulations and taxes on agriculturists (Spengler 1960, 4–5). According to the Physiocrats, the various restrictions and regulations imposed by the French government on production and business activities not only retarded industrial development in France in the seventeenth and early eighteenth centuries, but also militated against the natural order and individual self-interest. To the Physiocrats, since the peasant farmers had to pay a great deal of their produce to the landlords, they had very little incentive to expand their productivity in order to increase the national output.[2]

According to the Physiocrats, since the rules of nature governed human societies, human activities must be allowed to revert to the harmony of the natural laws. As such, every human being must enjoy the fruits of his or her own labor (i.e., laissez-faire, laissez-passer). They maintained that the primary goal of scientific studies is to discover the laws that guide and regulate the universe. They viewed industry and trade as being sterile.

ADAM SMITH AND THE CLASSICS ON ECONOMIC GROWTH

Classical liberalism, another name for classical doctrine, promotes personal liberty, private property ownership, individual initiative, and private enterprise, and argues against government interference in the economy and the affairs of people (Oser and Brue 1988, 47). Classical liberalism maintained that free competitive market forces guide production, exchange, and distribution in societies. As such, the economy is usually self-regulating, and always tending toward full-employment equilibrium (Oser and Brue 1988, 48). This is one of the primary reasons why classical doctrine subscribed to the view that the most critical duties of the government are national defense, public education, the maintenance of law and order, and the protection of property rights. When they perform effectively, the competitive market forces are expected to lead to the attainment of the most efficient allocation of resources and, hence, growth in the economy. Classical liberalism, therefore, held similar views to those of the Physiocrats in terms of the self-interested economic behavior of people. As such, the continuing promotion, preservation, and pursuit of self-interested behavior were deemed critical to economic growth and progress in societies. Classical liberalism maintained that if people were allowed to pursue their own self-interests they would, in the long run, promote that of society in general. That is, the progress of society and any welfare gains made are all byproducts of individual private actions based on self-interest. In general, classical liberalism insisted that national wealth is generated through such activities as agriculture, commerce, production, and international exchange (Oser and Brue 1988, 48).

The writings of Sir Dudley North (1641–1691), Richard Cantillon (1680–1734), and David Hume (1711–1776) served as the critical foundations for the development of classical liberal thinking. It is on these ideas that Adam Smith based his economic ideas and principles. Oser and Brue (1988, 48) point out that the applications of the theories of classical economics has led to capital accumulation and economic growth. It accorded businessmen and -women with prestige and hope regarding their contributions to the growth of national income. They were also assured of the opportunity to enjoy the fruits of their labor and hard work. Mercantilist restrictions were thrown overboard and replaced with classical liberalism, which opened further doors for extensive commerce and industrial activities. "By helping to remove the remnants of the feudal system, classical economics promoted business enterprise," and the primary result of this phenomenon was increased output (Oser and Brue 1988, 49).

About two centuries before economists began to formalize models and theories of economic growth, Adam Smith (1776) clearly noted that economic growth was fostered by the availability and efficient use of a society's capital stock, land, and labor. In the Smithian economy, capital accumulation, a *sine qua non* to economic progress, is made possible by the continuing postponement of present consumption in favor of future consumption. As such, the capital accumulation process depends on a significant amount of the combined thriftiness of individuals in society. Smith argued, therefore, that since parsimony (i.e., extreme frugality or stinginess) is the greatest cause of most increases in a society's capital stock, frugality (i.e., strong thriftiness and not being wasteful) is society's friend, and prodigality (i.e., being exceedingly or recklessly wasteful) is a strong enemy to capital accumulation in society. Smith also maintained that the private actions of individuals in society are the primary sources of economic growth (see Rogin 1956, 51–109; Arndt 1978, 7).

This is one of the primary reasons why Adam Smith always advocated for natural liberty. He pointed out, however, that the extent to which the effectiveness of labor can be carried out in terms of productivity is limited by the size of the available market. When the limit is reached, economic growth and progress may come to a grinding halt. In addition to this limitation of the market size, Smith contended that a large population and cutthroat competition among businessmen and -women would also lead to lower profits and economic stagnation in the long run, and that excessive restrictions on international trade could also lead to declining domestic productivity. As such, Smith argued that "no regulation of commerce can increase the quantity of industry in any society beyond what its capital can maintain" (quoted in Adelman 1961, 27). Smith did not ignore the relevance of the institutional framework of a society to the marginal productivity of its available inputs. He concluded, however, that the primary factor that determines economic growth is capital formation.

Obviously, the true engine of growth in the Smithian economy is capital accumulation. Smith therefore recommended that nations should do whatever is necessary to promote capital formation. Any successes achieved in this regard would facilitate the growth process of nations.[3] In Smith's view, division of labor usually leads to increased productivity. This, in turn, leads to greater output. This higher output calls forth higher wages—the real reason why increased per capita income is attained. As labor receives higher wages, the annual levels of consumption increase. The nation is, therefore, able to attain higher levels of societal wealth. As the national wealth increases, capital accumulation also escalates. This, in turn, leads to increased division of labor and the process repeats itself until society arrives at the steady state of economic growth.

David Ricardo (1937) also pointed out that output growth is affected by labor, land, and capital. In his analysis, Ricardo assumed that the production function is subject to the law of diminishing returns. Ricardo believed that, though it is possible that economic growth in society may reach a stationary state in the final analysis, it is quite possible for society to delay or push forward in an indefinite sense the time when this stationarity will be arrived at. He argued that this postponement can be achieved through improved and/or increased foreign trade, efficient exploitation of existing natural resources, and continuing technical progress (see Sraffa 1951; Hicks 1966, 260; Arndt 1978, 9). Ricardo's model of growth focuses on the agricultural sector (Sundrum 1990, 54). As such, land and labor were the two critical factors in Ricardo's model. While Ricardo viewed land as being fixed, he treated labor as a variable because it can be increased through population growth. The two critical factors that drive output growth, according to Ricardo, are the rate of growth of population and the wages fund. Ricardo maintained that variations in each of these variables will significantly affect the level of output growth in each country.

Other classical economists who wrote about growth include Malthus, John Stuart Mill, Say, and many others.[4] The classical liberal views were later challenged by Karl Marx and scholars who agreed with his views. The views of the Marxian scholars regarding the process of economic growth are presented and discussed in Chapter 4.

SCHUMPETER AND ECONOMIC GROWTH

Schumpeter (1949) was also very interested in comprehending the dynamism of the capitalist system and how it works. He presented a very strong and interesting

view about the significance of the process of innovation and the role of the entrepreneur in economic growth and development in the capitalist system. Schumpeter
(1949, 15) viewed the production process as being made up of a mixture of productive processes. To Schumpeter, both technical and social factors play a significant role in economic dynamics. "Thus, the growth of output depends upon the
rate of change of the productive factors, the rate of change of technology, and the
rate of change of the socio-cultural environment" (Adelman 1961, 95). In discussing the dynamic evolution of an economy, Schumpeter maintained that changes in
factor availabilities and the effects of social and technological changes are critical to the growth process.

In Schumpeter's (1949, 66–74) analysis, five different types of events can lead
to the process of development. These include the introduction of a new product, a
new technique of production, the development of a new market, the discovery of
new raw-material sources, and continuing changes in the organization and reorganization of industries (see also Adelman 1961, 100). To Schumpeter, economic
development is equivalent to sporadic technological changes. This whole process
is brought into motion, according to Schumpeter, by the entrepreneur who is engaged in invention and/or innovation. Improvements in techniques depend on the
magnitude of entrepreneurial activities taking place in society. This whole process
is propped up by the continuing supply of new entrepreneurs. Yet, according to
Schumpeter (1949, 228–230), only a few people possess these entrepreneurial
qualities and abilities of leadership. To Schumpeter, the bunching together of the
development of innovative activities of the entrepreneurial class is, therefore,
critical to the economic growth process. In a sense, Schumpeter viewed progress
as originating from the process of creative destruction. This process, according to
him, is promoted and propelled by innovation and continuing competition, each
of which significantly affects the intensity of the other.

A more critical review and study of the works of both Karl Marx and Schumpeter
reveals that both of these writers were concerned about understanding how economies grow over time (see details in Lewis 1955; Rostow 1960, 9; Hahn and Matthews
1964, 1; Arndt 1978, 34).

ARTHUR LEWIS AND ECONOMIC GROWTH

Lewis (1954) presented a model of economic growth that has come to be labeled the dualistic growth model (see Sundrum 1990, 69). By classifying a
nation's economy into two distinct sectors (i.e., the traditional and modern), Lewis
discusses how the traditional agricultural-based sector transforms to become the
modern advanced industrialized sector. In his discussions, Lewis argues that surplus labor exists in the traditional sector which can be withdrawn without any dire
consequences for productivity in the traditional agricultural sector. This surplus
labor, according to Lewis, will then be transferred into the modern sector and
given a wage rate equal to their marginal product. As more of this labor becomes
easily available to the modern sector, profits grow. The rate of growth of profits

leads to increased savings and continuing growth in the rate of capital accumulation. According to Lewis, as long as surplus labor exists in the traditional sector, this accumulation process will continue (given constant wage rates). The increasing rate of growth of capital accumulation will, in the long run, lead to the absorption of the surplus labor from the traditional sector.

This process of labor transfer from the traditional sector to the modern sector continues until marginal products in both sectors become equalized. As such, "when the process is completed, the center of gravity of the economy will have shifted from the traditional or agricultural sector to the modern or industrial sector" (Sundrum 1990, 70). As is therefore obvious, the dualistic model of growth discusses the critical role of surplus labor, a high propensity to save out of accrued profits from the modern sector, and capital accumulation as factors of economic growth. In this model, the growth process may arrive at a steady state when the existing surplus labor is exhausted.

Lewis (1955, 57) observed that "institutions promote or restrict growth according to the protection they accord to effort, according to the opportunities they provide for specialization, and according to the freedom of maneuver they permit." Lewis (1955, 60–61) noted further that while capital formation is one of the key conditions for economic growth, it requires the existence of conditions for the law of property to occur. To Lewis, such laws of property must furnish people the legal right to exclude others from utilizing certain resources. He noted that in cases where the state was either too weak or unwilling to protect property ownership, many communities declined in the past. Lewis (1955, 61) argued that property right is fundamental to economic growth because without it, most people would be unwilling to invest or engage in productive economic ventures. Lewis also argued that the withholding of rewards may diminish the growth potential. Problems arise when those who make continuing use of property are not the owners of property. Managers who are paid to take care of property or business may also perform very perfunctorily. When these things happen, rewards to the process of capital formation may decline and hence the growth rate. Lewis (1955, 63) argued further that "more importantly, perhaps, from the angle of economic growth, is the fact that the agents may neglect the property, if their income does not vary directly with the care they take; or even on the other hand may prolong its life improperly, in order to prolong their own employment, by reinvesting in the property part of the owner's profits which could more profitably be invested elsewhere." Lewis (1955, 68) is correct when he observes that "the human mind revolts against discipline, and no big organization can be run successfully without discipline, obedience and loyalty." He noted that trade facilitates growth through demand, which calls forth new commodities and the desire for hard work, and that "trade also brings new ideas—new patterns of consumption, new techniques, or new ideas of social relationships. . . . Trade also stimulates specialization, since the division of labor depends upon the extent of the market" (Lewis 1955, 70). Specialization in itself promotes output growth. Its sole limitation is therefore the size of the market (Smith 1776).

To Lewis (1955, 85), societies in which authority ceases to protect the rights of property owners also fail to experience economic growth. In the same way, when a society falls into the habit of giving its best jobs to people based on birth or relationship, it is quite possible that the best people may not fill the best and most sensitive positions. When this happens, productivity growth may also decline continuously. These beliefs led Lewis to argue that it may be necessary to do away with the ruling class if economic growth is to ensue in society.

The existing upper class usually opposes any changes that promise to diminish its wealth. In this case, economic growth can only ensue when a new ruling class that favors economic growth develops and controls events in society. It must be recalled that in certain cases, the replacement process may lead to struggles, huge losses of lives and property, and so on. For growth to ensue, therefore, it is critical to open up existing opportunities to all sections of the society. Lewis (1955, 89) pointed out, however, that continuing discrimination against groups might lead them to develop in many different directions. An excellent example is the case of the Jews in Western Europe, even before Hitler began his atrocities. Though they were severely despised, they concentrated on business and made huge sums of money.

In addition to all this, Lewis (1955, 90–101) argued that economic growth also needs freedom of markets in which men and women can freely purchase factor services. Every entrepreneur must be able to freely buy and sell factors of production. It must be possible for people to acquire and use land, labor, and capital. Lewis (1955, 101–141) presented a detailed analysis on how religion, slavery, the family, the organization of agriculture, and cottage industries affect the economic growth of nations.

GERSCHENKRON'S VIEWS ON ECONOMIC GROWTH

Gerschenkron (1962, 44) argued that nations whose industrial development has been delayed for a long period of time have greater chances of more explosive spurts of industrialization when the process begins in the long run. As such, in his views, the more backward countries could experience significant levels of industrialization if they would put in place an organized and properly directed program. Such a program could be facilitated by investment banks and the ongoing leadership of the state.

Gerschenkron (1962, 31–51) also argued that capital accumulation might not necessarily lead to economic growth and industrialization. For example, he pointed out that the industrial expansion of Germany was not necessarily due to any previously accumulated capital. Rather, the credit-creation policies and programs of the banking system led the way. In his view, the banks collected funds and made them easily available to entrepreneurs. In the case of Russia, Gerschenkron (1962, 45–66) noted that previously acquired capital was not the fundamental reason for Russia's violent industrial activities. Instead, the fiscal policies and strategies pursued by the Russian government led to the development of a great source of capital supply. While the importation of capital was very significant in Russia's industrial advancement, preindustrial wealth played an insignificant role. Although the ploughing back of profits played some role, Gerschenkron concluded that "all other sources do tend to pale into insignificance compared with the role of budgetary finance of the new and growing industrial enterprises. If a somewhat sweeping expression is permissible, one might say that original accumulation of capital was not a prerequisite of industrial development in major countries on the European continent."

In his discussion of the prerequisites of modern industrialization, Gerschenkron (1962, 47) asked the question, "Why did industrialization occur in Central Europe under the aegis of the banks and under the state in Eastern Europe?" To answer this question, he maintained that it was due to the varying conditions that existed in each region. As such, "what effectively prevented banks from engaging in industrial investment in the Russia of the nineteenth century was *inter alia* the impossibility of building up an effective system of long-term bank credit in a country where the standards of commercial honesty had been so low and where economic, and particularly, mercantile activities and deceit were regarded as inseparably connected. 'He who does not cheat does not sell,' taught the economic wisdom of the folklore." Because many people viewed well-organized and premeditated bankruptcies as normal in personal wealth creation and enrichment, governments prevented banks from engaging themselves in long-term credit activities (Gerschenkron 1962, 47–48). This is one of the primary reasons why the government of Russia engaged in activities to overcome the existing problems of industrial dishonesty. In the same way, since conditions in Central Europe were not only different, but also conducive to decentralization and banking finance, the banks played a greater role in the industrialization process. To Gerschenkron, industrial dishonesty was prevalent in Russia because of the institution of labor services. For example, serf-entrepreneurs deceived their owners in order to keep some gains for themselves; uncertainties regarding the peasants' property rights forced them to disrespect contractual obligations frequently; the dishonesty of Russian artisans and traders; and so on.

Gerschenkron (1962, 50–51) argued further that the lack of certain known prerequisites of industrialization may make it advantageous for a people to pursue an industrial program successfully. This lack may urge a people to act in effective ways to overcome the absence of critical factors that promote industrialization. Difficulties, problems, crises, and different forms of hindrances must, therefore, be viewed as opportunities for industrial progress (see also Ofori-Amoah and Adjibolosoo 1995). Gerschenkron (1962, 51) concluded, therefore, that

In viewing the historical record one cannot fail to be impressed with the ingenuity, originality, and flexibility with which backward countries tried to solve the specific problems of their industrial development. There is no a priori reason to suppose that the underdeveloped countries which today stand on the threshold of their industrial revolutions will show less creative adaptation in compensating for the absence of factors which in more fortunate countries may be said to have "preconditioned" the initial spurts of rapid industrial growth. One can only hope that in drafting the maps of their own industrial progress they will be eager to select those paths along which they will be able to keep down the cost and to increase the yield in terms of human welfare and human happiness.

Gerschenkron (1962, 61–62) pointed out that widespread social attitudes not only exerted a negative impact on the development of entrepreneurship, but also affected the pace of economic development of Russia. As such, he concluded that adverse attitudes toward entrepreneurs can delay the commencement of a nation's industrialization. He noted that economic growth in France was delayed by the nature of entrepreneurial behavior—conservative spirit, aversion to risk, dislike for practices of competition, greed for higher profits, and so on. Entrepreneurship in France was scorned and, as a result, the best people sought after the more traditionally respected careers rather than becoming entrepreneurs who were accorded lower status. It did not, however, completely stop the rapid industrialization in the 1890s.

TOYNBEE'S VIEW: CHALLENGES AND RESPONSES

Toynbee's views regarding the relationship between challenges and responses in terms of economic development and growth is quite intriguing. In his view, while small challenges in society may not produce any significant responses, the continuing accumulation of challenges in society will lead people to begin to devise workable solutions to them. As the volume of challenges increases, the society's responses to the tensions created lead to the design of procedures and/or rules for dealing with existing pertinent problems. Societies that respond in significant ways are able to overcome the prevailing problems. By so doing, they are able to move from one level of economic growth and development to another.

THE BEGINNINGS OF MATHEMATICAL MODELING OF GROWTH

The pioneering work on the rigorous mathematical formulations of economic growth theory and model building was started explicitly by Harrod in 1936. In his formulations, Harrod assumed the rates of growth of population and innovations as given (i.e., the natural rate of growth) and hence discussed the critical role of the savings rate, investment, and the capital stock. His pioneering work was extended by himself (1939, 1948) and Domar (1946, 1957). The results arrived at by both Harrod and Domar led many economists to argue that these conclusions were based on the typical assumptions they made. In light of this, Arndt (1978, 33–34) noted that this debate led to the evolution of the theory of economic growth. At this point in time, economists were being possessed by the spirit of mathematical model building to explain theoretically how economic growth occurs in nations. Rules, principles, and theories began to be formulated and established in the literature. Traditions and precedents were being set for economic growth modeling. A new dawn in the history of economic theory and model building was born. The way the existing pool of modern economists received this new stream of mathematical model building to explain how economic growth happens could be likened to discovering a motherlode that has panned out beautifully. Economists of different persuasions began to latch on to the concept of mathematical growth modeling. Believe it or not, the continuing mathematicization of the growth concept in economics flowered and bloomed like early spring tulips. New concepts and building blocks were defined and developed to keep the concept of economic growth in perspective. Hahn and Matthews (1964, 2) observed that many of these models forged mathematical relationships between economic growth and labor, saving, investment, technical progress, income distribution, capital stock, population, and so on. Any attempts to either validate or falsify existing models encouraged the formulation of newer models. As such, there does not seem to be an end in sight regarding economic growth modeling.

Most economic growth models were more concerned about discussions regarding the significance of critical variables to the growth process than they were about the human qualities of the people who bring the changes about. The plausibility of each model made it too difficult for other scholars to reject. Of course, the criterion for judging the validity of each newly proposed model was not how it accurately described the practical reality of the growth process and what makes it happen intuitively, but the mathematical beauty, rigor, and sophistication exhibited by the model(ist). This was what determined whether economists would accept or reject any proposed model or theory of growth. This obsession with grandiose mathematical growth modeling found a perfect and peaceful home in neoclassical economic theorizing and analysis.

NEOCLASSICAL ECONOMIC GROWTH THEORIES AND MODELS

The commencement of the neoclassical growth theory is rooted deeply in the marginalist revolution that began in the last half of the nineteenth century. In the views of Dixit (1990, 3), growth theory was officially birthed in 1956 when professor Robert M. Solow published his now-famous seminal paper, *A Contribution to the Theory of Economic Growth*, in which he presented his pioneering views on neoclassical economic growth theory. In this model, Solow, like Harrod, also assumed that both the propensity to save and the natural rate are exogenously given. The volume of work done on the neoclassical model of growth is too huge to be completely reviewed in this chapter. My objective here, therefore, is to present the basic thrust of the neoclassical economic growth model, and to point out and discuss how neoclassical growth-model theorists view the process of economic growth and how it happens. The interested reader who is curious about the advanced mathematical treatment of neoclassical economic growth theories and models should refer to the relevant scholarly work presented in the endnotes.[5]

Although the mathematical delineations and formulations of neoclassical economic growth theory are highly complicated, the message is rather simple. That is, neoclassical economic growth models suggest that growth in output is caused by growth in factor inputs (i.e., labor and capital), and growth in output is in relation to continuing growth in inputs (Gordon 1984, 571). This theory of growth is mainly concerned with how a nation can achieve the fastest rate of economic growth by depending on both continuing input and output growth rates. As such, the neoclassical growth model developed by Solow (1956, 65–94) and Swan (1956, 334–361) focuses on the relationship between the saving rate, the growth rate of the population, technical progress, and the standard of living of a people. The model also attempts to explain the forces and factors that affect the rate of economic growth of a nation. The model discusses whether economic growth will stabilize, accelerate, or cease (Abel, Bernanke, and Smith 1995, 194).

Neoclassical growth models are concerned with economic growth in relation to how changes in both labor and capital (including changes in the saving rate, investment rate, population growth, technical change, etc.) affect the rate of growth of output in the whole economy over a period of time. In neoclassical types of economic growth models, increases in the saving rate are expected to lead to increases in the capital–labor ratio, and, hence, an increase in national output, while an increase in population growth rate is viewed as leading to reductions in the capital–labor ratio, and, therefore, a decrease in total national output. In view of this postulation, neoclassical economic growth models usually argue that nations that desire to grow and also improve their long-term living standards must pursue policies that can lead to increases in the saving rate and decreases in the rate of growth of population. Productivity increases are also seen as leading to upward shifts in the production function and hence higher national output at any given capital–output ratio.

Since developing countries are viewed as not only suffering from low saving rates, but also from continuing increases in their population, it is always recommended to these countries that if they desire to achieve continuing economic growth they need to significantly reduce the rate of growth of their population and also strive to increase their saving rate. It is usually argued, from the neoclassical growth-model perspective, that unless these changes are forthcoming, very little can be achieved by way of economic growth in these countries. Besides, it is also a foregone conclusion that productivity increases may not last under situations of low capital–labor ratios, a low savings rate, and too-high rates of population growth. Productivity increases are also expected to increase the capital–labor ratio and hence lead to growing national output. This increase in output is a result of the continuing increases in productivity which also lead to increases in the savings rate. Abel, Bernanke, and Smith (1995, 206) pointed out that, "In the very long run, according to the neoclassical growth model, only these continuing increases in productivity hold the promise of perpetually better living standards. Thus we conclude that, in the long run, *the rate of productivity improvement is the dominant factor determining how quickly living standards rise*" (emphasis original).

The rate of growth of output is viewed as depending on the magnitudes of both capital and labor inputs available in the whole economy. The most basic form of these models is usually specified in the general Cobb–Douglas production functional form as

$$Q = AK^b L^{1-b} \tag{1}$$

In its basic form, the production function specified in Equation 1 suggests that real output depends on "an autonomous growth factor (A), expressed as an index, multiplied by a geometric weighted average of an index of Capital (K) and labor (L). The weights, b and 1 – b, add up to unity and also represent the elasticity of real GNP [gross national product] to an increase in either factor" (see Gordon 1984, 572). From Equation 1, the approximate relationship between the rates of growth of output, inputs, and productivity is derived as

$$\Delta Q/Q = \Delta A/A + b\ \Delta K/K + (1-b)\ \Delta L/L \tag{2}$$

where $\Delta Q/Q$ = the rate of growth of output; $\Delta K/K$ = the rate of growth of capital; $\Delta L/L$ = the rate of growth of labor; $\Delta A/A$ = the rate of growth of productivity; b = elasticity of output with respect to capital; and (1 – b) = elasticity of output with respect to the labor.

These elasticities (i.e., b and 1 – b) show the percentage increase in output as capital or labor inputs change by 1 percent. Equation 2 is usually referred to as the growth accounting equation because it distributes growth into its component parts (see details in Solow 1957, 312–320; Lithwick 1970; Denny et al. 1992, 584–603; Rao and Lempriere 1992; Costello 1993, 207–222; Abel, Bernanke, and Smith 1995, 186–194). Growth accounting is an empirical measure of the relative contributions of the rate of growth of each input to the rate of growth of total output. Usually, total factor productivity is derived as a residual after the contributions of capital and labor have been carefully accounted for. This residual is viewed to be the result of improvements in total factor productivity (Abel, Bernanke, and Smith 1995, 187). Total factor productivity is usually defined as the measure of the economy's overall efficiency (Krugman 1994). It is "the difference between the rate of growth of real product and the rate of growth of real factor input [i.e., capital and labor]" (Jorgenson 1995, 51–98; see also Stigler 1947; Abramovitz 1962, 764). Production functions that exhibit constant returns to scale portray changes in total factor productivity as shifts in the production function (Jorgenson 1995, 53).

Jorgenson (1995, xv–xvi) noted that Japan offers an excellent example of the Asian model of economic growth. This model reveals that investment is exceptionally critical in the years of continuing growth. Using postwar examples from both the United States and Japan, Jorgenson (1995) maintained that policies that stimulate capital formation also promote growth. He argued further that U.S. economic growth between 1948 and 1979 was due to increases in labor and capital.

He acknowledged that productivity growth was also important. His observations are probably based on the views of Tinbergen (1942) that the sources of productivity growth can be classified into two distinct groups—investment and productivity. In a similar way, Abramovitz (1956) and Solow (1957) argued that productivity growth contributed more to aggregate U.S. economic growth than labor resources and capital mobilization (see details in Jorgenson 1995, 1–23). Denison (1985) argued that the slowdown in U.S. productivity from the early 1970s to the 1990s was a result of falling productivity growth. His conclusions were confirmed by Jorgenson. Jorgenson (1995, 2) noted that "the decline in the rate of aggregate productivity growth accounted for 80% of the decline in the rate of growth of output."

In the neoclassical growth model, while increases in the savings rate are expected to lead to continuing growth in national output, population growth is always viewed as being negative in that it reduces the capital–output ratio and hence leads to declining national output. These views often lead to policy suggestions that recommend programs to increase the savings rate and others to lower the population growth rate in developing countries.

THE KEYNESIAN GROWTH THEORY

In the Keynesian theory, a very strong emphasis is placed on the continuing investment decisions made by entrepreneurs (Eltis 1973, 72). Entrepreneurial investment decisions are viewed as being independent of those made by savers. These investment and saving decisions usually determine how the profits being made would be shared between savers and investors. In the views of Kalecki (1954), where there are no investments being made in the economy, there will be no profits (see also Eltis 1973, 73). As such, high levels of entrepreneurial investment will promote increasing profits and, therefore, high returns to capital. This will lead to higher profits, which will in turn lead to higher investments and the process continues. Eltis (1973, 82) pointed out that "high investment would only lead to a high growth rate in the long run if it had a favorable effect in the rate of technical progress." It is, however, possible to attribute more technical progress to entrepreneurial investment than these technical progress functions allow for, and this is achieved by attributing much to the *animal spirits* of entrepreneurs. This idea of animal spirits was used by Keynes to illustrate the critical role of people in the economic growth and development process. Probably, Keynes used this term, animal spirits, not because of his naïveté, but because he lacked knowledge of a better or more appropriate term. A critical analysis of his views about what he called the animal spirits reveals that he was trying to describe the significance of personality characteristics in enterprise development. In his own words, Keynes (1936, 161–162) pointed out that people's decisions to engage themselves in activities aimed at the attainment of positive results is facilitated by their animal spirits—spontaneous urges to action rather than inaction. Thus, according to Keynes, "If the *animal spirits* are dimmed and the spontaneous optimism falters, having us to depend on nothing but a mathematical expectation, enterprise will fade and die" (quoted in Eltis 1973, 83 [italics added]).[6]

The implication of Keynes's analysis, viewed from the human quality perspective, is that while higher levels of human quality development will lead to growing investment, its decay or underdevelopment will diminish both savings and investment rates, therefore leading to declining output. Problems with the animal spirits in men and women can create formidable obstacles to the growth process (see also detailed analysis on this issue in Robinson 1962). Keynes, however, continued to point out that the law of diminishing returns may be at work (especially in the case of capital).

Commenting on Keynes's views regarding the effectiveness and resilience of the animal spirits in men and women, Eltis (1973, 84) noted that when a firm is faced with significant obstacles regarding its investment programs, its returns to capital may begin to fall. At this point in its development process, if the firm is owned and/or managed by faint-hearted people, they may revise their expectations downwards. If, however, the owner and/or management possess strong animal spirits, they will look for ingenious ways with which to successfully deal with the problem of diminishing returns. It is likely that when this task is completely accomplished, the firm may either invent or innovate new techniques for continuing survival and success.

It is, therefore, the case that businessmen and -women who have acquired the animal spirits will set higher goals for themselves and work assiduously to attain them. In the process of doing so, they would not allow problems and all forms of fear and failure to deter or discourage them from achieving their goals. These people are individual entrepreneurs who are prepared to persevere and stick to their goals and objectives no matter what happens in the long run. As goals are translated into reality, the growth rate will increase as expected (Eltis 1973, 84–85). Eltis pointed out clearly that in economies where low animal spirits prevail, low growth rates will be experienced. That is, growth cannot ensue and be sustained in the presence of human quality decay or underdevelopment. This is the same issue discussed by Leibenstein (1966), usually referred to as X-inefficiency.

NEO-KEYNESIAN MODELS OF GROWTH

These types of models present an eclectic view of development by drawing upon Schumpeterian and Marxian dynamics and combining them with contributions to growth theory in the 1930s through to the 1960s.[7] These models intensively discuss the significance of savings, investment, capital accumulation, and the rate of growth of labor to the rate of growth of per capita output. In the Neo-Keynesian models it is argued that the changes experienced in the desired capital–output ratios are the primary determinants of the warranted rate of accumulation. In cases where the continuing expansion in capital exceeds the rate of increases in production, the decline experienced in the capital–output ratio automatically leads to a fall in accumulation

(Adelman 1961, 116). As such, continuing increases in capital will lead to continuing increases in output. That is, both capital accumulation and the average productivity of capital are highly related. Jorgenson (1961), by relegating innovations to the background and focusing only on the rate of growth of population, derived several steady growth rates (see Hahn 1995, 86). Arrow (1962), by assuming that the rate of growth of population is constant and that productivity growth rate is endogenous, argued that productivity growth is a direct function of the growth rate of capital stock (see Hahn 1995, 86).

Hagen (1962, 11) observed the following about technological progress:

[It] consists of two steps: the discovery of new knowledge which makes possible an increase in the output of goods and services per unit labor, capital, and materials used in production; and the incorporation of that knowledge in productive processes. It includes the devising of more satisfying products as well as of more efficient methods of production. It includes the entire process of innovation, from an advance in pure science to its adaptation in engineering and its application in production. Within the realm of methods it includes not only scientific and technical advances but also the devising of new forms of organization or methods of procedure which make the society more efficient in production.

Hagen (1962, 12) noted that increases in income may originate from capital formation, rich natural resources, increases in the labor force, accelerating accumulation and the spread of scientific and technical knowledge, the decision to work many more hours, and many other possible factors. In Hagen's view, continuing economic growth is achieved only through continuing improvement in techniques and/or commodities. Hagen maintained that no other routes to the attainment of economic growth exist. He argued, therefore, that "if steady technological progress is occurring in any given society at a rate sufficient to more than compensate for increase in population, and if the behavior pattern of the society is such that the technological progress promises to continue, then in a sense the fundamental economic problem has been solved." As a result, Hagen (1962, 16) asked the following critical questions: "Why has technological progress appeared so spottily?" and "Why have various societies differed so much in the degree to which they have taken advantage?" In his answer to these questions, Hagen noted that the usual answers provided to these questions include geography and climate (Huntington 1915, 1945), religion (Weber 1930), personality (McClelland 1961), economic conditions, resistance to cultural changes, social and political change, concentration of leadership, creativity, and many others. In Hagen's (1962, 17) own view, it is clear that personal attitudes and/or personality traits permeate the innovating behaviors of entrepreneurs in the process of economic growth. Hagen maintained that it is not only necessary to know that personality traits affect the process of growth, but also to know and comprehend how such personalities come to exist in certain groups and not in others. It is also critical to clearly conceptualize how these are translated into technological advancement and economic progress in societies.

Sheshinski (1967) extended Arrow's (1962) model. Since then, not much work was done on growth theory until Romer (1986) resurrected the dying field of economic

growth theory. Lucas (1988) viewed increases in human capital as the major determining factors of economic growth. However, Hahn (1990), Grossman and
Helpman (1991), and Aghion and Howitt (1992) viewed research as the critical
factor that propels economic growth. Research is expected to lead to the development of new goods that are usually more desirable and more productive (Hahn
1995, 90). Romer (1986) and Grossman and Helpman (1991) assumed in their
models that returns to research are increasing. Hahn (1995, 90) observed that "as
knowledge increases, given inputs into the search activity can produce more
knowledge. But if the rate of growth of knowledge is not to tend to zero, there must
be constant or increasing returns to the stock of knowledge."

THE NEW GROWTH THEORY

The shortcomings of the neoclassical economic growth model have led many
scholars to try to find adequate ways of reformulating these models to include
explanations for productivity changes, which have hitherto been assumed to be
given. The pioneering work in this regard was begun by Romer (1986, 1002–
1037) and Lucas (1988, 3–42). According to Hahn (1995, 85), "Growth theory
flourished in the 1950s and 1960s, died, and has now been resurrected. Romer
(1986) led the way, but it needed Lucas's (1988) uncanny knack of creating followers to beget the now large and growing literature. The aim of the new growth
theories is to have an account of an economy's growth rate which is exogenous to
the theory." These new growth models focus on the role of knowledge, skills,
training, and the education of people (i.e., human capital development and/or acquisition). Investment in human capital may involve the development of health
facilities, training on the job, adult education, and the like (Thirlwall 1972, 113).
By introducing the human-capital variable into the neoclassical growth model, the
new growth theory, through empirical studies, has shown that a significant relationship exists between the rate of growth of the economy and the levels of education and literacy (see Mankiw, Romer, and Weil 1992, 407–438; Abel, Bernanke, and
Smith 1995, 209–210; Jorgenson 1995, xvii and Chapters 6 through 8).

Another aspect of the new growth models stresses the importance of technological innovation by private companies operating in the economy to productivity
growth (Abel, Bernanke, and Smith 1995, 210). Through R&D, a great deal of
discoveries are made. As such, through continuing learning by doing, innovations
may occur that will lead to productivity increases (Arrow 1962, 155–173). Thirlwall
(1972, 113) observed that continuing advancement in health care, education, and
skill acquisition have promoted rapid growth in productivity and labor incomes.
These achievements have also facilitated the development of highly sophisticated
and advanced technology. As is often argued in this case, a nation's capacity to
absorb physical capital may be hindered by its level of investment in human capital (Schultz 1961; Thirlwall 1972, 113).[8]

The main achievement of the new growth models is their revelation and confir-
mation that a significant role exists for national governments to play in the process

of economic growth and development. For example, any successes achieved by government policy in raising the savings rate may, in the long run, lead to improvements in living standards. This change may also lead to increases in investment in human capital, which will in turn lead to more innovations and hence growing output and the process of continuing economic growth will ensue (Abel, Bernanke, and Smith 1995, 210). The new growth models predict, therefore, that any increases in the savings rate might lead to greater gains than have been predicted by the traditional neoclassical economic growth model. The views of the new growth models completely mirror those of Thirlwall (1972, 109–116). According to Thirlwall (1972, 109), the betterment of the production process (i.e., advancement in technical progress) is a direct outcome of intensive investments in such activities as research, invention, development, and innovation. These ventures usually lead to the development and advancement of knowledge. In turn, the newly created knowledge is applied to enhance the production process. It is therefore clear that what is called the new growth theory is actually nothing new. The ideas the new growth theorists latch onto today were in existence long before Romer and Lucas developed what is currently being labeled as the new growth theory. In any case, the new growth models resurrected the views about the significance of invention, innovation, R&D, and investment in human capital to the economic growth process.

OTHER SCHOLARS ON ECONOMIC GROWTH MODELS

As noted, the literature on growth theory is extensive. As such, all of it cannot be reviewed exhaustively in this chapter. However, to conclude this review it is appropriate to briefly mention the contributions of some other scholars to this literature. Hla Myint noted that since market imperfections retard growth, policies aimed at dealing with these imperfections will promote the economic growth and development of nations. Weber emphasized the critical role of the entrepreneur in the economic growth process. McClelland and Hagen extended Weber's analysis and argued strongly regarding the entrepreneur's role in the economic growth and development process. People who possess a strong need for achievement are the individuals who serve as the primary engines for economic growth and development (McClelland 1961). Rostow (1960) propounded and discussed the stage theories of growth.

For many decades, the economic development programs of developing countries, especially those in Africa, Asia, and Latin America, have been based on the various views, models, and growth theories presented by economic growth theorists (see Adjibolosoo 1995a for a detailed discussion of some of these policy prescriptions).

The fact that the free market system is a great economic system cannot be denied. It is a system that encourages individual freedom. Yet, the pursuit of these policies in both developing and developed countries has not helped the working poor overcome their scarcity problem. In addition, neither the welfare nor the general human conditions of the workers have significantly increased. The system sometimes provides incentives to people to act in ways that would lead to the betterment of their own economic conditions. However, its operations usually lead to results that are not usually socially desirable. When this happens, the invisible hand leads astray. Thus, many scholars argue that it is important to search for solutions to its many problems. The socialists argue, however, that it is far better to develop an alternative system (i.e., socialism or communism) that will surpass and perform much better in dealing with the plights of workers and the scarcity problem than does the capitalist system.

If we all believe that the malfunctioning of the capitalist system sometimes makes life unbearable for those who suffer losses after an economic change, then there is the need to develop procedures to correct the maladies. Since blind or extreme fanaticism could rob society of the ability to observe the problems of the system, and therefore be detrimental to all people, all men and women need to join forces to find workable solutions to the problems of the capitalist system. It seems to be the case that those who appeal to Adam Smith's views regarding the laissez faire economic system usually misunderstand his views and concerns. As such, they make continuing errors in judgment and maintain that the capitalist system is the best known system that men and women can use to successfully deal with the attainment of individual liberty and also for overcoming the pertinent scarcity problem.

CONCLUSION

In this chapter, I have reviewed the main views regarding how economic growth happens in societies. Though many factors have been put forward as contributors to economic growth, the more critical ones that stand out from among the rest include capital accumulation, labor force, technical progress, savings, investment, technological advancement, invention, innovation, and entrepreneurs. These results have led to the various policy conclusions and recommendations presented in the chapter. Yet, as will be discussed in subsequent chapters, the pursuit of development planning, policies, programs, and projects based on these traditional economic growth theories and models has not led to any significant improvements in the economies of countries. This being the case, it must be admitted that something must be missing from these models. That is, either traditional economic growth theories and models are wrongly conceived and developed, or those who apply them to policy have misused them. I am inclined to believe that the theories and models are severely inadequate as far as existing conditions in many countries are concerned.

In view of these observations, traditional economic growth theories and models have denied the developing countries the opportunities to develop. They succeeded in keeping these economies in economic bondage and slavery. Any countries that actually desire to achieve long-lasting economic growth and development must rethink the prescriptions of traditional economic growth theories and models. When this process is thoroughly accomplished, I have no doubt that these developing countries will discover for themselves that personality characteristics are the primary sources of growth and the sole engine of economic development (Adjibolosoo 1995a, Chapter 5).

It must be pointed out that during the era of the industrial revolution, Britain had more than a mere abundance of inventors, innovators, entrepreneurs, risk-takers, capital, and other relevant raw materials. What happened in Britain during the era of the industrial revolution was a result of the availability of men and women who exercised a great deal of integrity, accountability, responsibility, commitment, and the like. Without people who possessed such critical human qualities, I doubt whether the industrial revolution could have begun in Britain in the first place. Recall that other places like Greece, Rome, Germany, France, Portugal, and Spain (just to mention a few) could rival Britain in terms of the availability of inventors, innovators, risk-takers, and entrepreneurs.[9] Yet the industrial revolution did not begin in these places. Though many scholars from almost all disciplines tried in the past to rationalize why this was the case, their conclusions usually leave many more unanswered questions than they sought to provide solutions for. They all failed to recognize that the primary difference was the magnitude of the existing differences in the human quality possessed by each country during that time. The failure of orthodox theorizing and policy making, instead of leading economists to rethink their views about what makes economic development happen, has rather led them to rationalize why their intended economic development plans, policies, programs, and projects do not achieve their intended objectives. Their rationalizations have led to the continuing advancement of plausible reasons aimed at providing explanations for the failure.

NOTES

1. See detailed presentation on Mercantilist theories of economic growth in Spengler (1960, 299–334).

2. All things being equal, one would think that the peasant farmers would have higher incentives to produce more because the landlords demand so much. That is, the break-even point was so high that the only way to profit would be to exceed the point set by the landlords by a great deal. Though this kind of reasoning is sensible, the peasant farmers did not rationalize the whole situation in this manner. Instead, they viewed the whole process as a means of exploitation. As such, they only produced that much. An alternative explanation is the *corvee*, which prevented the peasants from increasing yield by arbitrary and counterproductive rules imposed by landowners.

3. Adam Smith's theory of economic growth has been presented schematically in Ekelund and Herbert (1990, 121).

4. The interested reader should consult any textbook on the history of economic thought to read about the views of these classical writers. See, for example, Ekelund and Herbert (1990).

5. Some relevant references in this regard include the following: Solow (1956, 65–94; 1957, 313–320); Swan (1956, 334–361); Shell (1967); Sen (1970); Dixit (1973, 1976, 1990); Prescott (1988, 7–12); Hahn (1990). See also additional references in Note 8.

6. Keynes, in this case, is referring to human quality decay and/or underdevelopment in society. It is true that societies that are experiencing human quality decay and/or underdevelopment will find it too difficult to make economic growth and development happen. See Adjibolosoo (1995a) for a detailed discussion on this issue.

7. The issue regarding returns to education (i.e., investment in human capital) has been discussed by several scholars. Notable works in this area include Schultz (1961); Becker (1964); Bowman (1964); Blaug (1965).

8. Relevant literature in this area includes Tobin (1955, 103–115); Robinson (1956); Solow (1956, 65–94); Swan (1956, 334–361); Leibenstein (1957); Kaldor (1957, 591–624); Little (1957, 152–177); Champernowne (1958, 211–224); Power (1958, 34–51); Dusenberry (1958); Harrod (1959).

9. For a detailed discussion regarding the critical role of the entrepreneur in the development process, see Schumpeter (1934, 1943).

Chapter Four

CONFRONTING SCARCITY
THE SOCIALIST WAY

The Birth of Command Economic Systems and the Future of Capitalism

Since every individual or country is confronted by the problem of scarcity, great consideration is usually given to the development of procedures and mechanisms for dealing with it. In the history of humanity, different economic systems have been developed to deal with the scarcity problem and the four key economic questions it births. In modern times, three major alternative economic systems, usually referred to as capitalism, socialism, and the mixed economic systems are pursued by different societies to contain the scarcity problem. Each of these systems is just a means or method for providing answers to the basic economizing problem of scarcity. Each system makes rules and regulations concerning property ownership and how existing property and available resources can be used to improve the welfare of people in society.

In Chapter 3, our focus was on economic growth viewed from the capitalist perspective. It was clear from that chapter that in capitalist economies, societies try to deal with the scarcity problem by engaging themselves in economic activities aimed at promoting economic growth—a laissez-faire economic system. This is the case because the general belief in capitalist societies is that once a country's economy begins to grow, there will be a larger piece of economic pie to be distributed among its people, especially those who contribute to the production of output using their factors of production. Thus, economic growth has been viewed as the major means for dealing effectively with the scarcity problem. Above all, it is expected to lead to minimizing the number of poor people in society, thereby diminishing the intensity of the scarcity problem.

Yet, unfortunately, the ongoing pursuit of plans, policies, programs, and projects that are aimed at economic growth has not brought into existence the desired changes to the working class. For example, although these activities have led to significant increases in the magnitude of GDP of many nations (i.e., the developed and developing countries alike), the increases in GDP have not yet lessened the growing number and burdens of the poor people. In fact, in most capitalist countries, poor people have experienced and continue to suffer significant declines in their incomes and general welfare as their nations pursue policies and programs for economic growth.

The sordid plight of the poor people in these countries became much more evident during the era of the industrial revolution in the eighteenth century. During this era, while the capitalist system was excessively successful in expanding the boundaries of its own production possibility frontier and generating continuing significant increases in input productivity and turning out huge profits for the industrialists, the poor workers and their families were living under deplorable social and economic conditions.[1] The whole era was saturated with significant exploitation of the working class by industrial capitalists. Men were forced by their employers to work for no less than twelve or fifteen hours each day. In addition, women and children were excessively exploited. They were made to work under very poor conditions. While child labor was used in the factories, women were excessively exploited and abused in many different forms. For example, Robinson (1898, 2) noted the experience of a woman who worked in a textile mill in the early years of the nineteenth century. He recalled, "Hitherto woman had always been a money-saving, rather than a money-earning, member of the community, and her labor could command but a small return. If she worked out as a servant, or help, wages were from fifty cents to one dollar a week; if she went from house to house by the day to spin and weave, or as a tailoress, she could get by seventy-five cents a week and her meals. As a teacher her services were not in demand, and nearly all the arts, the professions and even the trades and industries were closed to her" (quoted in Perelman 1983, 36). Barrios de Chungra (1979, 44–45) documented a similar experience voiced by the wife of a twentieth-century miner from Bolivia: "The miner is doubly exploited? Because with such a small wage, the woman has to do much more in the home. And really that's unpaid work we're doing for the boss, isn't it? . . . The wage needed to pay us for what we do in the home, compared to the wages of a cook, a washerwoman, a baby-sitter, a servant, was much higher than what the men earned in the mine" (quoted in Perelman 1983, 37). Truly, due to the poor working conditions in the factories, men, women, and children suffered from terrible sicknesses and diseases. They had no other lives than having themselves toasted in the capitalist oven of work—the factory and its premises—in the attempt to vanquish the scarcity problem.

Indeed, although the capitalist system was extremely successful in expanding its productive capabilities, this achievement did not significantly help the working class to break away from their poor conditions of life and excessive lack of financial resources to provide substance for their families. Instead, the successes of the capitalist system diminished workers' abilities to deal successfully with the scarcity problem. While many rich capitalists were successful in providing enough for themselves and their families, the poor were denied this possibility. Thus, while to the rich industrialists the problem of scarcity was not necessarily that real, to the poor it created painful memories of hunger and destitution. To them, scarcity became a permanent part of daily life.

The problems and ongoing struggles for existence and daily suffering of the working class did not go unnoticed by Karl Marx and a few other scholars of the time. At this point in time, Karl Marx began to write about and highlight the plight of the workers. He decided to take capitalism, an already entrenched economic system, to task. In his writings he pointed out clearly that regardless of the significant achievements of the capitalist system, it would never improve the lot of workers. To Karl Marx, the industrial capitalist was much more concerned about the magnitude of his or her company's profit margin rather than the welfare of the employees who contribute to his or her financial success through their hard labor. With this conclusion in mind, Karl Marx embarked on a lifelong crusade to write and speak about the poor conditions of workers and to provide them with ideas regarding how they could help themselves overcome the severe problems being created for them by industrial capitalists.

In view of these observations, this chapter presents, in a nutshell, Karl Marx's conceptualization of capitalist development. Note, however, that since many volumes have already been written on Marxian economic theory, this chapter does not intend to reproduce the existing literature. Instead, the chapter places its emphasis on Karl Marx's views regarding capitalist development, its inability to deal successfully with the scarcity problem, and its imminent demise. The chapter also presents a few ideas regarding how the socialist economic system could lead the working class successfully into the communist society and then help them to overcome the ongoing scarcity problem.

Recall that socialist or command economic systems are both centralized and planned. They do not necessarily allow for private property ownership. The means of production are owned by the state (i.e., society). Unlike the free-market system, where private individuals make production and consumption decisions, socialism is based on extensive planning as determined and operated by the state. For example, in the former Soviet Union, the Gosplan was the government arm that gave oversight to a complicated system of socialist production processes. In the past, this system was subscribed to by mostly eastern European countries and also a handful of countries in Africa, Asia, and Latin America. Since socialism is perceived as being excessively detrimental to individual liberty and human rights, western democracies not only look down on it, but also do everything possible to avoid anything associated with it or to prevent people from embracing its ideology.[2]

KARL MARX: HIS CRITIQUE OF CAPITALISM

In his development of the foundation principles of Marxian economic theory, Karl Marx (1818–1883) discussed and analyzed the inherent contradictions in capitalism.[3] Lenin (1870–1924) analyzed the weaknesses and strengths of monopoly capitalism and imperialism and presented ideas about how people can successfully revolt against it. Joseph Stalin (1879–1959) brought into focus the socialist foundations required for developing Soviet power. Using Marxian ideas and supported by many Chinese at the time of the cultural revolution, Mao Tse-Tung (1893–1976) carried out a successful socialist revolution against the old capitalist order in China.[4] Gurley (1979, 5) noted, "Marx supplied the critique of the 'old' [capitalist] society, Lenin the revolutionary means to overthrow it, Stalin the socialist foundations of Soviet power, and Mao the newer, 'higher' socialist society. Together, the four of them have shaped and defined contemporary Marxism, in theory and in revolutionary practice."

In what follows, we will proceed by discussing Marx's view about the future of the capitalist transnational company. Karl Marx, discussing the capitalist development process, argued that as capital accumulation increases, the rate of profit tends to decline. This fall in the rate of profits leads to a continuing chain of events that finally promotes misery, oppression, exploitation, and so on. As this process escalates, a revolution of the working-class becomes imminent. Indeed, the growing numbers of the working-class secure a solid foundation for such a revolution. In the final analysis, the "centralization of the means of production and socialization of labor at last reach a point where they become incompatible with their capitalist integument. This integument is burst asunder. The nail of capitalist private property has been fully hammered in. The expropriators are expropriated" (Marx 1906, 1:837 [originally published in 1867]).

In this passage, Marx suggests that capitalists cannot fool labor forever. The growing suffering, impoverishment, and degradation suffered by labor will one day be rebelled against by suffering workers. When the workers become fully aware of the exploitation and misery that the capitalist unleashes on them, they will strive as hard as possible to redeem themselves out of the financial bondage into which they have been pushed by insensitive capitalists. At the time when their education is properly done and completed, they will rise up, unite together, and fight for their rights, privileges, and freedom. When this happens, the capitalist, who had always enjoyed life at the expense of the working poor, will have to trade places with labor. The large army of the existing labor force will seize power from the bourgeoisie and be able to set up their own institutions that would see to the reorganization, management, and direction of the working force to achieve and promote the best possible world for themselves. Society will then begin to move toward the perfect communist society (i.e., utopia).

Marx's conception of capitalist development is vividly clarified by Fusfeld (1986), who observed that by taking exploitation of labor as the starting point, workers end up with insufficient buying power. At the same time, the capitalist pursues a massive program aimed at capital accumulation. Thus, since workers are unable to purchase all the products of the capitalist firm, a severe glut develops. This phenomenon then facilitates a chain of events that leads to falling prices, increasing unemployment, declining profits, and stagnation of the capital accumulation process. As these crises deepen, the capitalist system, according to Karl Marx, cannot survive any further. According to Marx, the capitalist's imperative is to continue to accumulate. This accumulation process leads to a phenomenal increase in the capital–labor ratio. However, the constant rate of growth of the surplus value would eventually lead to a decline in profits over time. Thus, in order to avert this grim process of profit deterioration, the capitalist has to make labor work harder and do more overtime. In this way, labor is continually exploited and rendered more and more impoverished over time. Thus, the simultaneous deterioration of profits and worker impoverishment is expected to lead finally to a Marxian form of ruin. The nail that seals the casket of capitalism would already have been fastened, preparing it to be buried. In the final analysis, the expropriators are expropriated.

Staley (1989) gave a detailed analysis regarding how this process is expected to lead to the final demise of capitalism. He noted that the growing poverty of workers denies them the ability to purchase the capitalist's products. Thus, by working many hours to generate more surplus value for the capitalist, "the worker becomes a mere appendage of the machine, unable to develop his full potentiality, and in this sense capitalism impoverishes the worker [i.e., increases the scarcity problem] no matter how high his real income" (Staley 1989).

Marx argued that the continuous generation of business cycles by capitalist business and economic activities would lead to a nasty situation within which the big transnational corporations would swallow the smaller businesses. He maintained that larger companies would not only gain more financial resources and physical property and hence continue to survive, but ownership of industry would become concentrated in the hands of a few—strongly centralized. As this process gathers momentum, according to Marx, the capitalist class grows richer and richer while the proletariat not only grows in power unnoticed by the bourgeoisie, but also increases in numbers. In the final analysis, when the crises reach a stage where the impoverished working class can no longer bear their problems and ongoing exploitation, difficulties, and oppression as dished out to them by the rich and privileged capitalist class, they (i.e., the workers) finally revolt, seize power, begin a new socialist order, and then a communist society in the long run. Again, capitalism would have killed itself (see also Fusfeld 1986, 65). Marx's conception and vision of capitalist development are shown schematically in Figure 4.1.

In Figure 4.1, note the various stages of capitalist development. The process begins at Stage I, where labor is severely exploited. This process goes through Stages II through V, where the working class is alienated and dehumanized in terms of personal and social relationships. When labor is fully depleted and becomes highly aware of its exploitation, society goes through a massive unstoppable revolution, being led by avowed and unrelenting communists in Stage VI. Finally, in Stage VII, a brand new communist society is born.[5] At this point, Marx believed that all major struggles of humanity (i.e., humanity against nature and

Figure 4.1
Marx's Conception of the Capitalist Development Process

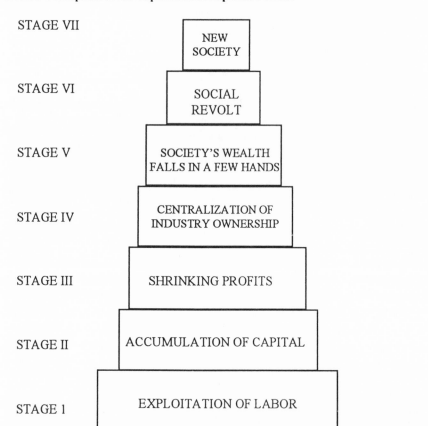

STAGE VII — NEW SOCIETY

STAGE VI — SOCIAL REVOLT

STAGE V — SOCIETY'S WEALTH FALLS IN A FEW HANDS

STAGE IV — CENTRALIZATION OF INDUSTRY OWNERSHIP

STAGE III — SHRINKING PROFITS

STAGE II — ACCUMULATION OF CAPITAL

STAGE 1 — EXPLOITATION OF LABOR

humanity against each other) would be terminated; abundance and not scarcity, equality rather than inequality, justice rather than injustice (i.e., classlessness), and freedom instead of bondage would reign in the new communist society (see Fusfeld 1986, 68).

Sweezy (1942) strongly believed that capitalist crises cannot be solved by financial restructuring. He maintained that continuing fluctuations in the rate of profits are sufficient to create intense crises for the capitalist system up to a point that it cannot contain. Fluctuations in profits are expected to lead to production crises. Like Karl Marx, Sweezy maintained that the process of capitalist accumulation will usually lead to declining profits. As this process continues, the capitalist crises will escalate until the day when it finally succumbs to degradation. In one of his comments on Marx, Sweezy pointed out that, in cases where the reserve army is exhausted due to continuing competition for labor services among capitalists, rising wages would lead to significant declines in the magnitude of the surplus values. As such, the ensuing crises will finally lead to lags in the capital accumulation process. Worst of all, Marx suggested that the development and growth of labor power would lead to the payment of higher wages to labor. The implications of this new development, Marx believed, would be a reduction in the total value of capitalist accumulation. A bitter antagonism between labor and the capitalists develops in the long run. This is a result of declining profits. The law of declining profits suggests that the capitalist crises may not easily be resolved, though Marx left the possibility that the crises have the potential to resolve themselves some of the time.

It seems quite clear, therefore, that it was this process of declining reserve army, rising wages, and reduced profitability (the cause of the crises) that Marx had in mind when he formulated his well-known criticism of underconsumption theories in Volume 2 of *Capital*. The crises are always precisely preceded by a period in which wages rise generally and the working class actually gets a larger share of the annual product intended for consumption.

In cases where each sector or industry is disproportionately affected by severe depressions, the crises in the capitalist system can create massive crises and problems that can choke off capitalist growth. Once these crises consume a vital industry or sector of the economy, Marx and his followers believed that problems in this industry or sector would easily be passed on to other industries and sectors that depend on it. Crises that permeate the rest of the economy might lead to significant reductions in production, decline in profits, shrinking accumulation of capital, and, finally, the demise of the capitalist economic system.

Wright (1978), after having carefully studied and analyzed the capitalist conceptualizations, suggested that Marxist underconsumption theory has the following four basic propositions:

1. There exists a strong tendency for the absolute value of the surplus value to increase in capitalist societies. In a similar way, as labor productivity increases its value also increases simultaneously.

2. There exists some variance between the production of the surplus value and its realization. This is so because, while capitalists desire to minimize the wage bill in order to increase the magnitude of the surplus value, this desire usually militates against the rate of growth of effective demand and purchasing power. This phenomenon usually forces effective demand to lag behind the rate of growth of the surplus value. However, effective demand can be generated through government purchases, the development of new (global) markets, institutionalization of consumer credit, and so on. If these are not done, some portion of the surplus value may not be attained by the capitalist.

3. The inability of capitalists to attain all the expected surplus value may show itself in lower (declining) profits, which in turn may lead to bankruptcies, falling investment, growing unemployment, and so on. If effective demand is not quickly restored through some of the programs specified in item 2, the state of capitalist operation may worsen.

4. Underconsumptionist characteristics become more acute at the monopoly stage of capitalist development. This is so because under monopoly there is a great tendency for the surplus value to grow in size. When this occurs, the capitalist corporation is plagued by problems of underconsumption.

In many circumstances, Marxian economists believe that the crises in the capitalist economy not only come as a result of declining profits, but also from underconsumption of the masses or the consuming public. In the light of this belief, Sweezy (1942, 160) suggested that, since the development of capitalism is completely tied to profits, any lags in effective (consumption) demand will not only lead to continuing gluts, but also limit further expansion. Thus, these crises will not only serve as interruptions to the economic life, but also act as the trigger mechanism of social problems and class struggles in society. Marx suggests that the rate of profits is highly affected by class struggles. In this case, while workers struggle to better and improve their welfare and living standards, capitalists make sure that they also strive hard enough to maintain the total value of their surplus value.

In view of all these observations, it is not all that difficult to perceive the struggles that capitalism is expected to go through as it rises or grows towards maturity. However, in its striving for growth and survival, Marxists suggest that capitalism will experience a great deal of birthing crises and growing pains, whose severity will be more than it can bear. In the final analysis, it will succumb to communism (see details in Marx 1906, 2:443). Thus, to Sweezy, the demise of capitalism is as sure as the rising and the setting of the sun. There is nothing capitalists can do to avert the destruction of their operations. Regardless of what they do, they may only achieve infinitesimal successes in delaying the day of doom. This phenomenon would, however, not abort the birth of the new child, socialism, which would grow up and mature into communism, the real adulthood of capitalism.

In general, the heart of Marxian economic theory can be summarized as follows:

1. To Marx, capitalism is simply a historically determined mode of production.

2. The Marxian analysis focuses on the increasing contradiction between the productive forces and the social relations of production that shows itself in the crises and struggles between the bourgeoisie and the proletariat.

3. Marx's critique of the capitalist mode focuses on the prediction of the imminent overthrow of the bourgeoisie by the proletariat.

4. Marx maintains that capital is not a "thing." Rather, it is "a definite social relation which belongs to a specific historical formation of society" (Gurley 1979, 32). Its four major forms are industrial, trading, lending, and renting capital.

5. According to Marx, capital, in the social forms of instruments of labor, raw materials, and labor power, produces surplus value in the production sphere; in the social forms of commodities and money, realizes surplus value for the capitalist class in the sphere of circulation; and in the social forms of merchants' industrial (trading) capital, interest-bearing (lending) capital, and landed (renting) capital, distributes the surplus value among industrial, commercial, financial, and landed capitalists (Gurley 1979, 32).

6. Surplus value comes from industrial profits, commercial profits, interest, and rent. In Marx's view, although the creation of surplus value occurs in the production sphere, its realization happens in the circulation sphere (i.e., the sale of commodities at their value). The surplus value is the difference between the cost of maintaining and reproducing the laborer and his or her family (i.e., socially accepted standard of living) and the price at which the commodities produced are sold. Workers sell their labor power to capitalists, who in turn use it to get commodities which are usually sold at values greater than what has been paid for the use of labor power. As such, the primary source of surplus value is labor power. The capitalist receives the surplus value because he or she owns the means of production. The magnitude of the existing surplus value is the measure of labor power exploitation by the capitalist. Indeed, the capitalist firm uses labor power to produce commodities and generates a surplus value by selling them at significantly higher prices than paid to labor.

7. The gross value of commodity is the sum of Constant Capital (c), the socially necessary labor time of both capital goods and raw materials used in the production process (also viewed as indirect labor, a cooperant factor); Variable Capital (v), the value of direct labor employed in the production process (wages, in conjunction with machines and raw materials); and Surplus Value (s), part of the value produced by labor, but not received (i.e., profits, interest, and rent). These three, according to Marx, constitute the gross value of the product. That is, $C = c + v + s$. The full value of $v + s$ is produced by labor. Yet labor receives only v. The capitalist, the owner of capital, takes all of s for him- or herself (i.e., the magnitude of exploitation).

Marx viewed capital accumulation as a process that transforms the workplace into an environment that not only lords it over the employees and makes them nonentities, but also destroys the employee's self-worth, self-respect, and ability to be human. In addition, while capital accumulation increases the net worth of the industrialist, it increases the "misery, agony of toil, slavery, ignorance, brutality and mental degradation" of the worker (see Gurley 1979, 41). Marx believed and argued that poverty and misery are not necessary due to the negligence of capitalism. Instead, they are its unavoidable progenies. Marx sees human beings in capitalist societies as being continuously alienated from the products they produce, the fruits of their own labor, from others, and from themselves. They lose control over their own products and creations. They are usually deprived of their own powers and personal dignity. They believe that this power is enshrined elsewhere (i.e., outside themselves). In this process of alienation, people lose their inner self and allow themselves to be ruled, controlled, directed, and tossed to and fro by outside powers. As such, they yield themselves to continuing subjugation and manipulation—they are filled with a sense of powerlessness and passivity. Gurley (1979, 44) observed, "According to Marx, the laborer exists to satisfy the needs of capital; material wealth does not exist to satisfy the need of the laborer to develop into a complete human being." As such, the capitalist exacerbates the problem of scarcity rather than minimizing it. It is a death trap for workers. These observations form the actual basis for Marx's primary message regarding the process of capitalist accumulation and growth.

KARL MARX AND MARXIAN GROWTH THEORIES

Karl Marx's view about economic growth is not only complex, but based on a set of assumptions. These assumptions are made in relation to the nature of the production function, the nature of innovation, and how capital accumulation ensues in societies (Adelman 1961, 60). The various changes in wages and the maladjustment prevalent in the whole economy lead to the whole system being very explosive (Adelman 1961, 60). Taking a cue from Karl Marx's labor theory of value, it can be argued that, to Marx, the sole driving force of growth in the economy is labor. As such, the chief determinant of the rate of capital accumulation, according to Marx, is the size of surplus value. All other things depend on the conditions of labor and the magnitude of the remuneration it receives from capitalists. Marx argued that the relations of production are always changing. From his Hegelian perspective, Marx viewed the whole world as being full of processes that are always in a state of flux. As such, it is the continuing changes that lead to what one might call the progressive development (Adelman 1961, 63).

Karl Marx argued that at the various stages of capitalist development the material productive forces act in continuing contradiction with the already entrenched productive relationships. The continuing clash of these forces and structures leads to changes in the existing economic foundation, leading to a total transformation of the whole superstructure (Marx 1904, 11). From the conceptualizations of Karl Marx and Frederick Engels, production relations are viewed as evolving through at least four stages. These include primitive communism, slavery, feudalism, and capitalism. At every stage of the evolutionary and growth processes, existing systems and productive structures that could no longer meet the needs and demands of society were replaced over time. As such, the Marxian view of change is enshrined in the continuing struggles between the existing classes due to contradictions inherent in the system (Adelman 1961, 67–68). This being the case, Marx argued that the capitalist system has its own seeds of destruction rooted in its very nature. In conclusion, from the Marxian perspective, "Development can occur only as a result of an exogenous shock, the essential effect of which is to change the initial conditions in such a way that self-sustained growth takes place" (Adelman 1961, 91).

COMMUNISM AND THE CONTAINMENT OF SCARCITY

Marx argued that the continuation of the impoverishment of labor would lead to lower purchasing power, making it impossible for labor to purchase the goods and services put on the market. The apparent decline in effective demand would in turn lead to declining sales and lower profits. Over time, the demise of capitalism would finally arrive. The bourgeoisie would be overthrown and the proletariat would take over. Thus, in his philosophical thinking, scientific socialism will indeed become the inevitable intermittent state of the development of capitalism. In the final analysis, communism, a classless state, would take over as the new flawless society, a society within which all injustice, inequity, discrimination, unfairness, scarcity, and other forms of exploitation would no longer be experienced. The leaders of the revolution would indeed do away with these problems and propel society toward a perfect state of work and happiness. The joy and feeling of being well treated would create many incentives for everyone to work at his or her best. Scarcity would have been successfully dealt with in a collective manner. This would be the case because, as the Marxian rule has it, from each according to his or her ability and to each according to his or her need. This Marxian principle of output (income) generation and distribution is expected to lead socialist societies into a new era of plenty for everyone, a society in which there will neither be any lacks nor exploitation. The economizing problem, scarcity, would be vanquished completely. Those who produce more than they personally need will subsidize the needs of those who produce less than they need to survive. Indeed, everyone will have the requisite amount of resources to survive on. Since everybody's needs will be fully satisfied, there will be real human joy and fulfillment in a communist society (see details in Figure 4.1).

Indeed, the Marxian view of capitalism seems to suggest that capitalism increases the degree of intensity of scarcity rather than minimizes it. Its ongoing problems create more lacks and lead to continuing decline in factor incomes and hence the inability to deal successfully with the basic economic problem—scarcity. In reality, the major Marxian debates and analysis of capitalist crises have always focused on four critical hindrances to the capitalist accumulation process. These include the rising organic composition of capital, the problem of realizing the surplus value, a low or declining rate of exploration resulting from rising wages, and the contradictory role of state accumulation (see details in Figure 4.1).[6]

In their written manifesto for the communist party, Marx and Engels described in detail the problems and suffering of the working classes. Their observations and views reveal that there is no way capitalism can help solve the social, economic, and political problems of the people. To them, if people are to rise above their pertinent problems of scarcity and human suffering, a drastic change in society has to occur. This change must place all the means of production back in the hands of the working class. Such a process will return all the means of production to all workers under a common property ownership system. By so doing, a communist society will see to it that there will never ever be an occasion in such a society where some are excessively rich and have more than they need and others suffer from severe lacks and abject poverty. When this becomes a reality in the new communist society, the working men and women all over the world would have created for themselves a perfect society in which no one would experience the slightest level of scarcity. Indeed, no one would take undue advantage of others in a communist society (see the development process in Figure 4.1).

To achieve this objective, Marx and Engels outlined in *The Communist Manifesto* the following critical steps that must be taken and implemented:[7]

1. Abolish property in land and apply all rents of land to public purposes.
2. Impose a heavy progressive or graduated income tax on the wealthy.
3. Abolish all rights of inheritance.
4. Seize the property of all rebels and immigrants.
5. Centralize all credit in the hands of the state through national banks and exclusive monopoly.
6. Centralize all means of transportation and communications in the hands of the state. Let the state own all means of production and factories.
7. Cultivate all wastelands and improve the productive capability of all lands that are excessively barren.
8. Establish industrial armies for agricultural purposes.
9. Combine agriculture with industries for the purpose of increasing their productivities. Abolish any distinctions between town and country through programs aimed at equal distribution of population.
10. Provide free education through the public school system for all children. Abolish child labor in the factories.

Societies that take these steps are expected to transform a socialist state and usher it into the desired (utopian) communist society. This is the society in which no one is expected to suffer from the problems of scarcity. Capitalist exploitation and its untold suppression of the working class would have been vanquished. The existing bridges of human struggles and suffering would have been burned down completely. No trails of their previous existence would be left to remain standing as monumental reminders of past afflictions.

Yet, unfortunately, as world events have revealed since the later half of the 1980s, the socialist agenda has suffered some severe blows. The Berlin Wall came tumbling down. The former Soviet Union has already been dismantled. Communist China is currently revamping its socialist plans, policies, programs, and projects. North Korea is still under authoritarian communist rule. Socialist Cuba is not only struggling to make ends meet for its citizens, but also reeling under intensive scarcity problems. In these societies, hunger and human suffering in their many forms are well-known to the working class. These people cannot make ends meet. The glorious socialist and communist agenda has not only faltered, but has also left behind it trails of bewilderment, betrayal, sicknesses, confusion, overexploitation, corruption, deceitfulness, and so on. A passionate dream to achieve resource abundance has gone sour. All over the world, current events are continuously revealing that the socialist system has a long way to go to achieve its intended objectives. Many scholars are beginning to doubt whether command economic systems have what it will take to completely overcome the scarcity problem and human suffering.

Regardless of what positive achievements might have been made in socialist and communist societies to date, it must be pointed out that some of the worst cases of human-rights abuse, continuing denial of personal freedom, inequity in income distribution, leadership corruption in its various forms, unlawful incarceration of advocates of human rights and social justice, senseless torture and imprisonment of political opponents, and the like have occurred in socialist and communist countries as well as capitalist countries. In many of these countries, dissenting voices have been brutally silenced. Millions of people have been shot, hanged, beaten, dragged on city streets, and so on. The irony, however, is that the socialist system is supposed to prepare people for a better life of peace, tranquillity, and abundance. It seems to be the case that the cries of Thomas Jefferson, Jeremy Bentham, James Stuart Mill, Martin Luther King, Jr., Mahatma Ghandi, John Stuart Mill, Mother Theresa, Nelson Mandela, and many others against the maltreatment of other human beings fell on the deaf ears of modern revolutionaries in all countries (i.e., socialist, communist, and capitalist alike). These observations point to the fact that the socialist system is neither better nor much more promising than the capitalist one. Regardless of its ideological stipulations and beauty, socialism and communism have also fallen short of their promises to the working class of the world. Socialism and communism do not have what it will take to solve the problems of scarcity. These observations, in fact, bring many questions into mind. Two most critical and pressing questions, therefore, are as follows: (1) Why has socialism failed to help the working class to successfully overcome the scarcity problem? and (2) Why is capitalism not yet dead as suggested by Karl Marx and his followers?

In Chapter 5, diverse evidence is presented to substantiate the fact that, as a viable economic system, capitalism cannot easily disappear as suggested by Marxian theorists. The growing forces behind capitalism are isolated and exhaustively discussed. In the light of these discussions, we will realize why the rise and growth of the transnational company significantly contributes to the successes of an economic system that has its own built-in mechanisms to cushion crises. Indeed, it seems that many Marxists continue to make predictions based mostly on their ideologies rather than on critically surveyed or observed real-life phenomena. This is not to suggest that all their predictions about the relationships between the bourgeoisie and the proletariat are wrong, but that they do not normally possess the perfect foresight they think they have. This blindness on their part has been vividly illustrated by an observation made by Frederick Engels himself in 1868 regarding military technology. Brennan (1968, 2) quoted Engels as saying the following:

The Franco–Prussian War (1870–1871) marked a turning point which was of entirely new significance. In the first place the weapons used have reached such a stage of perfection that further progress which would have any revolutionizing influence is no longer possible. Once armies have guns which can hit a battalion at any range at which it can be distinguished, and rifles which are equally effective for hitting individual men, while loading them takes less time than aiming, then all further improvements are more or less unimportant for field warfare. The era of evolution is therefore, in essentials, closed in this direction.

How much poorer could the foresight of a revolutionary be? Engels thought and believed that it was not possible to improve upon the existing military technology of his day any further. Historical evidence has, however, proven him wrong. It is, therefore, not surprising that some of the main predictions of Marxian theories have already been falsified by historical evidence and stylized facts.

After having pursued a socialist or communist agenda for many decades, most socialist states are now aware that their agenda of emancipation did very little to contain the SEPE problems. The economizing problem, scarcity, is much more entrenched today in these societies than at the time when a few vocal revolutionaries forcefully usurped power and placed their societies on a socialist or communist diet of economic growth and development. It is the case, however, that regardless of how scholars view socialist theory and its failure to bring about human progress in the desired direction, this theory has made some contributions to all humanity. In reality, some of the most important aspects and contributions of Marxism to the human race include the following:

1. Marxism suggests that a viable social order and political economy needs to provide people with dignity and relevant opportunities through which people can overcome the problem of scarcity and survive in life.

2. Marxism has been successful in articulating and describing in vivid terms the moral problems of all humanity—especially as evidenced in capitalism.

3. Marxism has offered humanity a theoretical framework for analyzing the critical SEPE problems prevalent in every society.

4. Marxism not only raises the hopes of suffering people, but also provides them with the justifications for political or revolutionary action. That is, in cases where people have come to perceive that they have been oppressed for far too long, they are able to learn about the various alternative ways to deal with their pertinent problems.

5. Marxism has not only revealed to the leaders and people of socialist states that the pursuit of mere ideologies does not necessarily deal successfully with both the SEPE and scarcity problems, but also that ideologies do not get things done by themselves. Instead, people using ideologies make progress or failure happen in society.[8]

CONCLUSION

The socialist challenge to the capitalist system is not only real, but also scary to many adherents of the capitalist system. Indeed, socialism has provided many suffering people with a framework through which they can view and analyze their problems and associated difficulties. The Marxian analysis has created a situation that has led to what many economists have come to know today as the mixed economic system (see details in Chapter 5). As can be argued, regardless of the setbacks to and the failures of the socialist agenda, it has significantly contributed to the many changes being experienced today in the capitalist agenda of economic growth and development.

Ideas and ideologies usually sound wonderful. Thus, it is usually the case that those who hold ideas often think that they are better poised to achieve greater results than those who do not have any such ideas. It is also the case that, in politics, when one party is on the throne, ruling, opposition parties always think and believe that they could do a better job of ruling than the party in power. Yet when reality strikes and one of these opposition parties is voted into office and given the mandate to rule, its leaders usually end their terms of office severely devastated or destroyed. All along the way, they fall into similar traps regarding conflicts of interest, the mismangement, misapplication, and misappropriation of public funds, political greed, system exploitation, double dipping, sexual scandals, and the like. It is only at that point in time that they learn and comprehend that it is not easy to deal with SEPE problems. There is always more to these problems than most people with basic ideas think.

Indeed, Karl Marx and his followers believed that they had correctly identified the pertinent SEPE problems of every human society. They were also convinced that they were successful in determining the requisite solutions to these problems. Yet when it comes to practical applications of their designed solutions, most programs based on their suggested solutions fall flat on their faces. As such, the pronouncement made by Marxian economists regarding the demise of the capitalist system has not yet happened and may not even in the longer term. In fact, current events seem to be suggesting otherwise. Capitalism is, however, experiencing significant transformation. In view of this, it is legitimate to proceed from here to find out why events did not turn out as suggested by Karl Marx and his followers. This is what forms the content of Chapter 5.

NOTES

1. See details in *The Communist Manifesto*, Section I, "Bourgeoisie and Proletarians" (Marx and Engels 1955).

2. Of course, we need to be aware that some countries have had great successes with some variations of socialism (i.e., the Scandinavian countries).

3. Since this chapter is not necessarily concerned with the details of the life story of Karl Marx, readers who are interested in it may consult Gurley (1979), Fusfeld (1986), Ingersoll and Matthews (1991), and McCullough (1995). References to relevant sections on Karl Marx in standard textbooks on the history of economic thought would also be useful.

4. For a more detailed discussion of these individuals, see Gurley (1979).

5. This whole process, from the Marxian perspective, can be likened to the cycle of development of a fly. Since a fly's development process is ordained by nature, it can neither be stayed nor escaped. What Marx forgot to take into consideration, however, is that, in the fly's environment, predators might be successful in short-circuiting the total development of this fly into adulthood. This ignorance on his part led him to propose a doomed path for capitalist development. In his mind there was no force powerful enough to rescue an ailing and declining method of production. It is, however, not quite clear what actually made Marx perceive the capitalist developmental process the way he did.

6. For details, refer to Wright (1978) and Ross and Trachte (1990) and the references thereof.

7. These points are also listed in Colander and Landreth (1995, 22–23).

8. See Adjibolosoo (1995a) for details on this view.

CHAPTER FIVE

THE CAPITALIST RESPONSE

New Strategies and Programs for Growth and Development

Capitalism has been viewed as being filled with its own seeds of destruction. According to Karl Marx, capitalism as a means of production would collapse some day. Joseph Schumpeter, an intelligent and very well-read economist, did not believe that capitalism would survive for long. To him, the evolution of big business, big governments, and big labor unions will lead finally to the annihilation of the capitalist mode of production (see details in Fusfeld 1986, 133–140). Many other socialist and Marxian scholars held similar views (and some still do today). Summarizing the Marxian views regarding the final demise of capitalism, Heilbroner (1986, 171) observed the following:

Karl Marx pronounced his sentence of doom on capitalism in the *Manifesto* of 1848; the system was diagnosed as the victim of an incurable disease, and although no timetable was given, it was presumed to be close enough to its final death struggle for the next of kin— the Communists—to listen avidly for the last gasp that would signal their inheritance of power. Even before the appearance of *Capital* in 1867, the death watch had begun, and with each bout of speculative fever or each siege of industrial depression, the hopeful drew nearer to the deathbed and told each other that the moment of Final Revolution would now be soon at hand. But the system did not die. True, many of the Marxist laws of motion were verified by the march of events; big business did grow bigger and recurrent depressions and unemployment did plague society. But along with these confirmations of the prognosis of doom, another highly important and portentously phrased Marxist symptom was remarkable by its absence: the "increasing misery" of the proletariat failed to increase.

As is obvious from this quote, the demise of capitalism has not yet happened. Capitalism as a mode of production did not yield easily to its own seeds of destruction as

predicted by the Marxian laws of motion. The system has been able to deal successfully with its inherent problems and difficulties. Indeed, the ingenuity of the capitalist in dealing effectively with some key problems has marveled many. As such, the
turnaround of events needs detailed explanations. The primary objective of this
chapter is to explain why the capitalist system did not die as predicted by Marxian
scholars. To accomplish this task, real-life evidence and stylized data are used.

MINIMIZING EMPLOYEE MISERY

The challenges posed to the capitalist system by the pronouncements and
propositions of Marxian scholars forced capitalists as well as scholars from the
West to begin to search for relevant solutions to the inherent problems of the capitalist system. The socialist challenge, in reality, can be viewed as a significant
wake-up call to the capitalists to get their act together. In their response to the
socialist challenge, capitalists set out with plans, policies, programs, and projects
aimed at helping improve the well-being of their employees. At the same time,
they also engaged themselves in extensive R&D activities aimed at expanding the
frontiers of the capitalist business. As such, the capitalist agenda for dealing with
its own problems and difficulties led to the development of many different technologies, systems, and programs that have been used to circumvent the imminent
demise as predicted by Marxian laws of motion.

Since Marx wrote his treatise in the volumes referred to as *Capital*, the world is
yet to experience the institutionalization of dictatorships in Western capitalistic
democracies. Though we have all experienced the setting up of dictatorships in
many developing countries through very violent and bloody *coups d'etat*, we are
yet to experience such events in Western capitalist societies. In these societies,
governments have not only been changed by orderly democratic elections, but also
are hardly ever unlawfully forced out of office. The balloting process has served
as the primary and highly acceptable way for individuals to request a change of
government if they are dissatisfied with it. Even when individuals are not happy
about the ruling government, they have the freedom to speak their mind without
being harassed, as is the case under dictatorial regimes.

Given that all these programs are well-organized, instituted, and carefully ex-
ecuted to the benefit of every individual, why would workers want to rebel, set up
their own work programs, and form a government for themselves? If capitalism
were not a dynamic system, it could easily collapse. All through the decades it has
been strongly successful in developing techniques and using relevant institutions
to deal with crisis situations. My prediction is that as we enter into the twenty-first
century and beyond, many more such programs will be developed and used to help
improve the welfare and working conditions of all workers.

In addition to these developments, the modern-day company worker enjoys an
extended political democracy in that he or she enjoys voting rights and plays a key
role in the evolution of national economic, social, and political policies. In a sense,

the militancy of labor has made it become a strong force to reckon with in the political arena.

In a similar way, economic growth, development, and progress have helped in alleviating industrial problems perceived and pointed out by Karl Marx. Goudzwaard (1979) noted that "the technology of production advanced so rapidly that the time had come to profitably manufacture products of only a few varieties in such great quantities and consequently at such low cost that the masses of society could afford them." Whitehead (1926) suggested that Marx's intelligence was unable to perceive the ability of capitalism to innovate and invent. In its struggle for survival, R&D has become an integral part of the modern industrial corporation. It is through these projects that corporations' innovative and inventive tentacles have been well-developed and widely spread to perpetuate the survival of the capitalistic free-enterprise economic system.

If one is a Marxist, it is not all that difficult to enumerate a series of items that constitute the commencing points of the capitalist crisis, including the growing and escalating immiseration of the proletariat, the inability of the system to deal with the growing crisis, the exclusion of the working class from the bourgeoisie class, societal polarization, growing resentment of the ruling class and the bourgeoisie by the proletariat, dictatorial rules and regimes (see details in Chapter 4). Indeed, if the capitalist system actually comes under partial fire from all these simultaneously, it may find it rather difficult to cope. From these discussions and perspectives, one would agree that crisis situations can lead to the destruction of the capitalist system.

If Karl Marx were totally right in his historical and philosophical thought and accompanying prophecy about the demise of capitalism, the world should have seen the annihilation of capitalism by now (or at least continue to expect the day of doom for capitalism). However, this has not been the case so far. For over a century, since Marx's prophecy regarding the annihilation of capitalism, capitalism seems to grow from vigor to vigor, regardless of its difficulties and the many criticisms leveled against it by its opponents. To the Marxists, this is extremely frustrating and discouraging because it delays and holds back the day of Marxian redemption and salvation for the working classes of the world. In what follows, I present a detailed discussion to substantiate the fact that Karl Marx and his followers did not fully foresee the dawn of new developments, innovations, and inventions that would come into being to aid and facilitate the growth, transformation, and survival of capitalism and the transnational companies (TNCs).

Given all these presuppositions, a basic question is whether or not Marx was really aware of the fact that certain changes and developments could come into being to divert the path and/or process of capitalist development that he thought would lead to the demise of capitalism. The answer to this question is yes. He was aware of the fact that political and social changes could affect the direction of his postulations (see Fusfeld 1986).

However, since Marx had his own conception of what he imagined and believed the state of society in the final analysis to be, he was not really open in his vision to perceive how new developments might render some of his prophecies false. Thus, even though he believed that certain developments might surface, they would not be sufficiently powerful to rescue capitalism from its cold bed of sickness and the unavoidable path to destruction. To him, the developmental process of capitalism toward its destruction is like the act of leading a sheep to the slaughter house, where it would definitely be butchered regardless of intervening circumstances that might strive to either halt or delay the death process.

In what follows, I discuss a series of practical steps that TNCs and domestic businesses have taken through the years to fuel and invigorate the strength and power of capitalism. It can be argued that like Malthus, who made some shortsighted proclamations about the state of world population growth and national productivity (though he has been proven right in some circumstances), Marx was oblivious to the new developments to be brought into reality by capitalist R&D to foster transnational business growth and development.

Glyn and Sutcliffe (1971, 1972) also argued that the share of labor of the total output has been on the increase. According to them this observed phenomenon has been the British experience since the mid-1960s. In their view, the increase experienced by labor in its share of output is due to strong bargaining power that labor has attained in recent years. However, many new developments in the system have helped hedge capitalism and capitalist business ventures against some of these Marxian propositions.

As many developments have taken place in capitalist societies, many utterances of Marx, in connection to the state of labor, seems to have been vitiated. For example, in capitalist economies, the growth and strength of labor unions have been so great that these unions have gained power and recognition from management and business owners. Trade unions have blossomed in the last few decades and have strong bargaining powers which are used to obtain the best for their members. They bargain for higher wages, Medicare, fringe benefits, flexible and/or reduced working hours, better working conditions, safety regulations, and much else. Success in this area has led in many cases to a vast reduction in the levels of antagonism and strife between top management and employees. Participatory management has allowed labor to have significant input into the running of the company.

From this perspective, it is obvious that the working class is able to participate in the benefits of the growing wealth and abundance of capitalist societies. For this reason, the working class has not seen itself as being completely impoverished as predicted by Marx. Profit and product sharing agreements between workers and big corporations like IBM, Ford Motors, General Motors, and many others have helped their workers to take home a larger net income than was the case in earlier years (i.e., during the industrial revolution). In addition, some of these companies have well-organized and well-designed welfare programs for their employees and families. Some of these companies have not only instituted self-improvement educational training programs for their employees, but also have begun to develop and support daycare programs for the children of their employees.

For example, unlike the period of the industrial revolution when many children were abused and misused, some modern companies are gradually putting resources toward the education and training of the children of their employees. These days, quite a large number of companies continue to contribute to the daycare expenses of their employees. In other circumstances, money is placed in scholarship funds designed solely for the education of the children of deserving employees. This is very encouraging to many employees today, because while they are at work they know that their infant children are being cared for by professional people. In addition, their older children go to the best schools and the school fees are paid by the scholarship funds instituted by their employers.

In addition to these company-tailored welfare programs, national governments have also developed and instituted welfare and income security programs to cater to the needs of their citizens. For example, in Canada, such welfare programs as demogrants, guaranteed income, unemployment insurance, social insurance, and social assistance have become pervasive (see details in Chapter 6). The federal government of Canada spends a lot of financial resources on health, social welfare, education, defense, and so on. All these programs have reduced the financial burden of industrial workers. In the modern world, many companies and governments provide funds and opportunities for unemployed people to retrain themselves in order to reenter the labor market.

In many Western societies like Canada, Germany, the United States, the United Kingdom, and France, governments have developed and promoted unemployment insurance programs. These income schemes are designed to cater to workers who lose their jobs unexpectedly. The contributions into these funds are made by both employers and employees. When an employee loses his or her job, the necessary steps are taken to make application for unemployment insurance. This program actually serves as a cushion against the devastating impact of unemployment and its traumatic experiences. The program reduces the difficulties unemployed people experience. To every employee, the unemployment insurance program gives financial relief and hope for the future.

Other similar programs are the disability and old-age pension payments (see details in Chapter 6). These programs have been successfully organized to provide people who have become incapacitated to have at least some income flow throughout the time of difficulties. Unlike the era of the industrial revolution when one had to earn almost all income spent, these income programs alleviate the burden of insufficient income when physical disability strikes. Pension plans provide adequate comfort to retired employees. It is not only satisfying to know that one has a constant stream of income to fall back on when one has retired from the labor force, but it also provides a great deal of peace and security to the individual. Its availability usually reduces the feeling of insecurity and self-pity during retirement years. Some employees look forward to their retirement period with a great deal of joy, expectation, and hope. The ongoing changes in advanced countries' economies may, however, change this scenario for the worse.

The Marxian hypothesis is that the variance between labor and the capitalist will continue to escalate until labor takes over completely from the capitalist. In this way, the expropriators are expected to be expropriated. However, the realities, as revealed in the historical records of capitalism, are revealing that this may not be the case. New developments taking place in the area of labor–management relations continue to point to the fact that there are unique and positive changes. Relationships are improving. Conditions under which labor functions are being improved dramatically. As these conditions change for the better and the labor force anticipates higher incomes due to growing average productivity, there is always the tendency to perform at one's best. Workers are working smarter rather than harder these days.

A case in point is the American NUCOR Corporation that specializes in steel production. In this company, many things are done to help improve relationships between labor and management. NUCOR does not distinguish between general workers and management when it comes to such issues as where to have refreshment, rest, and so on. Both management and general workers use all available resources without discrimination. Individual workers are rewarded according to their productivity. Workers are not only provided with good pay, but are also offered incentives based on teamwork. NUCOR has developed and established a "no layoff" policy. That is, employees are scarcely laid off. During recessionary time periods, workers take a small percentage cut in pay in order to make it possible for the company to adjust and live successfully through periods of recession. This works well for every worker.

Every worker at NUCOR is almost a jack of all trades. NUCOR encourages and emphasizes a flexible work force that is able to undertake any job function outside its own area of specialization and expertise. This is not only a great asset to the company; it also provides every worker with the freedom to move from one performance area to another as occasion demands. All these observations and many others not documented here point to the fact that, over the years, labor–management relations tend to improve rather than deteriorate. In circumstances where the trend may lead to deterioration, a third party comes in to arbitrate between the two groups. Product sharing arrangements are exciting and encouraging to both labor and management.

Employee performance appraisal involves the outlining of meaningful performance levels and designing procedures for performance evaluation which are employed to determine how much additional remuneration to offer to employees and also to identify what areas need be improved. By so doing, most employees are given the opportunity to learn to improve on their performance and future development. This development has led to the creation of significant hopes for all employees. In addition, performance appraisal procedures have also made it possible for employees to realize that there are opportunities for professional development and promotions to higher positions with their accompanying monetary and status gains. Thus, workers are able to identify themselves with companies they work for and are proud to see to their welfare and success.

Well-organized and well-executed performance appraisal procedures have the potential for providing relevant information to both management and employees. They create a proper work environment within which employees can be motivated to improve performance and quality.

The modern corporation has therefore allowed employees to seek their own welfare in a corporate setting. Grievance procedures have created avenues for workers to approach management and share their concerns and difficulties with them. Incentive compensation programs in corporations have led to increased bonuses and profit sharing arrangements. All these developments have reduced the magnitude of the ill-feeling of workers in regard to exploitation and abuse. It is fascinating to know that, in some cases, each employee has the chance to determine and design his or her own compensation package. For example, Cominco, a British Columbian mining company, allows its employees to choose their own benefits packages.

Unlike the days of the industrial revolution, where there were few industrial safety programs, the modern corporation has created safety devices in the workplace. Workers' Compensation Boards have been instituted to oversee some of these programs in most developed capitalist economies. For example, in Canada, Workers' Compensation Acts and the Canadian Safety Code have been in full force for many years. While the Workers' Compensation Acts make sure that individual workers are duly and justly compensated for any injuries sustained, the Canadian Safety Code outlines the fundamental safety programs that must necessarily be put in place in the industrial workplace. The Canadian Safety Code also outlines several procedures concerning how various injury problems and difficulties must be dealt with. It is easy to note that in areas where these programs are in place, workers feel safer and therefore are much more willing to work harder for the success of their corporations.

One of the greatest achievements made is the concept of flexi-time for most workers in the big corporations. This development is exciting to many workers because it provides them with the opportunity to decide on their own work schedules and hours of work. These days, many workers have the chance to settle work shifts that are suitable for them. The good thing about this is that the worker is able to select time schedules that fit neatly into all other schedules and programs of the day. Above all, not only do these workers have the freedom to make these selections, they also can switch schedules easily with their colleagues in times when such switches become necessary, useful, and convenient for all who are involved.

One great advantage of flexi-time work schedules is that they provide the worker with the chance to fit other items like educational programs (i.e., training, seminars, conferences, etc.) into their daily schedules. Many workers can now take evening classes and still work. In certain circumstances, work schedules are selected so that willing employees can attend day and night classes, if they so desire. Indeed, this is a satisfying and refreshing opportunity for every worker who experiences it. The worker is no longer devoted solely to a life of work, but also sets aside time for personal development through part-time educational programs.

In view of this, it is obvious that there have been significant changes to working conditions since the era of the industrial revolution. Programs that have been developed in the last fifty years have given hope to many employees.

Flexi-time work schedules have not only allowed workers to improve on their individual skills, but have also given them the opportunity to learn new skills. In a similar way, the newly acquired skills pave the way for employees to earn higher incomes from the use of these skills. I argue that such increases in employee incomes and benefits have led to huge improvements in the relationships between management and employees. The rivalry between these groups is, however, not over yet.

The old view that "employees are money-making machines" is dwindling and gradually dying out. Employers are not always solely concerned with maximizing profit as such, but are gradually realizing that improvements in working conditions will in the long run lead to increases in productivity and returns. As they continue to put more and more resources into employee educational programs, they will sooner or later reap the hidden benefits.

Innovation and technical changes have also led to improvements in worker conditions. Even though some labor-saving innovations and technical changes have occurred, we notice that some of these changes have reduced the stress and strain on the employee. Machines have not only led to the reduction of the number of hours an employee can put into the production process, but have also led to increased productivity and job satisfaction. It can be argued, therefore, that the modern-day employee does not necessarily have to put fourteen to eighteen hours per day into the production process. In some circumstances, the employee is only expected to press electrical buttons to set the machines and robots to work. Even though this development has not yet widely spread into all sectors of the economy, it is true that its inception is a great achievement and one hopes that workers in all industries can benefit from it.

THE SURVIVAL AND GROWTH OF THE CAPITALIST COMPANY

Karl Marx's analysis of capitalism and prediction of its final demise seem to have concentrated on certain factors to the detriment and neglect of others. He carefully and incisively discussed the destructive processes of capitalism without giving any significant consideration to other positive changes that might occur to perpetuate capitalist economic systems. Indeed, Marx failed to recognize the colossal growth that was about to take place in primitive capitalism. Capitalistic business activities grew from unlimited to limited liability companies. Marx unfortunately did not foresee how technological advancement could lead to lower production costs, which would in turn allow the masses to purchase goods and services produced by capitalists. He also failed to foresee the evolution of financial systems and their accompanying product lines. These developments have led to the falsification of Marx's prophecy concerning the demise of the capitalist TNC and its economic system.

THE ABILITY TO SURVIVE

One of the greatest gifts that every living thing possesses is the ability to survive in its habitat. This principle of life has been illustrated by nature itself and is seen all around us. For example, in the wide world of animals, every animal consistently strives to survive in its habitat, though preying animals constantly lord it over weaker, nonpreying ones. It is exciting to know that mother nature has equipped each of these animals with interesting tools, skills, and techniques for survival in its own environment. In a similar way, in the plant kingdom all plants vie for water, nutrients, and sunlight. Each of these plants does its best to obtain each of these items to survive.

One of the most interesting observations in all this drama is the survival instinct (ability) that human beings, animals, and plants possess. Regardless of the environmental conditions, each of these living things does its best to survive in its habitat among all others. The continuing striving for survival can either be competitive or cooperative. The greater one's sensitivity and ability to survive, the faster the development of survival techniques and procedures. Those plants that reproduce larger amounts of offspring have greater chances of survival than those with fewer offspring. Thus, where the question of survival comes into play, the probability of survival is higher for plants and animals with larger number of offspring than those with scanty numbers (Stebbins 1971, 68).

It has also been observed by many geneticists that organisms that have developed, maintained, and improved upon their methods of taking care of their young have higher chances of survival in their habitat. This is mostly the case when these species produce few offspring and spend most of their energies to care for the young ones. This makes intuitive sense because, for survival, every little thing requires a high degree of protection from its predators and enemies. In addition, the care from its parents in terms of food is essential for its growth and development. It seems evident, therefore, that excellent care for and protection of offspring are required for survival in every habitat within which each living thing finds itself.

A vine that grows among huge deciduous forest trees may have to strive for water, soil nutrients, and sunlight to survive. Any such vine that is unable to develop its own ability to acquire these basic needs may die or be dwarfed in its habitat. Thus, the survival instinct usually makes these vines strive to improve on their climbing or creeping abilities in order to climb up the branches of the bigger and more dependable plants as fast as they are able to reach the sunshine. Even though this climbing process, leading to the top of the highest trees for sunlight, may take a long time to accomplish, the determination of each vine makes its survival possible. The story of human beings, plants, and animals is similar. All these observations seem to confirm the view, "survival of the fittest." Stebbins (1971, 68) observed the following:

Another type of competition which very commonly leads to natural selection is the superior ability of an organism to take advantage of its surrounding medium, so that it grows faster and crowds out its less successful competitors. This kind of competition is very common in plants. If not removed from a field, weeds will grow faster than the crop which has been planted, and, although they rarely kill the crop plants outright, they often reduce or eliminate their ability to make seeds and reproduce. In many of the warmer parts of the United States, Bermuda grass (*Cynodon dactylon*) will establish itself in lawns. Because it can make more efficient use of the soil, water, and temperature regime available to it, this weedy grass will often crowd out and actually kill the more desirable but less tough lawn grass. Among animals this type of competition has been recorded in sedentary forms such as barnacles.

When we observe either plants or animals that seem to run out of things to do to survive, we realize that their end will come sooner or later. It is a well-known fact that there are serious diseases, sicknesses, and other accidental phenomena that can terminate the life of any living things abruptly. In cases where these problems are solved and diseases healed, life continues toward growth and maturity. Living things that resist inimical environmental changes have greater chances of survival. That is, these living things develop the ability to adapt to changing environmental circumstances and conditions. They are able to develop and maintain immunities against viruses, germs, and so on.

Thus, changing environmental conditions lead all living things to develop ways and means for survival and perpetration of their kind. They do not succumb easily to the vagaries of the weather and climate, but do their best to maintain life and living. It is through this process that some living things develop newer characteristics (through mutations) different from those of their parents in order to survive comfortably in a changing and probably perpetually harsh environment. These changing characteristics may promote survival by means of their reproduction systems or resilience to changing environmental conditions.

In what follows, I discuss some of the major developments by capitalist businesses to boost and to encourage business activities in a capitalist economy. The aim is to show that the innovative, inventive, and creative powers of capitalism are so strong that they seem to deal successfully with its own problems. In the discussions, I will draw parallels between the survival of the capitalist TNC and the animal and plant worlds.

THE DYNAMISM OF CAPITALISM

Social, economic, and political institutions also behave like plants and animals. An avowed human-created system may die if those who manage it are unable to either deal with existing inherent problems or fail to devise techniques to improve on its performances and adapt it to its existing environment. Human-created institutions come and go as long as they fail to serve the needs of society progressively. In a similar way, if they fail to develop techniques to solve existing problems, they are exterminated. In light of these principles, Karl Marx, after having carefully scrutinized capitalism and its inherent problems, difficulties, and crises, could not foresee how correctly capitalism could solve its deeply rooted problems success-fully. His staunch belief in the process of dialectical materialism led him to the strong conviction and conclusion that the inherent seeds of destruction in capital-ism, once sown, could no longer be dealt with successfully. This belief led him to prophesy that, in the long run, capitalism would destroy itself and be replaced by socialism and hence communism (see details in Chapter 4). It appears, therefore, that Karl Marx did not think carefully about the fact that capitalism could develop structures that would prevent its own destruction. Had he given deeper thought to this issue in the light of examples from the plant and animal kingdoms, he would probably have come out with a much more different theory regarding the final state of capitalism.

Over the years, as the battle between capitalism and socialism ensued, capital-ism realized its difficulties, identified its problems, and began to put relevant structures in place to deal with them. People in capitalist societies do not always fail to perceive that capitalism, an inanimate economic system with its own insti-tutions, needs to be organized and run by people to face its problems and difficul-ties head-on. Rather, capitalists have developed and erected structures and procedures to help the system to both maintain and perpetuate growth and devel-opment. Weisskopf (1979) pointed out that

Production is organized and investment is undertaken by capitalists in order to make prof-its; a fall in the average rate of profits—and consequently in the expected profitability of new investment—is bound sooner or later to discourage such new investment. This is a major determinant of both the level and the rate of growth of aggregate output and em-ployment. Thus it is quite reasonable on theoretical grounds to argue that a falling rate of profits will ultimately lead—via profit expectations and the rate of investment—to an eco-nomic crisis in which the levels and rates of growth of output and employment are de-pressed.

Note, however, that this phenomenon does not necessarily have to lead either to a crisis situation or to the destruction of the capitalist business. The falling rate of profits has the tendency to act as a signal to the management of the capitalist firm to reevaluate its business performance and activities. This event is more or less like a stock-taking process whereby the managers and leaders of the capitalist TNC examine their company's tactical and long-term plans and goals. In this way, any existing bottlenecks are usually identified and carefully dealt with appropri-ately. It is only companies whose management is unable to discover what the sources of the declining profit are that run into serious economic difficulties. It is therefore a great mistake to think that declining profits always implies an unsolv-able crisis situation for the capitalist company. Even though the transnational capi-talist company may experience significant declines for a long period of time, there is always the chance for its leadership to reorganize its plans and programs to ef-fectively deal with both escalating business problems and expected crises. The death of the company is not accepted as an easy way out. It is usually resisted and fought against through new ideas and programs and ongoing reorganization. In recent years, the various responses to existing crises situations at General Motors, Chrysler, and many other capitalist companies are excellent examples of how the capitalist firm works to overcome its problems.

Most Marxists speak and write as if all crises and problems have no solutions. Sometimes they argue as if every crisis leads to destruction regardless of what the management of the TNC may do to contain it. It is by this belief that they are usually misled to reach such wrong conclusions regarding the demise of the capitalist system. They fail to realize that most capitalist business institutions, through the ingenuity of their management and workforce, develop and possess crisis-management procedures, technologies, and tools. This development seems to have eluded the imaginations and intellects of many Marxists. No wonder most of their predictions are far wide of the mark.

A few scholars have observed that the capitalist owner of the transnational company does not allow its business to be easily destroyed by crises resulting from declining profits. Even if declining profits begin to create problems and crises for the capitalist, there is always ongoing attempts to contain them. For example, Ross and Trachte (1990, 30) suggested that if systemic features exist in capitalism that lead to continuing decline in profits, the capitalist will do everything possible to fight them. "Such pressures will be resisted. The institutional forms of investor resistance to such tendencies may be successful in a given moment of development. The resultant institutional innovations may fall short of transformation to another mode of production, yet, over time, produce change in the way capitalism functions. Such a sequence would mask empirical manifestation of declining rates of profit; yet simultaneously propel the system toward a new variant of capitalism." It is an undeniable fact that every living thing and institution has the power and the will to survive by dealing with its problems and crises. During crisis situations, the strong will to survive always leads the management of capitalist TNCs to develop new ways and methods for success in business. In all these situations, the capitalist transnational company remains strong and powerful in the global village (see detailed discussion in Chapter 7). Its traditional way of doing things is either revised, transformed, or discarded to ensure the survival of the capitalist business enterprise.

One powerful tool for the survival of TNCs is restructuring of existing operations and systems. Restructuring is usually undertaken to either control and contain the crisis or to mitigate and neutralize it. In this way, the behavior of capitalist TNCs mimics that of plants and animals that do all they can in order to continuously receive sufficient soil nutrients, water, air, and the proper amounts of sunshine to survive. Just as a plant may have to bend its stem, roots, or branches in order to obtain its basic necessities of life, so also does the capitalist transnational company. As a system of production, it continuously arms itself with new methods, new developments, new innovations, new inventions, new technologies, and new ideas to deal with its problems and difficulties. As a business enterprise, it strives to survive to serve the needs of its owners. Though its survival may not be beneficial to all people in society, business tycoons in capitalist societies make sure that the capitalist legacy that was passed on to them by their predecessors does not die. Its mantle is passed on to future generations who are also expected to do likewise. This is one basic reason why the system does not break down suddenly and die when it begins to experience crisis.

It is therefore more enlightening to view every economic crisis in the capitalist economic system as a major source of challenge which, when tackled appropriately, leads to excellent restructuring and the development of new procedures to deal with such crises. History has proven this observation to be true. If it were not so, all major crises (i.e., the 1929–1930 Great Depression, the 1973 and the 1979–1982 energy crises, and many others) experienced in capitalist economic systems should have led to the actual collapse of global business operations.

Global capitalists in every society behave like ants in their colony. As is well-known, ants usually drag any food item into their storehouses for current or future use. In circumstances where obstacles exist, ants try many different ways and work continuously until they are able to carry the food item to where they want it to be stored. They are not usually deterred by encumbrances they meet during their transportation process. These obstacles are usually viewed by the ants as challenges that must be faced up to and overcome. These little insects usually devise new procedures (technologies of effective and efficient transportation?) to bypass obstacles along their transportation routes. The global capitalist's behavior can be likened to that of these ants. Like ants, the global capitalist is a problem solver. Faced with severe difficulties and problems, the capitalist does not attempt to duck or avoid them. The problems and crises are squarely faced and dealt with in the most appropriate and meaningful way. In situations where redirection is required due to necessities, the capitalist does not hesitate to do so. Braudel (1979) suggested the following:

The long-term is made up of a succession of repeated movements, with variations and revivals, periods of decline, adaptation, or stagnation—what sociologists would describe as structuration, destructuration and restructuration. Sometimes too there are major breaks with the past and the industrial revolution was certainly one such, but I would maintain, rightly or wrongly, that throughout even this formidable transformation, capitalism remained essentially true to itself. Is it not in the nature of capitalism, a sort of rule of the game, that it thrives on change, drawing strength from it, being ready at any moment to expand or contract itself to the dimensions of all-enveloping context which, as we have seen, limits in every period the possibilities of the human economy everywhere in the world?

Turning weaknesses, problems, and crises into strengths is what global capitalism is all about. Indeed, to survive, it must. As will become obvious in subsequent sections of this chapter, modern-day corporations originating from the capitalist economic system (just like their predecessors from the twelfth century to today) do not specialize in any specific business or economic activity. They plunge themselves into almost every sector of the economy. Sometimes entry into a specific sector comes as a result of a severe and devastating crisis in another. When this happens, the global business manager is apt to shift resources into other more lucrative and promising sectors of the whole economy. Braudel (1979) noted further that

When the first fantastic profits of the cotton boom in Britain fell, in the face of competition, to 2% or 3%, the accumulated capital was diverted to other industries, steel and railways for instance; to an even greater extent though, there was a return to finance capitalism, to banking, to more speculation than ever on the stock exchange, to major international trade, to the profits derived from exploration of the colonies, to government loans, etc. . . . Its sphere of action has undoubtedly widened, since all sectors of the economy are now open to it and in particular it has very largely penetrated that of production . . . and since it does have the freedom to choose, capitalism can always change horses in mid-stream—the secret of its vitality.

Buist (1974) argued that even though capitalism does get sick every now and then, it surely never dies. Even though some business opportunities and ventures may be annihilated, new doors are usually opened for both new and old capitalist businesses. Those companies that survive are able to continue to grow and above all nurture the system toward continuous survival. Thus, for the ardent global-capitalist business manager, the ability to improvise and innovate, the aptness to adapt to changing business climate, the ingenuity to foster new ideas and/or ventures, the will to exist and defend freedom and private property ownership, and so on have all served as the unfailing fuel in its engine of survival, growth, and development.

THE DRIVING FORCES: TURNING WEAKNESS INTO STRENGTH

As noted in the preceding discussions, it is extremely important to add a few more items that can be considered as part and parcel of driving forces of the capitalist system. From the extended analysis presented, the principal tools usually employed by the capitalist corporation to deal with its crisis situations and problems are presented in the following sections.

The Process of Creative Destruction

It seems to be the case that most crises arising in capitalist economies are endogenous in that they are created by the production process. During this process, some capital is destroyed in various ways and forms. However, it is through this that new capital (investment) is generated. As the system strives to recreate and improve on its own performance, it goes through some form of creative destructive process. This process is able to foster capitalist growth and development rather than destruction. It is the case that during this process, as long as the rate at which new capital is created through the development and discovery of new investment opportunities is greater than the rate at which old capital is used up (depreciation), the capitalist system shows no weak signs of being destroyed. It is usually the case that in the capitalist economy the learning process is not only dynamic, but also leads to the creation of more opportunities than it has used up.

The process of creative destruction would only lead to the destruction of the capitalist business and its economic activities if capitalist societies were environments (worlds) within which there is no learning. This is usually the case because, in such a world, as soon as any investment opportunity is used up, the capital stock of that society remains idle. Thus, by the time all productive opportunities are all used up, the society will all of a sudden be faced with a situation of huge piles of idle capital that cannot be used for any productive activities. In such a society, this phenomenon brings into being the decay and the demise of business opportunities and activities. This is actually a prediction of neoclassical growth theory that takes the law of diminishing returns into account. That is, as the stock of capital grows and piles up, the resulting marginal product of each additional (successive) unit of capital acquired declines over time, approaching zero. It is therefore the case that in societies where there is little or no learning, capitalism would grow and thrive as long as investment opportunities are not used up. At their depletion, the system collapses. Unfortunately for the Marxists, this is not the case in the capitalist societies we know of.

In most capitalist societies, there is a continuous influx of learning and the development of new information and knowledge that make the capitalist corporation continue to survive. Lipsey, Purvis, and Steiner (1991, 824–825) observed that, in the world where there is effective learning taking place, "Researchers develop basic ideas for new ways of producing existing products or wholly new products. Firms spend money to develop these ideas into usable form. Together such research and development (R&D) provides a fund of new investment opportunities. When learning occurs, what matters is how rapidly the MEC [marginal efficiency of capital] schedule shifts relative to the amount of capital investment being undertaken."

In view of these observations, it can be argued that the Marxian view of capitalist development is actually couched on the classical view of economic growth. This view, however, fails to recognize that future technological innovation and advancement have the power and potentiality to keep and maintain the growth viability of the capitalist system. The capitalist economic system has the power and ability to generate new investment opportunities through R&D as fast as existing productive opportunities are being used up. Indeed, the creative destructive process may not necessarily lead to the annihilation of the capitalist economic system and its business corporations.

Competition

Growing global competition among transnational companies is also a strong driving force behind capitalist survival. Global capitalism has successfully situated capital all over the world to take advantage of raw materials, lower labor costs, and political stability. Because of the fierceness of global competition, each firm strives to innovate new products, improve upon quality, train and educate its labor force, and also devise new technologies to help reduce production costs. Thus, the fear of losing one's market share serves as a stimulating force, urging the capitalist corporation to grow and face up to the challenges of escalating global competition. As is usually the case, some inefficient companies are driven out of the competition. But for the survivors, the drive is always for survival.

Mobility of Capital (Domestic and Global)

Global capitalism has one great advantage. That is its growing ability to move from one area of lower returns, political instability, higher labor costs, and so on to other areas where these factors are more favorable. Thus, the chance and freedom for the transnational company to be mobile provides a vehicle that helps in the survival and establishment process of capitalist global business. Even within the same country, the capitalist corporation is able to do likewise. Again, observe that capitalists act in practical ways by situating their capital resources in much more productive areas. The opportunity to do so is in itself a survival dynamic that underlies the capitalist growth and development process.

Subsidiaries and Acquisitions

The ability of the transnational corporation to develop many subsidiaries and opportunities as its own viable offspring having the power and capacity to survive is strong and effective. The larger the number of subsidiaries developed or acquired by a particular transnational corporation, the higher the likelihood of success and survival by successfully dealing with crises situations in one or more areas.

The Differential Rates of Profits and Losses

The differential rates of profits and losses in each subsidiary or unit of the transnational corporation not only creates a greater chance of company survival, but also reveals that the less successful subsidiaries may not necessarily die in a crisis situation, but are usually aided by the more successful ones with higher profits. Even when the severity of the crisis leads to the death of some subsidiaries, the system may not necessarily collapse, except in cases where the ensuing crisis annihilates all subsidiaries and the parent company simultaneously. This scenario is, however, highly unlikely.

The Changing Concerns, Needs, and Problems of Society

Every society has its own concerns, needs, and problems. For this reason, any TNC that desires to be successful in the global marketplace must effectively and efficiently address these concerns, needs, and problems of the society in question.

Worst of all, these concerns, needs, and problems are dynamic rather than static. In view of this observation, it is clear that the TNC not only has to concern itself with these issues of the society under consideration, but must also be aware of the various changes taking place on a daily basis in each of these areas. The TNC, by trying to help society deal with its pertinent needs and problems by providing the relevant goods and services, must also monitor the various changes that take place in the areas of concerns, needs, and problems.

TNCs that are concerned about maintaining their global market shares must always recognize the changing needs of the society in which they do business. This is one way whereby new technology is developed to serve the needs of society. Note that transnational companies that are not abreast with the changing needs of society will have no future in the global marketplace.

The Development of New and Improved Procedures

Many capitalist TNCs are continuously developing, updating, and evolving better procedures for organizing, managing, and nurturing newly established or acquired subsidiaries. Some corporations develop and concentrate on fewer subsidiaries to cater effectively for them.

TNCs usually concentrate on subsidiaries that are more resilient to changing demand and market shares through the strong competition in the specific industry. Unprofitable ventures are usually sold and the proceeds redirected and rechannelled into other more productive and lucrative ventures.

New Methods of Business Adaptation

TNCs are in the habit of developing new ways and methods to increase their adaptability in the open and fierce competitive marketplace. Their characteristics and ways of doing business are in a state of ongoing flux and movement in order to accommodate daily problems and crises. The global company changes its behavior and traditional ways of operation to suit current competitive market conditions.

In capitalist societies, some businesses and companies have been in operation for many years. During all these years, efforts have been made and resources used to establish the business. Given the record of these long histories, it is not all that easy for owners of a company to let it die without having done their best to save and protect it. In many cases, different programs and activities are undertaken to ensure that the long-established business reputation is maintained.

As noted elsewhere, the TNC is always open to new ideas and better ways for organizing and carrying out business and economic activities. The older businesses are always more than willing to try new ideas that can be of assistance to them to help improve their sales and profit margins. Sometimes such businesses encourage their employees to attend informative conferences where they could come across new ideas that can be exploited and utilized for the benefit of the company. Businesses also organize their own internal competition for ideas. Thus, as long as the TNC is able to develop and follow through with new and relevant ideas, it will continue to improve its own business performance for success and survival. In many cases, these ideas are not only developed in relation to product innovation or invention, but also in the areas of efficient business management, global and domestic marketing, sales financing, business diversification, and so on. It is a real challenge for the business to strive to survive in this way.

One of the greatest flexibilities of global capitalism is the willingness and commitment to change. Capitalist businesses that were established many years ago have now learned that times and circumstances are changing. The characteristics of various market segments served are also changing day by day. Businesses that came into existence a few years ago also know that while some of the needs they came to serve have disappeared (or are disappearing), others are growing in strength. Thus, by recognizing these changes, many businesses continue to make desired changes that are necessary for survival and company effectiveness. It is what the customer desires that must be provided. Even though this process usually exerts too much strain on the corporation, it protects itself against obsolescence by becoming committed to meaningful changes that maintain its relevance and viability in modern society. In view of this, Naisbitt (1982, 87–88) noted the following:

The kinds of changes that are forcing us to think long-term, however, are so pervasive and so powerful that what is really required is that we completely rethink our businesses as part of the shift to the long-term. One way to do this is by applying the "Law of the Situation." The Law of the Situation is a term coined in 1904 by Mary Parker Follett, the first management consultant in the United States. She had a window-shade company as a client and persuaded its owners they were really in the light-control business. That realization expanded their opportunities enormously. The Law of the Situation asks the question "what business are you really in?"

The implication of this law is that as business conditions and consumer demands, tastes, and preferences change, the business unit has to reevaluate its usefulness and viability in the initial services and products with which it began the business. When this task is successfully accomplished in view of the ongoing changes that occur in the global business environment, it is likely that the TNC may reorganize and reconceptualize its purpose and hence reposition itself.

There is also the commitment to create a more vital new image as global conditions require. For example, any company that has gained a bad reputation in the community because of crooked business deals in the past, can improve its image by changing its business strategies, policies, and attitudes. If in the past it was noted for the ruthless exploitation of consumers through the setting of higher prices, it can restrain itself from doing so. If it has been accused of environmental pollution and destruction, it can change this image over time by getting involved with programs aimed at environmental cleanliness. Participation in the economy in this way will usually lead people to observe and applaud the new commitments of the business. This phenomenal change will lead to attitude alterations on the part of consumers. Thus, by developing and utilizing more effective ways of carrying out its business goals, the corporation is able to win the approbation of its customers. Indeed, businesses that behave in this manner have the ability and power to fly through stormy and very destructive business clouds.

This is what it means to say that a business has a great deal of flexibility and sensitivity. It is flexible in terms of its own organization and production and the kinds of goods and services offered, and it is sensitive in that it responds to the needs and desires of customers (both new and old). To significantly benefit from the qualities of flexibility and sensitivity, many TNCs continue to conduct a series of market and consumer surveys every year (or within a well-defined time period) in order to obtain relevant information for the planning process. For example, most fast-food restaurants exhibit their flexibility and sensitivity to customers by not preparing food items in advance, waiting until the actual order is placed by the customer. The attempt is always made to satisfy the customer by offering exactly what he or she orders. This is usually the case because a satisfied customer is a repeat customer. Customer service is, therefore, a vital part of the survival strategy. It is the determination to survive as a business that forces each capitalist business to act in this way. In view of these observations, it can be argued that the capitalist business thrives during crisis situations. Roll (1964, 21) noted that "the systems of philosophy . . . continue to live; and whenever critical convulsions occur in the economic system, their influence grows. When belief in established institutions and practices decline, the search for comprehensive philosophies of life and rival policies compete in the name of one or another . . ."

It is therefore the case that crisis and its accompanying rate of growth of the capitalist business venture are twins. One cannot be observed without the other. The rate of growth of one might lead to ongoing changes in the other. Regardless of which one precedes the other, it cannot be said with strong confidence which change paves the way for the other. The reason the corporation's influence grows over time is that, after having overcome a crisis situation, it puts in place relevant and effective tools and structures to overcome the conditions that brought about the crisis situation in the first place. The global capitalist's vigor and enthusiasm to survive must not be underestimated. Capitalism as an economic system will continue to build structures that will help it maintain itself in every regard. Wright (1978) noted, "The growth on a massive scale of consumer credit, built-in obsolescence of many consumer durables, the wide range of state interventions in the economy of the Keynesian variety, and so forth, all represent conscious strategies to increase the rate of unproductive demand and thus avoid realization/underconsumption crises. . . . These solutions themselves create new problems which the capitalist economy is only beginning to face."

One cannot envisage how easy it will be for capitalists to not continue to develop and use effective survival tools. As a matter of fact, capitalist companies that fail to devise new procedures to deal successfully with existing problems and crises will go bankrupt in the long run. As noted, no scholars naïvely argue that the failure of one or two businesses in capitalist societies is a sign that the system will be totally destroyed. Recalling our discussion on the survival instinct of plants and animals, we note again that the death of a single plant of a species does not necessarily imply the death of all others of that species family. Others that are successful in adapting to harsh environmental conditions will indeed be among the survivors. Their species may therefore exist for a very long time. In the word of Wright (1978), it is always true that "Real capitalists are under constant pressure to innovate because of competition with other capitalists, not simply class struggle with workers, and in the competitive struggle it does not matter whether costs are cut by savings on labor or on constant capital. . . . In fact, a strong argument can be made which suggests that in advanced capitalist economies, there should be a tendency for an increase to occur in the pressures for capital-saving innovations relative to labor-saving technological innovations." In addition to all these developments, one must not gloss over the many developments that have led to improvements in employee living conditions.

DIVERSIFICATION OF BUSINESS AND ECONOMIC ACTIVITIES

In the recent past, many modern-day business corporations became engaged in programs of business diversification. Many businesses today spread their business operating tentacles into all kinds of markets and business ventures. The basic reason for doing so is to avoid the danger of putting one's financial resources into a single and volatile venture. The more highly diversified a company is, the greater the chances of financial success (as long as the company does not spread itself too thin). This is so because, while some elements of certain investment portfolios in certain sectors of the economy may not be doing well, others will be very successful. Returns from these successful ventures of the business can be used to cover the losses of other unproductive ones.

Corporations are also into holding assets in other businesses and several sectors of the whole economy. This has led to an increase in industrial diversification of production. For example, giant corporations in the modern era continue to invest in different productive ventures. Thus, when one area of business investment is sagging, another booming one is able to make up for the losses incurred in declining businesses. It is therefore not uncommon to observe one particular company getting involved in such areas of the economy as banking, insurance, agro-business, fruit plantation, fast food, furniture, electrical appliances, grocery store chains, photography, and many others.

The ingenuity of global capitalism in this regard should be commended, because its strong innovative and inventive powers serve as bypasses to the roadblocks pointed out by Karl Marx. It is either able to deal effectively with its problems or able to devise ways and means for riding over the shoulders of its pertinent business problems and seeds of destruction. The tools employed by global capitalist TNCs for this bypass surgery include R&D, ongoing market surveys, inventions, and innovation. Through these tools, global capitalism is able to identify some of the key areas of the economy that may be promising for successful business ventures. Corporations that are committed to these programs usually end up diversifying their business activities. Note, however, that diversification is a program that demands much care, caution, and careful planning.

Although the principle of business diversification is not a new one, it has been successfully and effectively used by major corporations in the twentieth century. The fear of business failure because of declining demand in various sectors of the economy and industries serves as incentive for businesses to look for other areas of investment where they are not known to be traditionally involved. This development eluded the intelligence of those who believed that the global capitalist company is not capable of rising above its problems and inherent difficulties. Examples of companies that have engaged themselves in massive diversification programs include General Electric Company, Ford Motor Company, Boeing Company, Motorola, IBM, and many others. Each of these companies has its own international marketing programs, strategies, sales promotion techniques, company credit and financing schemes, and so on. All these programs are used by each company to effectively deal with some of the inherent problems of the capitalist system.

Because of the availability of these financial systems and diversification schemes, businesses have developed a series of procedures to help step up aggregate demand for their goods and services. For example, many companies try to encourage individual consumers to purchase gift items for family members and friends. Such festivities as Mother's Day, Father's Day, Valentine's Day, Easter, Christmas, and many others are all taken advantage of by businesses. These festivals reveal the times of the year when demand grows for certain goods and services. Thus, by popularizing and promoting such activities, businesses are able to keep aggregate demand as high as possible throughout the year. Effective advertising programs, filled with enticing messages, bring in informed consumers to purchase goods and services.

All these phenomena reveal that the goal of the global corporation is no longer concentrated on profit maximization alone, but also on securing the survival of the business enterprise. Goudzwaard (1979) noted, "When the business enterprise emancipated itself from the influence of individual investors and developed into a going concern, the goal of a maximum profit also had to be surrendered. In its place we encounter a new dominant good, namely, securing the continued existence of the corporation or—to employ current jargon—system maintenance. Profit maximization as a rule becomes of secondary importance except in situations where a certain minimum profit level is threatened" (see also Galbraith 1968).

This reveals that corporations usually act in direct and positive ways to maintain growing demand and their own success and survival. Modern-day corporations do not live at the mercy of historical fluctuations in the aggregate demand for their products. They act in conscious ways to keep the company going.

Once again, Karl Marx failed to envisage this phenomenal development in the financial organization in capitalistic economies. His argument that workers would be so impoverished that they would not be able to purchase the goods and services produced by industrialists is no longer relevant in the modern era. This is so because consumers who possess credit cards can use them to obtain goods and services they normally could not have purchased because of lack of sufficient financial resources. Capitalism, therefore, thrives in the environment of well-developed and well-organized financial systems.

The development of general credit systems has allowed banks to finance capitalist production as long as individual consumers are willing to take these loans to finance their own day-to-day purchases. It therefore removes uncertainties and fluctuations in the demand facing the modern corporation. Consumers can easily finance many items they desire to purchase according to their own wish. In what follows I discuss, in detail, specific company financial systems that have led to phenomenal improvements in the cash flow of each of the companies under study.

Company credit or finance schemes have been successful for two basic reasons. First, each of these schemes offers its customers lower interest rates than those available in the traditional banking institutions and credit unions. The lower interest rates usually serve as a means of luring consumers to take loans through company financial schemes rather than through the banks and credit unions. Second, these company credit schemes are not as rigorous as those of the banks and credit unions. The individual does not necessarily have to go through credit checks and intensive scrutiny in order to qualify to use any of these schemes. Customers of these companies could even be granted credit (loans) for purposes and purchases other than the products of the company granting the credit. Indeed, if each of these companies is able to continuously maintain its credit systems and makes them feasible and easily accessible to many more customers, its sales volume and profits would continue to climb.

In general, Karl Marx's point of poverty depriving workers and consumers of the ability to buy goods and services is no longer tenable in all cases. Corporations have now created the opportunities for everyone who desires to buy goods and services to acquire them now and pay later. These days, the individual consumer does not necessarily have to have the required funds available on hand before purchasing any items. All he or she needs to do is to approach the dealer or manufacturer and ask for financing. Usually, companies are ready to finance individual purchases as long as the credit-risk rating is identified and taken into consideration.

These ingenious financial developments have not only revealed the power and ability of capitalist corporations to succeed, but also the striving to survive, grow, and develop. What they have not achieved, however, is getting rid of the scarcity problem. In addition, one cannot argue conclusively that these developments have actually helped people to improve on their own well-being. These issues will be taken up in subsequent chapters.

CONCLUSION

It must be pointed out that most of these new developments were not perceived by Karl Marx at the time he conceptualized and crystallized his views about capitalist development. In reality, many things have (so far) taken a different route than suggested by Marx. The capitalist's instinct and drive for survival have been growing stronger and stronger in giant corporations throughout the years. It seems that, as new problems surface, most viable companies devise their own techniques to deal with them. As these techniques become more effective and efficient, other companies jump on the bandwagon and use these same (or similar) techniques to foster the survival of their own business and economic ventures. Indeed, as long as companies are able to respond to changing market conditions, it is not all that easy to support Marx's view concerning the final demise of capitalism.

In the final analysis, however, the face, nature, and state of the capitalist economic system will continue to change. This, in itself, is a reasonable proposition in that the system survives by developing and designing new procedures for dealing with observed problems and difficulties. As these new procedures are put in place, the nature and characteristics of the capitalist system are transformed day by day. One hundred years from now, all things being equal (i.e., the human race continues to exist on planet Earth), the capitalist economic system may not experience any physical and violent revolutions whereby the proletariat will overthrow the bourgeoisie and establish their own socialist state and finally a communist rule. Its character, however, will be changed completely. This will be the case because the capitalist economy will always continue to deal with and, above all, accommodate changes that occur in its free-market environment. A physical revolution is not necessarily required (or mandatory) for effective and workable changes to be effected in the capitalist economic system. The behavior and organizations of TNCs faintly reveal what the future will be.

CHAPTER SIX

FURTHER HUMAN ATTEMPTS AT SOCIAL ENGINEERING AND GLOBAL DEVELOPMENT

In this world, both men and women not only like to enjoy their lives, but also try to make the best out of it. "Pleasure" is what most men and women seek and go after; however, they hate anything that inflicts severe pain and suffering. Indeed, many human activities are designed and geared toward the attainment of these purposes. To maximize pleasure and minimize pain is a must for most people. The burning desire to achieve these objectives is increasingly controlling and directing most human attempts to have full control of these. Scarcity, the central focus of the economizing problem has also contributed in many significant ways toward people's desire to deal with pleasure and pain. For many centuries, men and women have tried to come up with different types of programs to enhance human welfare.

In view of this, every society continuously engages itself in efforts aimed at promoting and advancing the borders of social engineering. These attempts have led, in many cases, to significant ideas, theories, and principles that have led to new inventions and innovations. As is well-known to everyone (see details in Chapters 4 and 5), the technological achievements of humanity are incredible. The gains made in the areas of transportation, telecommunications, electronics, computers, dieting, physical exercises, health, medicine, knowledge, ideologies, military surveillance and intelligence, artificial intelligence, education and training, food, and many others are beyond our wildest expectations or imaginations.

For many generations, humanity has tried in many different ways to relentlessly search for solutions to its pertinent social, economic, political, and cultural problems. The ideas of national reconciliation (South Africa), multiculturalism (Canada), melting pot (the United States), collective national identity (Africa and Eastern Europe), and so on have been tried as measures to deal with visible racial tensions in many countries. Every year, many plans, policies, programs, and projects are fashioned and implemented to solve social, economic, political, and cultural problems. Governments are in the habit of funding huge research and development programs. Completed research programs usually lead to findings that are used as the primary basis for the formulation of theories and principles regarding existing problems. These theories and principles usually serve as the actual foundations for all social, economic, and political policies.

In this chapter, a selected group of programs aimed at social engineering are defined and analyzed in detail. Evidence of the continuing failure of human institutions and systems is also presented and critically examined. Conventional attempts made to rationalize the continuing failure of these programs are also highlighted. The concept of the human factor (HF) is introduced in this chapter. Its significant role in determining the magnitude of the ongoing failures and problems of the social, economic, political, and educational institutions in society is discussed in detail in Chapter 8.

While these SEPE problems have persisted for centuries, men and women have never ceased to look for relevant solutions. In fact, in cases where people feel that they have found answers to existing hindrances to social, economic, political, and cultural progress, several other problems are birthed. Indeed, since human pain and suffering are undesirable, human ingenuity is being used to search for solutions to deal with all human problems successfully. It seems to me that while all humanity is somehow locked up in a world that is infested with ongoing difficulties and challenges, the solutions sought by most societies have been powered by intellectualized personal ideologies that are usually too frail to perform their intended tasks. Yet the battle to obtain actual solutions has not only been raging for generations, it has also been carried in many directions. Humanity is always devising new technologies and methodologies to help deal with the human predicament successfully.

In this search process, men and women have developed and designed many academic disciplines to facilitate and enhance the human search for solutions. People go to educational and training institutions to acquire knowledge that is expected to generate good understanding of and solutions to human problems. In this regard, models, theories, and principles created in such fields as political science, sociology, economics, history, religious studies, mathematics, chemistry, physics, biology, languages, psychology, psychiatry, medicine, engineering, artificial intelligence, computer science, electronics, and the like have all been appealed to and used to design specific solutions.

The ongoing search for workable solutions has led to the growing deification of specific economic systems (i.e., either capitalism or socialism or both), political systems, science, and technology in different parts of the world. Since the search process has never been minimized, it has led to significant developments in human theorizing all through history. For example, the industrial revolution not only brought solutions to certain old problems, it has also birthed new and more complicated problems. During the era of the industrial revolution, men and women not only developed new technologies, but also improved and perfected existing ones. New institutional structures evolved to facilitate the growing intercourse among all humanity. Legal systems were evolved and used to promote law and order in society. Property rights also come into being and are continuously being improved to enhance human interactions. Systems, institutions, methodologies, and technologies also continue to evolve. They are used to facilitate human performance. In a world filled with many choices, plans, policies, programs, and projects, complicated strategies are formulated and utilized to deal with existing problems on an ongoing basis. Social, economic, and political choices are made using many different criteria.

The recent explosion in the field of electronics has led to new developments in the area of data creation, transmission, and storage (see details in Chapter 5). Indeed, great efforts and energy are expensed on the invention and innovation of new technology to help facilitate the accomplishment of tasks in an effective and efficient manner. Huge sums of money have been poured into R&D in this area. In terms of competition among companies for greater market shares, each transnational company focuses on product design, manufacture, and distribution. Each company continuously races against time to ensure that loyal customers are kept happy.

SOCIAL ENGINEERING AND ITS SIGNIFICANCE

The concept of social engineering (SE) is extremely critical. Social engineering refers to the use and application of the discoveries and conclusions arrived at by both social and physical scientists in solving the day-to-day social, economic, and political problems that prevail in societies. Its goal is to help improve the existing state of the human condition by preparing men and women to engage in a life of service to all humanity. As such, SE is expected to produce people who are servant leaders—ready to promote and foster the humanness of all humanity. As such, SE, as a process, is aimed at developing people whose presence in society will lead to quality human relationships that are capable of enhancing the quality of life, human welfare, and freedom from the impact of overemphasis on personal self-interest that is capable of promoting destructive criminal behavior in society. SE involves the design, development, construction, and utilization of institutions, technologies, systems, ideologies, theories, principles, and the like to help people acquire the HF necessary for building the desired society.

[The HF] refers to a spectrum of personality characteristics and other dimensions of human performance that enable social, economic, and political institutions to function, and remain functional, over time. Such dimensions sustain the workings and application of the rule of law, disciplined labor force, a just legal system, political harmony, respect for human dignity and the sanctity of life, social welfare, and so on. Social, economic, and political institutions cannot function effectively without being upheld by a network of committed persons who stand firmly by them. Such persons must strongly believe in, and continually affirm, the ideals of the society. The dimensions and attributes encompassed in the HF include far more than mere human resource development and human capital acquisition through education and training. HF attributes include dedication, responsibility, and accountability in implementing measures towards development. It is these attributes, or the lack of them, which contribute to the successful or unsuccessful development of societies. The relevant HF must be capable of blending together social values and technical skills for the success of the development process. (Adjibolosoo 1994b, 26)

The six primary components of the HF are spiritual capital, moral capital, aesthetic capital, human capital, human abilities, and human potentials. Table 6.1 presents a summary description for each HF component with illustrative examples to further clarify what each component entails. Adjibolosoo (1995a) noted that "the HF constitutes the intangible asset or liability of humanity. A properly developed HF animates, guides and encourages people to perform specific functions that are required of them in their tasks assigned by society [business organization]." These people are not only strongly duty-conscious, but also highly self-fulfilled.

Indeed, from the HF perspective, social engineering is the process whereby a society is able to employ education systems, training programs, and mentoring techniques, including other available agents of socialization, to assist men and women to acquire the necessary human qualities (i.e., the HF) that every society, community, and organization needs for efficient and effective performance. SE must always and necessarily be aimed at altering problem situations in society through the creation and use of intensive HF development programs. Social engineers and thinkers must of necessity contrive and operate plans, policies, programs, and projects for nation building through intensive HF development schemes. In a sense, SE is the ingenious practical application of knowledge gained, principles derived, and wisdom culled from the intensive study of both artificial and natural phenomena to foster HF development for the evolution of an efficient and effective social contract.

The continuing acquiescence among members of society to bind themselves together to organize and run society to promote the interests and benefits of its citizens is one of the most important foundations of the social contract (SC). Social contracts are agreements (either written [formal] or unwritten [informal] between agents in society regarding how they must relate to each other and what constitutes acceptable or unacceptable behavior in relation to production, distribution, exchange, consumption, economic activities, business dealings, and many others. They are usually enforceable by law. They therefore constitute relevant stipulations regarding the commitment of members of society to do as prescribed or not to do as proscribed. That is, they exist to restrain people from engaging themselves in certain types of behavior that may jeopardize the peaceful and harmonious coexistence of people in society. It is aimed at developing, securing, and promoting the rights, privileges, and responsibilities of everyone who belongs to the community, society, or organization. These agreements are rooted in foundational principles that are acceptable to everyone who is a party to the social contract and possesses a vested interest in it. SCs are not necessarily static. They change according to the

Table 6.1
The Composition of the Human Factor

HF (Type of capital)	Description
Spiritual Capital	It is the aspect of the human personality that is usually in tune with the universal laws and principles of human life. It sees beyond what the five senses are able to grasp and furnishes the individual with insight into the nonmaterial world.
Moral Capital	It represents habits and attitudes of the human heart that are based on universal principles regarding right or wrong. It refers to the qualities individuals possess that lead them to conform or not conform to universal principles of life. Its constituents include integrity, humility, justice, charity, patience, honesty, sensitivity, fairness, etc.
Aesthetic Capital	A deep sense of and love for beauty. It includes a strong passion for music, art drama, and other artistic capacities (imagination and creativity are strong components).
Human Capital	The know-how and acquired skills (i.e., technical, conceptual, intellectual, analytic, and communications), human experiences, knowledge, intelligence, physical well-being, emotional health, etc.
Human Abilities	These constitute the power or capacity of an individual to competently undertake projects or effectively perform tasks requiring mental and physical effort. They are required for the effective use of human capital. Examples include wisdom, vision, commitment, determination, diligence, courage, accountability, judgment, responsibility, competence, motivation, human energy, optimism, endurance, self-control, objectivity, reliability, adaptability, alertness, etc.
Human Potentials	They are the human talents that may or may not be harnessed and employed for human utilization. These may be referred to as the unused dimensions of the HF.

Source: Adjibolosoo (1995a).

times, availability of knowledge, and new information, understanding, events, and so on. SCs are necessary but not sufficient for the building, organizing, managing, and running of good societies. It can be argued from the HF perspective that the effectiveness of a people's social control systems is significantly dependent of the quality of their HF characteristics.

Cultural engineering (CE), an inherent process of SE, mainly focuses on procedures aimed at the attainment of continuing improvements in the sum total of a people's way of life. It is a basic process whose goal is to reform a people's culture and make it more relevant to the tasks of the day. CE is, therefore, a human attempt at SE aimed at the continuing study, evaluation, questioning, and revising of a people's existing culture with the primary objective of discovering its shortcomings and shortsightedness and then correcting observable deficiencies in order to strengthen the culture and equip it to solve day-to-day problems more efficiently.

In the next section, I take a detailed look at the various conventional programs that have been used in many countries to deal with the problems that plague the social, economic, and political institutions and systems. Their efficiency and effectiveness are later discussed in detail.

SPECIFIC PROGRAMS AIMED AT SOCIAL ENGINEERING

As pointed out in Chapter 1, the scarcity problem has affected human behavior in many different ways. This problem has led to many inventions, innovations, and developments that have both created pleasure and pain for all humanity. Before we proceed to discuss some of these programs, it is necessary to define the nature of some of them in general terms. This section presents definitions for social institutions and social systems. These definitions are necessary for the author and reader to dialogue on a level playing field.

Social Institutions

These are firmly established human practices that portray how people in different societies carry on their general modes of living. Their general structure is usually indicative of the people's behavior, relationships, and interactions as they relate to production, exchange, and consumption in their specific society. These institutions are the repositories for the varying rules and regulations concerning procreation (i.e., love, marriage, and the family), education (i.e., schools, colleges, universities, etc.), religion (Animism, Christianity, Hinduism, Islam, etc.), and the like. Social institutions function through well-established and organized customs, laws, beliefs, and so on. Viewed from this perspective, the organization and function of social, economic, and political institutions are reflections of a people's way of life—culture.

The *family* is expected to perform many different functions. In recent years, the debate regarding the definition and duties of the family has been on the increase. We do not concern ourselves with this debate in this chapter. We must note, however, that most scholars agree that the family must nurture and socialize the newborn (see Murdock 1949; Reiss 1980). This being the case, the family is also expected to provide a sense of emotional support, security, belongingness, and personal worth to its offspring (Stark 1992, 378). It is often argued that when the family is able to carry out its duties successfully it will be able to prepare young people for a better life of service to themselves and to society at large. Whether the family has been very successful or not in discharging its expected duties is an issue discussed in detail in Chapter 8.

Religious institutions have also been at the forefront of helping develop values and ethical systems on which people should base their behavior and action. Since the beginning of time, men and women have always sought detailed explanations for natural phenomena that they are unable to comprehend through their physical senses. In many countries, people have come to hold different religious views, beliefs, principles, and so on. As noted by Stark (1992, 406), "All religions have one feature in common: they always involve answers to *questions about ultimate meaning*, such as, Does life have a purpose? Why are we here? Is death the end? Why do we suffer? Does justice exist? . . . Hence, religion has been defined as socially organized beliefs and activities offering solutions to questions of ultimate meaning" (emphasis original). Since this is too broad a definition of religion, and, as such, may include ideologies such as communism as religion, other sociologists have narrowed down the definition by pointing out that religion concerns itself with the existence of the supernatural and the ability of men and women who practice religion to invoke the power, authority, wisdom, and assistance of the gods (see details in Spiro 1966; Berger 1967; Stark 1981, 1992; Stark and Bainbridge 1985).

Many religions also go beyond these basic questions and offer their adherents views regarding the desires of the supernatural and its expectations from human beings. By legitimizing certain norms, religion gives hope to people regarding the existence of life after death. According to Stark (1992, 408–409), "By specifying what the gods require of humans, *religions in effect regulate human behavior by formulating rules about how we must and must not act.* Such rules of behavior, of course, are social norms. Religions explain why certain norms exist and why they should be obeyed. For norms to be obeyed, most members of a society must believe that the norms are proper and right" (emphasis original). In view of these observations, it becomes clear how religions can pull together people in society and encourage them to live lives that are acceptable to the gods. The recognition of divine sanctions gives more credence to the establishment and operation of other social institutions (Stark 1992, 409). The moral communities that are brought about by religion may promote conformity to social norms and regulations. Sociological research has shown that teenagers who hold to forms of religion are less likely to engage in deviant behavior than those who do not subscribe to any religious views (see Stark, Doyle, and Rushing 1983a; 1983b; Stark 1992). Of course, this is not to suggest that people who do not subscribe to religious views do not adhere to social norms. In fact, research suggests this is not the case (see Hirschi and Stark 1969).

Indeed, this being the case, continuing decline in people's subscription to religious views may lead to significant social, economic, and political problems in society. Such societies are also likely to experience severe HF decay. The experience of HF decay or underdevelopment in societies may lead to severe problems in relation to social, economic, and political institutions.

Political institutions and the state, in the same way, have a great deal to do with human performance in society. In general, government is expected to see to it that citizens make the best use of national resources. In cases where resources are just left, in the sense of "free for all," society may experience the problem of the "tragedy of the commons." This is a terrible economic situation in which to place a whole society because it leads to the depletion of existing resources. In the event it occurs, it may escalate the scarcity problem in the future. In a sense the state and, for that matter, political institutions exist to make sure that certain things are made available and also maintained in society. In a laissez-faire (free-market) economic system, Adam Smith (1776) argued that it is the government's duty to not only administer rule in the state, but also to see to the defense of the nation from outside intruders. In the same way, the government is expected to provide relevant machinery that is required for the maintenance of law and order in society. In this regard, the state is duty-bound to promulgate the necessary rules and regulations for running the nation. Nations whose governments are relatively weak and therefore fail to make sure that law and order prevail will be faced with complex social, economic, and political problems.

The government is necessary in most societies because everyone needs to be protected from harm that may be inflicted upon them by others in society. In the same way, individual property has to be protected. In cases where private individuals may not find it profitable to produce certain products that the whole society may need, it is the function of government to ensure that these commodities (i.e., public or collective goods) are made available to all people. Examples of such items include highways, bridges, dams, parks, and so on.

Scholars such as Max Weber (1946), Nozick (1974), and many others have viewed the state as being the sole entity that assumes monopoly rights and decides who should wield and exercise authority and power in society. The government exercises its acquired monopoly power and authority to decide which public goods and services are to be produced and who should receive them. Hobbes (1956) noted that if organized coercion (by the government) does not exist in society certain individuals may engage in private coercion—"the war of all against all." In the absence of organized collective security programs, a society may experience anarchy. Hobbes noted that, "During the time men live without a common power to keep them all in awe, they are in that condition which is called war . . . where every man is enemy to every man. . . . In such condition, there is no place for industry; because the fruit thereof is uncertain: and consequently no [agri]culture . . . no society; and which is worst of all, continual fear, and danger of violent death; and the life of man, solitary, poor, nasty, brutish, and short" (quoted in Stark 1992, 440). That is, societies that fail to provide security for people in terms of their lives and property will not experience true freedom. This is why it seems to be necessary that for everyone to enjoy his or her freedom to the greatest degree, he or she must know that that freedom stretches as far as possible, but ends very quickly where others' begins. The American constitution was designed to foster and promote individual liberty, justice, internal peace, human welfare, protection, and so on.

All presidents of the United States are expected to uphold these principles, values, and virtues. Failure to do so would be a complete betrayal of the constitution.

True and productive *education* is a process concerned with the acquisition of knowledge, the development of the ability to reason and judge, and the preparation of people for life through HF development programs. Through effective schooling, individuals are expected to gain a great deal of knowledge that will be relevant to them in their future employment. In a sense, education must be viewed as a means of socialization. It is the traditional belief that people with higher levels of education will increase their individual competence levels. It is expected that most people will learn to play certain roles that are commensurate with their educational attainment (Meyer 1977; Stark 1992, 489). Education must prepare people for life. In this case, the educational systems is not only expected to equip people with knowledge and skills that will help them to acquire well-paying jobs, but also to help them to acquire relevant human qualities that will make them become productive citizens. Men and women who are citizens of a nation must be properly educated to acquire and exhibit positive human qualities that will make them become good leaders, mothers, fathers, husbands, wives, lawyers, doctors, engineers, priests, and so on. Lee Kwan Yew of Singapore once noted the following:

The first subject concerns good citizenship and nationhood. What kind of man or woman does a child grow up to be after 10–12 years of schooling? Is he a worthy citizen, guided by decent moral precepts? Have his teachers and principals set him good examples? Imparting knowledge to pass examinations, and later to do a job, these are important. However, the litmus test of a good education is whether it nurtures good citizens who can live, work, contend and cooperate in a civilized way. Is he loyal and patriotic? Is he, when the need arises, a good soldier, ready to defend his country, and so protect his wife and children, and his fellow citizens? Is he filial, respectful to elders, law-abiding, humane, and responsible? Does he take care of his wife and children, and his parents? Is he a good neighbor and a trustworthy friend? Is he tolerant of Singaporeans of different religion? Is he clean, neat, punctual, and well-mannered? (quoted in Hill and Kwen Fee 1995, 89–90)

Societies that are truly concerned about preparing people for a life of service to society and themselves need to constantly revisit their educational and training curriculum and other related programs and activities in all their institutions of learning. They need to see to it that the curricula have the capability to develop the caliber of people required for successful nation building.

Training is a specialized process that is usually aimed at instructing and disciplining people to acquire specific skills, qualities, and so on for specific duties or functions in some art, vocation, or profession. *Mentoring* is the process whereby experts in specific arts, vocations, professions, and so on take individuals under their wing with the view of educating and training them through advice, counseling, suggestions, and role modeling in order to prepare them to function effectively and efficiently in their duties or functions. Both training and mentoring programs must complement the educational process.

Education systems, training programs, and mentoring techniques help society to develop its HF and the necessary leadership—the primary requisites of social, economic, political, and intellectual development. Regardless of what forms they take, if they fail to develop the HF in any society, that society will have no meaningful future. These programs must be precise in their attempt to develop the caliber of leadership and people who are required for the running (and the resuscitation, where applicable) of failing social, economic, and political institutions. These will be people who are full of knowledge, understanding, wisdom, courage, integrity, and the like to keep society afloat.

For the purposes of this chapter, *social systems* are viewed to be the developed and organized doctrines, principles, rules, and theories that serve as the foundations on which social institutions operate. They prescribe and proscribe various schemes, methods, and procedures that determine how social institutions must carry on their functions and programs. As social systems evolve, they are developed through critical social and scientific studies, analyses, and the examination of available data and information about human behavior, natural phenomena, and so on. As is always the case, most societies function by means of invented or innovative procedures, structures, programs, and systems. Some of these include the following.

Social sanctions and rewards (SSR) are statutory provisions that allow for the awarding of rewards or the imposition of punishments on individuals who violate or promote social contracts, societal rules and regulations, and the like. For example, while sanctions are used to disapprove and discourage certain activities or behavior, rewards are instituted to encourage acceptable behavior and activity. Their goal is to see to the proper functioning of society.

The legal system is one of the greatest means of social control ever designed by all humanity. Many people continue to advocate for development, implementation, and improvement in the legal system of their societies. Legal systems enact and promulgate laws, rules, and regulations that are used to promote the better functioning of society. Cohen (1971, 105) defined law as "a statement which specifies that an action will incur penalty, in threat or in fact, by a human agency—as distinct from a supernatural agency—and that involves a predetermined, specified penalty (loss of life, limb, freedom of movement, privileges, rights, or possessions) that is commensurate with the infraction." As such, the legal system is employed to keep people in check regarding what they can or cannot do in society. The terms of socially sanctioned human behavior are stipulated in the laws of society.

In places where the HF is developed, one would expect effective and efficient legal systems. When people know that their legal system is usually successful in adjudicating cases brought before it, they keep their own individual actions in check. This is not to suggest that in such societies every person is a good citizen in terms of being law abiding. Deviant behavior may still occur in such societies as long as people do not have profitable means with which they can overcome the scarcity problem they face every day. A society's legal system, when well organized and operated by its own citizens, can serve as an excellent means of social control.

However, in the face of continuing HF decay or underdevelopment, legal systems may experience severe difficulties and problems. Problems being experienced in the legal systems of such countries as Canada, the United States, Britain, France, Germany, and so on are all due to the fact that these countries are currently going through the experience of HF decay or underdevelopment.

TYPES OF AVAILABLE ASSISTANCE TO THE NEEDY

In many developed countries, governments are in the habit of putting in place specific programs to help the needy and the aged. These programs are usually aimed at reducing problems of abject poverty and criminal activities. The traditional belief is that when people are unable to care for themselves because they lack decent employment, they may turn to criminal activities (i.e., drug trafficking, prostitution, armed robbery, stealing, swindling, etc.). This is usually the case because when people are faced with the belief that their current financial situation denies them the ability to successfully deal with the scarcity problem, they are tempted to engage in other forms of behavior that may help them to circumvent this problem. Some of the people who find themselves in such circumstances do not necessarily care about whether the means they use to make ends meet are socially acceptable or not. All they want to do is to keep themselves alive and also enjoy good food, clothing, and housing.

The establishment and operation of these programs can, therefore, be viewed as palliative measures aimed at alleviating the financial difficulties of those who are either disadvantaged in many regards or people who might have been displaced in the labor market because of various circumstances beyond their individual control. In what follows, a few examples of these programs are presented. Their goals and tasks are presented and briefly discussed.

Social Insurance (SI). This is a contractual arrangement made by governments to promote or guarantee the welfare of citizens in society. Examples involve health-care insurance, unemployment insurance, social and financial assistance, and so on. They fulfill pressing needs that, when left unprovided for, may create more difficult problems for society.

Social Services (SS). These involve the provision of utilities, public goods, and activities that otherwise would not have been provided, either because they exhibit no visible signs of profitability to encourage private production or the working poor cannot afford to pay for them should they be asked to. SS is sometimes extended to deal with pressing social problems. Some examples are providing recreational facilities for the youth and teenage hangouts; drugs, condoms, needles, and syringes to drug addicts and prostitutes; and many others. Governments are the major providers of these services.

Social Security (SOS). To ensure a reasonable future for individuals when they retire from active worklife, these public programs guarantee both social welfare and economic security for people in the senior years of life. Financial contributions to this fund are made by both employers and employees. SOS acts like a social safety net for the aged when they no longer actively participate in the labor force to generate income. When properly organized, its objective is to guarantee the aged a reasonable standard of living, *ceteris paribus*. Above all, it tries to provide security for all people in society.

Social Work (SW).   To maintain or improve social conditions, governments are in the habit of creating and funding specialized services and activities to help the poor, disadvantaged, minorities, disabled people, and so on. Social welfare and social assistance are therefore made available to a class of people who otherwise could not provide such services for themselves, either because of disabilities or lack of relevant skills to participate in the market economy.

Technology.   This is one of the means by which societies try to provide for themselves and also solve existing pertinent problems. In recent years, many people have depended on technology to protect their homes and property, monitor employee performance on the job and production processes, trace and track criminals and their activities, and so on. Society has come to trust science and technology and believes that these hold the golden keys for solving humanity's social, economic, and political problems.

As is evident from these definitions, these programs are developed and organized by societies to help them achieve the best welfare and living standards for themselves. The whole society depends on the effectiveness of these programs and procedures to achieve social cohesion, economic progress and political liberty. They also exist to foster social security, safety, protection, and peaceful coexistence (i.e., social harmony). Above all, their successes and effectiveness are expected to always foster improved social welfare, economic development and growth, political stability, and intellectual (academic) freedom. Given these developments in society, one may want to know the effectiveness with which some of these programs have helped social institutions and systems to perform throughout the centuries.

CONVENTIONAL SOLUTIONS TO THE SEPE PROBLEMS

The design and development of conventional solutions to problems in society are usually based on the perspectives of different social scientists who have come out with generalized conclusions from their research of social phenomenon. Weinberg and Rubington (1973, 301) noted, "When violated expectations are constituted as a social problem, laymen, sociologists, and professional problem-solvers begin thinking about them, using a perspective and often devising solutions which their perspective suggests to them." Indeed, when one surveys previous and current policies, programs, and projects that are aimed at dealing with social, economic, and political problems in society, one immediately realizes that these are often based on the perspectives the experts brought with them to the problem. This procedure sometimes leads to suggested remedies that the experts have come to believe are those that will deal successfully with the problems. From the perspective of social pathologists, individuals who engage in deviant behavior due to poorly regulated personal impulses ought to be regulated and prevented from engaging in such behavior that destroys social tranquillity (Bernard, Ottenberg, and Redl 1973, 26–39; Slater 1973, 40–52; Morris 1973, 53–63; Reich 1973, 64–78). Scholars such as Davis (1973, 85–98), Gordon (1973, 99–109), and Toffler (1973, 122–133) discuss how social disorganization could create many problems in society. From social disorganization's theoretical perspective, when the social system is destabilized and flung into continuing disequilibrium by such events as conflicts in culture, anomie, lack of rules, and so on, a society will experience many problems and difficulties. Such factors, when not dealt with effectively, may lead to the disintegration of the existing social order. The experts argue that the best way to deal with the situation is to slow down the rate at which change is happening in society. It is suggested that by developing rules and regulations that will help bring together all the various forces and agents that are bringing the change about, the social order may be brought back into coherent and consistent equilibrium.

Carmichael and Hamilton (1973, 143–151), Piven and Cloward (1973, 152–159), Cantarow et al. (1973, 160–168), and Weisberg (1973, 169–177) discuss the issue of value conflict and how it leads to ongoing social problems. The argument from the value-conflict perspective is that the differing values held by different groups in society usually lead to explosions and clashes. These clashes may erupt due to the fact that certain groups may begin to feel that they are being discriminated against and, as such, are being denied critical opportunities they need to successfully deal with the scarcity problem that confronts them. Examples of such value conflicts include the now defunct apartheid policies of South Africa, the denial of opportunities to Blacks in the United States, and so on. Other minorities and women who have suffered similar plights often experienced the problem of value conflicts. In such struggles, all parties to the squabbling usually suffer huge damages of property loss or the death of many of their members. Another example is the Tiananmen Square incident between Chinese (communist) authorities and Chinese students. In such situations, solutions are usually more of a compromise than the flexing of muscles. Where this does not work effectively, such struggles can drag on for generations. Any concessions granted by the dominant groups to the minority groups may help alleviate or minimize the intensity of the conflicts. In most cases, such concessions may succeed by lulling the conflict into temporal slumber. As historical evidence and stylized data reveal, many nations have tried to resolve problems originating from value conflicts by extending certain privileges to minority groups and by enacting laws to proscribe certain inflammatory behavior on the part of the major group.

Deviant behavior can come from many different angles. Cloward (1973, 186–199), Knight (1973, 200–211), Rubington (1973, 212–219), and Johnson and Cressey (1973, 220–242) discuss the theory of deviant behavior. In this case, deviant behavior relates to situations where the individual decides to act contrary to the accepted societal norm. In some cases, this behavior is deliberate and is engaged in rebellion against authority. Individuals who break the rules, threrefore, utilize illegal means to achieve their intended objectives. In reality, deviant behavior can be viewed as the means used by an individual or group of individuals to deal with the scarcity problem (in cases where stealing of property or money or the robbery of a financial institution is concerned). Individuals who are usually the victims in these cases may force the authorities to enact and enforce regulations to prevent future deviant behavior. In this case, the critical solution is the establishment and enforcement of the law. Those who believe in this type of solution are usually convinced that the existence of stringent laws in society will lead to reduction in deviant behavior in society (see details in Chapter 8).

The final perspective on the causes of social problems is called labeling. Scholars such as Grinspoon (1973, 252–269), Schur (1973, 270–276), Laing (1973, 277–286), and Weinberg and Williams (1973, 287–298) discuss this issue. These scholars note that the problem of labeling originates when officials of certain critical agencies of social control, interest groups, or social classes decide by themselves to view certain behaviors, actions, activities, and so on as social problems. In their continuing attempts to control these problems, those who have labeled them as problems promote their views regarding why they have come to view them as such. Their labeling of certain behavior of others as social problems often leads to explosive situations and may also lead to ongoing social problems. To deal with situations of this nature, a reclassification may have to be carried out.

APPLICATIONS OF THESE VIEWS TO REAL-LIFE CASES

In the United States Congress, senators and representatives from both the Democratic and Republican parties have all argued in favor of crime bills. Yet in all these attempts to establish laws to proscribe certain kinds of criminal activity, they ignore the real foundational causes of the problems prevailing in American society: HF decay and underdevelopment. For example, the American Senate passed a crime bill in November 1993. To carry the bill through to execution, 20 billion dollars were voted to put more police on the streets and to foster punishment and prevention (see *The Economist* 1994, 25). The bill is expected to do the following:

1. Help police to ride over constitutional and legal barriers.
2. Facilitate the search for drugs and weapons.
3. Establish the "three strikes rule" (i.e., by being arrested three times for criminal activities, one could be locked up for life).
4. Deny prisoners the opportunity to participate in weight training at the taxpayers' expense.
5. Alter the death-row appeals processes.

In addition to this, community policing is a brand new concept that is gaining wide popularity and acceptance. Many communities are turning to it and hope that it will be successful in combating crime in their neighborhood. The crime bill is expected to strengthen community policing. New prisons are to be built, mandatory minimum sentences are to be upheld by judges and enforced by the police, and the death penalty is expected to be extended to cover criminal activities it has hitherto ignored (refer to *The Economist* 1994, 25).

Economists usually view criminal activity as a utility-maximization problem (Becker 1962, 1–13; 1965, 493–517; 1971, 50–64). Economists argue that the decision to engage in criminal activity is made when the individual carefully weighs the expected costs and benefits of engaging in criminal activity. Whether the individual indulges in any criminal activity or not is, as the argument goes, dependent on the net expected gains and the magnitude of the probability of apprehension. As such, many economists believe that such a decision can be influenced by the magnitude of the accompanying rewards and punishments. It is this view that has promoted policies aimed at increasing expenditure on anti-crime programs. That is, those who hold this view maintain that by spending more on police education, training, and operations, and courts and prisons, the problem of crime will be minimized. About 90 billion dollars were spent on these three categories in 1993 in the United States (*Business Week* 1993, 72–73; see also Chapter 9).

It has become a generally accepted belief that by spending huge sums of money on security alarms and guard systems, private citizens may increase their own safety. It has been reported that Americans spent approximately 65 billion dollars on such systems in 1993 (see *Business Week* 1993, 72 and Chapter 9). Yet the magazine's estimates revealed that criminal activities cost Americans approximately 425 billion dollars each year (see Chapter 9). *Business Week* (1993, 78–79) pointed out that a cost-effective plan for reducing crime must include (1) improving enforcement, (2) focusing on punishment, (3) controlling drug-related crime, (4) expanded job training, (5) supporting neighborhood safety, and (6) lessening levels of violence.

Additional evidence abounds regarding the difficulties of social institutions. Police dogs, helicopters, vigilante groups, high-powered electronic cameras, and many other devices are being used extensively to combat socially deviant behavior.

OTHER RELATED EXAMPLES OF POLICIES AND PROGRAMS

The following is a list of policies and programs in use today:

1. Changing the law
2. Channeling huge sums of money into social programs
   social assistance
   unemployment insurance
   building and making teenage hangouts available
   prison rehabilitation programs
   job training and skill-acquisition programs

3. Pursuing community policing programs to raise the awareness of increased probability of apprehension

4. Building more prisons

5. Providing needles and syringes to users

6. Legalizing drugs

7. United Nations programs
   decade of the child
   globalization of human rights
   controlling population
   economic and military sanctions

8. Business involvement and programs
   total quality management
   process reengineering
   quality circles
   management by objectives
   employee empowerment

9. Problem accommodation

Regardless of the intensity of these policies and programs and the huge financial resources being channeled into them, society seems to be achieving very insignificant results. This is very puzzling because, though the results from these policies and programs are not that encouraging, governments and international organizations still continue to channel huge resources into them. It seems, therefore, that by behaving in this manner, authorities are suggesting that they are extremely ignorant about the real causes of problems plaguing societies all over the world. In what follows, I discuss available empirical evidence to support the view that human institutions, systems, plans, policies, programs, and projects are continuously failing to accomplish their intended tasks. My hope is that this discussion will serve as an eye-opener to the reader that if society continues to deal with its pertinent problems the way it has been doing it all along it may end up compounding the intensity of the human predicament (see Figure 8.1).

CONCLUSION

Political economy is not only an academic discipline, but also a relevant and meaningful body of knowledge that helps humanity to improve its well-being. The careful study of the principles of the global political economy and the application of the relevant knowledge gained can help improve the physical condition of all humanity.

Human knowledge of the principles of the social order and the global political economy is able to help us design policies that can help us know how to use these resources wisely. Since human life is affected by the principles of the social order and the global political economy, these principles must be learned, understood, and used to the best advantage of all humanity. The social order and the global political economic system must have the power to effectively deal with major economic problems of the day. It is my understanding that by subscribing to a humanistic political economic system, humanity will deal effectively with some of these problems.

THE EVOLVING ELECTRONICALLY WIRED GLOBAL VILLAGE

Its Development and Implications

As many of us are aware, the world is gradually being transformed into a global village. Technological developments and advancements, improved electronic devices, the electronic mail system and its assessories, and well-organized transport and telecommunications systems continually remind humanity that we are more of a well-connected global village than scattered and severely disjoined countries. Disasters in one country have the tendency of impacting the economies and lives of other nations. Humanity is therefore being reminded day by day by natural and humanly created events that its many habitats are intricately intertwined and expected to function that way. In view of these observations, the main objective of this chapter is to present an evolutionary model to explain the development of the global village. Major implications of this process are pointed out and then briefly discussed. The issues raised can be directly exploited by transnational companies for corporate strategy and by national leaders for development plans, policies, programs, and projects.

The concept of the village is quite an intriguing one because it illustrates the situation of people living in an area usually deemed to be smaller than a town. In reality, a village can have a number of people ranging from a family of two to a little less than one thousand. In this situation, the lives of all members of the village are intricately intertwined. Almost every person knows all other people in the village. Information about what is happening in the village is known (almost instantaneously) to all villagers. In some cases, the chief or king or queen of the village uses a town crier who, with the gong-gong (in addition to his or her voice), informs the people about the chief's policies and suggestions when it is necessary.[1] In some villages in many African countries, talking drums are used to communicate messages to the subjects.

In terms of economic activities, villagers in many cases develop systems whereby they can help each other to engage in such activities as farming, fishing, brewing, and the like. First, one observes two or more villagers gather together to plan regarding either their farming or building or other projects. This group of people then decides on how they must tackle the labor shortage problem. That is, at their initial meeting, they all decide unanimously in what order they must go to the farm of each member to help in digging the soil and planting the seeds. After this process is completed on one person's farm, they proceed to the next person's farm until, in complete succession, the group is able to complete work on every member's farm before the rains begin.

Financially speaking, villagers have their own income security systems. These are developed to assist each member to build a strong and sufficient financial base. Their concept of financing members in the group is simple. That is, a group of concerned individual villagers get together and decide on how much each person must contribute to a common purse. Once this is done, the money is either given to one individual member or a group of individuals for their use. It is then determined that at an agreed upon time all individuals must collect money (a second round) to be distributed to other members. This process continues until every person receives his or her share and then the process is repeated as many times as desired.

There are no securities or guarantees regarding whether individuals who receive the funds initially will continue to be supportive of the goals of the financial union. The only sources of security and guarantee are the personal trust, integrity, and loyalty each member has. In addition, an intended default can have severe ramifications on a person's character and integrity in the village. If this happens, the whole village gets to know about it. The individual concerned is usually ostracized. Thus, in the village setting, people do things in conjunction with others. No single individual is self-sufficient because everyone's livelihood is tied to those of others. The activities or behavior of one or few people affects the lives and businesses of others. Every person treats others as if they are close relatives. Everybody else is somebody else's brother's or sister's keeper. Regardless of these positive aspects, occasional acts of crime, violence, hatred, and so on are not uncommon in the village. By exploiting the basic concept of the village, this chapter describes and analyzes the concept of the global village and its development.

GLOBAL AGENTS OF CHANGE AND
EVOLUTION-INDUCING PROCESSES

In the past, many nations played adversarial roles in that they were constantly at war (whether cold or hot) with other nations. Nationalistic behaviors have contributed to more bellicose attitudes among different countries. The distrust between the superpowers (the United States and the USSR) has led to artificial demarcation of the world into two ideological camps (of capitalism and socialism), each viewing the other with mistrust and suspicion, always searching for social, economic, political, and technological strategies to outwit the other.

Regardless of the intensity of these ideological struggles, the invisible hand has been at work for many centuries trying to make humanity realize that economic successes and improved welfare standards can be attained for the whole world when all nations pull together side by side. Humanity is, therefore, reminded day by day by natural and humanly created events (i.e., earthquakes, famine, floods, wars, oil spills, environmental degradation, ethnic strife, etc.) that its many habitats are intricately intertwined. In view of these observations, it can be argued that the realization that naturally or artificially created events in one nation can affect every facet of life in other countries creates the feeling that the many habitats of humanity are, therefore, little fragments of a whole. This perception sets in motion an evolutionary process that calls for concerted joint efforts which, in turn, lead to the creation of various means for either adaptating to or solving the problems and dealing with the numerous concerns of all humanity. It is this realization which is shrinking the size of the world in terms of time, space, and distance, and hence promoting the development of the global village.

In what follows, some of the key factors that are facilitating the evolutionary process of the global village are presented and discussed. The evolution process is summarized in Figure 7.1.

THE GROWING ROLE OF ENVIRONMENTALISM

For many years, many nations have been ignorant about the fact that the natural environments of all people are interrelated. For this reason, many thought that hazards created by other nations would not affect them in any way. It cannot be denied that changes in the ecosystem in different countries affect life in others. The destruction of rain forests (i.e., in the Amazon) and temperate forests (i.e., in British Columbia) is bound to have debilitating impacts on life in other nations. Because of the fact that people all over the world have begun to become increasingly aware of this, there is a joint effort to preserve the ecosystem in all nations. For this reason, other nations have a say in what other countries decide to do with their atmosphere, plant life, and other natural resources.

The destruction of the ozone layer through excessive industrial activities in many advanced countries is of a great concern to all humanity. Not only is pollution (in its various forms) drawing nation states (i.e., Canada and the United States) together to find ways and means for dealing with artificially created pollutants, but increasing acid rain is also of concern to all humanity. Decisions made in one country or geographical area (i.e., industrial disasters, short-sighted industrial policies, or other localized events) influence other people. For example, in the recent past, radiation from Chernobyl finally reached Finland and caused a great deal of havoc. In the same way, the Exxon Valdez oil spill caused severe destruction to marine life in different countries. Acid rain caused by pollution from the United States affects life in Canada and vice versa. For these reasons, many nations are getting more and more concerned about the welfare, economics, politics, hunger, and so on, of other countries.

Figure 7.1
The Evolution of the Global Village

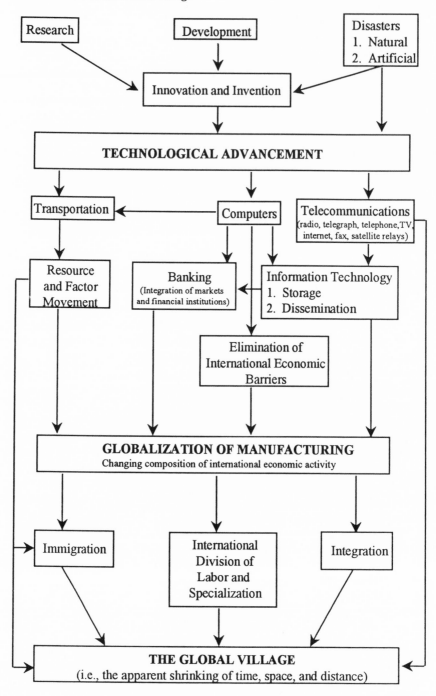

The survival of local economic activities in the global economy depends on what others do in their countries. For example, in the Canadian fishing industry, local fishermen are affected by pressures from the rest of the world. Toxins such as furans and dioxins produced by paper and pulp mills have sometimes affected fishing waters leading to their closures. The irony of these closures is that firms producing these toxins operate in different geographical areas. The different pressures and problems originating from different geographical sources impact lives and economic activities in different parts of the world. This is because of the fact that nations are becoming increasingly dependent on each other and are less and less self-sufficient. Since these problems of environmental degradation cannot be solved by nation states in isolation, international forums are being organized to discuss how the problem must be addressed in the global sense.

The major developments that are contributing to the growing concerns for the environment and its quality include the alteration of energy exchange, destruction of land and its quality, deforestation, and contamination of rivers and underground water supplies on a global scale. As long as these continue to escalate at a rapid pace, calls for global efforts to deal with these problems will continue to come from all corners of the globe.

INFORMATION TECHNOLOGY AND TELECOMMUNICATIONS

Throughout the centuries, the methods for disseminating information have changed drastically. For example, in ancient Greece, people had to run miles from one location to another (for many days) to deliver important messages to those living in different parts of the country. Phidepedis, for example, ran twenty-six miles to communicate Greek victory in war.

The idea of mailing letters developed later and people could send messages by means of letters that took many days or even months to arrive at their destinations. Improved information technology and telecommunications procedures have produced massive advances in this century. Messages sent through the telegraph, telegram, wireless, telex, Internet, faxes, and so on evolved over time as humanity strived to develop more efficient means for communicating ideas, views, events, and so on (see details in Figure 7.1).

Today, it can hardly be denied that information technology has made considerable advances in many directions. Well-developed fax machines are able to transmit volumes of information from one spot to another instantaneously. Fiber optics and satellite relay systems have helped humanity to enhance international communication techniques. Teleconferencing, electronic mailing, and telemarketing systems are effective means of communication. It is no longer the case that people have to wait for days before they can have relevant information they need. The television, video, radio, and the like help people to be well-informed (instantaneously) as events take place. The power of these information gadgets in communicating information to people in the four corners of the world is phenomenal (see Figure 7.1). It is becoming more and more a reality that a chief executive officer (CEO), a politican, a university professor, or any other person can attend meetings, conferences or roundtable discussion sessions in, for example, Ottawa at nine o'clock in the morning and be on time for similar meetings or programs at two o'clock in the afternoon in Vancouver. Indeed, technology is making it increasingly easy for people to do business globally regardless of where they live or where their business headquarters are located.

Media coverage has been extensive, fast, and effective regardless of the information being relayed, time, space, and distance. Millions of daily, weekly, and monthly papers, magazines, and journals have been developed and are being effectively used to communicate information to most people. Effective and efficient media coverage makes it possible for most people to be abreast and up to date with current information. The evolution of satellite relays, fiber optics, the Internet, television, and video systems have made effective educational instruction across the globe possible. Optical-fiber cables have the capability of carrying 10 thousand times as much information as copper cable with a speed 1 thousand times greater. Blackwell (1990) noted, "When local and backbone networks are linked, the all-fiber systems promise cleaner, quieter voice communications and virtually error-free data transmission."

British Columbia Telephone Company (BC Tel) is providing its customers a new device called the Voice Mail. This telephone technology is able to answer all telephone calls from all over the world for both individuals and businesses throughout the year. This technology is able to direct all your calls to a required location. The AT&T Enhanced Fax System allows businesses to send messages through the AT&T exchange. Through the use of this system, AT&T sends your messages to all your customers (Findley 1990a, 1990b). Facsimile machines intermarry a photocopier and a telephone in order to transmit information. It has been noted that the total number of fax machines used in Canada rose from 200 thousand in December 1988 to 340 thousand in March 1989 (see The Royal Bank of Canada 1989, 15). As of now, there exist portable fax machines that can link individuals to their cellular phones. Naisbitt (1982) observed that the development and use of advanced information technology has altered the process of communication significantly. For example, in the information age, huge volumes of data are transmitted very easily and much faster than ever before. In the view of Naisbitt (1982), "The new technology has opened up new information channels with wider range and greater sophistication. It has shortened the distance between sender and receiver and increased the velocity of the information flow. But most importantly, it has collapsed the information float."

In previous decades, most business, economic, political, and social communications were done through letters, notes, memos, and the like. Usually, these took many days to reach the receiver. For this reason, it took a great deal of time for certain crucial decisions to be made concerning the issues concerned. However, thanks to improved information technology, electronically mailed letters, Internet systems, memos, and notes reach their receivers in seconds. Thus, decisions can now be made in less than no time. Information technology has led to a drastic reduction in the time span between people and places.

It is becoming increasingly possible for students in, say, Japan to sit in a classroom in their own country and listen to an American professor give lectures or teach courses in economics, psychology, physics, mathematics, and so on. This phenomenon is not only reserved for international instruction alone—it can also be used in the same country to reach rural dwellers. News reporters utilize similar systems for reporting purposes. As these systems continue to be developed and improved upon, the world will continually shrink in size and may be reduced into a global village. In an information age, information-disseminating bureaus are able to provide end-users with the relevant information they require. These developments not only make relevant information available to those who need it, but also minimize the danger of not being aware of relevant information for crucial decisions. For lawyers, this will improve their performance and enhance their effectiveness. The on-line services are also useful to doctors, engineers, teachers, businesspeople, government personnel (especially intelligence officers), and many others.

The growing availability of information technology and instruments will not only encourage teleconferencing, but will also support telecommuting. Workers would like to find themselves working in different circumstances and conditions. Regardless of where the branch offices are located, the technique of telecommuting would allow many of them to tap into the mainframe computing systems in their respective offices and be able to accomplish exactly the same tasks as when they were in their own offices located at the company cites. In a similar way, corporation managers can easily get their secretaries to prepare relevant documents while they are home and electronically mail the output to their bosses at desired locations. In view of all these developments, Naisbitt (1982) suggested that in the age of computers all humanity lives in a world that is being more and more connected together by a massive electronic superhighway rather than extensive physical roads, highways, and motor vehicles. In his view, just as the motorcar was the basic *sine qua non* for the passing industrial society, so will electronics serve as the kingpin and the lifeblood of the post-industrial electronically wired global village. These developments in the modern world will continue to affect our conceptualization of time, space, and distance. Not only will we be able to accomplish tasks much more quickly than before, but also reduce (apparently) the distance between us and other locations through powerful electronic means. This will also lead to significant declines in the amount of time used to accomplish work and relevant projects. All these developments and many others would not have been possible without the invention and continuous improvements in computer technology and telecommunications systems.

The new silicon technology, software systems, and electronic transmission have all contributed in immense ways to effective information processing, storage, and dissemination. These are done at high speeds (Olson 1988). The use of microelectronics (the science of storing millions of transistors and electronic components on silicon chips) is revolutionizing the storage of information. This fascinating science has a strong promise of aiding humanity to store volumes of written work for safe storage for hundreds of years. In addition, the science of photonics will continue to facilitate the transmittal of information over long distances to different nations in a short time. The science of photonics is able to help humanity to send volumes of the printed page to different parts of the world over thousands of kilometers of fiberglass within seconds.

The development of the Smart Card is another great technological breakthrough for all humanity. It is the microchip advancement that makes it possible for individuals to store useful data and information on a plastic card. Such information may include personal and medical records, insurance information, personal data, and so on. Because of the huge memory capacity of this card, an individual consumer or business can store budgets, banking activities, and the like. It is expected that the card can also be used to open doors and start cars. This impressive development promises to revolutionize international business in the global village (see the *Royal Bank Reporter* 1989, 19).

Computers have enhanced secretarial duties in the office. This has influenced the efficiency, effectiveness, and amount of work being done in the office. The computer has assisted chief executive officers, managers, and secretaries to pull out relevant information on demand, given the required input to the system. It can hardly be denied that computers not only provide a wealth of information to people of all walks of life, but also stimulate creativity.

High-tech developments are not just revolutionizing our lives and the way we do things, they are also drawing us closer and closer together over time, space, and distance (see Figure 7.1). New high-tech developments and projections promise extensive changes in the way we conduct business, our social lives, and economic activities. The *Royal Bank Reporter* (1989, 3) noted the following imminent technological developments that will change our lives and bring all humanity closer together forever:

1. The debit card will make it possible for those who possess it to charge all their purchases on the spot to their bank accounts (refer to the section on banking for details).
2. Video phones will send and receive messages on the phone in such a way that the parties involved can see each other as they talk on the phone.
3. High-definition television (HDTV) will provide sharper and brighter images.
4. The home information system will make it easier for individuals to pay bills, buy tickets, send and receive mail, do correspondence courses, and be able to access information through the computer over a single phone line at home.
5. Teleshopping will allow people to select and buy items using their computer and telephone lines and items bought would be delivered at one's doorstep.
6. The electronic car, with video map display, will help people locate destinations easily inside and outside cities.

The successful implementation of these technological developments will facilitate the evolutionary process of the global village (refer to Figure 7.1).

THE GROWING IMPACT OF TRANSPORTATION SYSTEMS

Transportation systems began to change dramatically when improved shipping, automobiles, and airplanes began to come on the scene. This ushered in increased contact between merchants and consumers of all nations. Even though distances between different countries remain the same, travel time has been greatly reduced by flight engineering and technology. The recently developed British Concord exhibits a tremendous speed ability. This development has apparently rendered cities of different countries into suburbs as if they belong to one country. Distance is no longer a barrier. For example, presidents, prime ministers, world organization leaders, and business chief executives can plan and arrange for different meetings in different cities or countries and be able to attend all these meetings in a single day. This is made possible by computerization of air travel systems. Electronic reservation systems have completely changed the conduct and functioning of air travel.

Passengers do not really need to wait for several months before they can get seats on planes traveling to their destinations. It used to be the case that many airlines conveying passengers and freight over great distances depended on jumbo jets like Boeing's 747. Yet these are excessively expensive to operate during off seasons when the planes are sometimes half or less than half full. The new transportation technology, however, is making it possible for aircraft manufacturers to produce smaller efficient aircraft that can convey a small number of passengers from one area to another with a large frequency of flights. For example, Kenneth Labich (1990) noted that unlike the Boeing 747 which carries about 700 passengers, the Boeing 767–800 ER carries about 210 passengers. This makes it easier for airline companies to undertake many more frequent flights with small volumes of passengers and freight carried each time.

These new machines have made it possible for some airline companies (i.e., American Airlines) to follow fragmentation strategy on various routes. This development has allowed businesspeople and tourists to make more frequent contacts with the rest of the world. Indeed, American Airlines is at the forefront of this type of air travel (see Labich 1990, 40–48). In view of these developments, it is clear that the speed and the ease with which people can travel from one area of the globe to another are contributing to the apparent shrinking size of the world. All these development will finally lead to the shortening of miles into microseconds. Travel would be accomplished in a short period of time, saving a lot of time for everyone who travels to do other things. Indeed, the development and use of superjets, supersonic jets, superfreighters, metroplanes, and the various means for the transportation of ballistic missiles will significantly reduce the amount of time required to move critical items, war gear, and other kinds of machines from areas of production to where they are needed and used. The magnitude of physical distances across the oceans and different countries will sooner or later seem like mere provinces or regions. Similarly, continents will become little more than nation states.

As we enter into the twenty-first century, transportation systems will play a significant role in global relationships. All aspects of human life, such as economic, business, social, and political, will be affected in many significant ways. The feeling of closeness and togetherness among all humanity regardless of geographical locations will be much deeper than we have ever before imagined or actually recognized. Other factors that are helping forge the global village include new developments in banking and finance, continuing global immigration and strong family ties, common global problems, and the growing awareness of international debt (see details in Figure 7.1).

GLOBALIZATION OF MANUFACTURING
AND GLOBAL BUSINESS ACTIVITY

The growing volume of international trade and business also reveals the extent of interdependence among countries. It is now clear that as countries observe the massive involvement of their companies in international trade and business they can no longer stand aloof to watch events in other countries unfold. The stability of jobs, prices, and the economies of countries are affected by conditions (i.e., social, political, economic, etc.) in others. National governments are getting more and more concerned about economic policies of other nations. As political relationships between nations improve, growing technological progress continues, changing demographic trends persist, and accelerating economic growth ensues year after year, the evolutionary process of the global village will escalate.

The global manufacturing process is a strong force in the evolution of the global village. Since the industrial revolution, the production of goods and services has assumed new dimensions. Humanity is realizing that the manufacture of a single product involves the use of inputs and other resources from the four corners of the world. An excellent illustration of this observation is that given by Dicken (1986, 304) in connection to the production of the Ford Escort (in Europe). The various parts used in the manufacture of the Ford Escort come from over fifteen countries. For example, while Austria supplies the tires, radiator, and heater hoses, Canada supplies the glass and radio. As such, it will be a great disaster if two or three countries fail to supply Ford Escort producers the required input materials.

Cast in the global village concept, countries that supply Ford Escort assemblers in Halewood (United Kingdom) and Saarlouis (Federal Republic of Germany) can be treated as if they are just different municipalities of one huge city or different regions of a single country. The global interdependency revealed in this international production process is an excellent illustration of the globalization of manufacturing and the concept of the global village (see Figure 7.1). It is no longer possible for countries to think and believe that they can be self-sufficient. For now, whether or not we like it, humanity lives in a global village. These developments explain why many advanced countries do not like the idea of sanctions. Sanctions hurt those who impose them because most of their industries depend on resources from other nations. For example, Naisbitt (1982) noted the following:

Production sharing, as Peter Drucker has said, will be the prevailing form of worldwide economic integration. Auto makers are not the only ones to recognize its potential. So have baseball mitt manufacturers: 95 percent of the baseball mitts used in the great American pastime are made in Japan. But they are made from American cowhide, which is shipped to Brazil for tanning before it goes to Japan to be made into baseball mitts. Shoes are often shipped among several countries in the course of production. Before Japan began making microprocessing chips, the only thing made in Japan on a hand-held electric calculator was the nameplate that said "Made in Japan"; the electronic chips came from the United States. They were assembled in Singapore, Indonesia, or Nigeria, and the steel housing came from India. The "Made in Japan" label was tacked on the calculator when it arrived in Yokohama or Kobe.

Just as the production of an item requires inputs and other resources from different parts of the world, so also are all economies vulnerable to shocks that originate from other countries. These shocks, because of international political and economic interconnections, can cause significant reverberations whose repercussions can embrace the whole world within a short period of time.

The oil crises of the 1970s, 1980s, and 1990s (as a result of the Gulf War) have produced similar repercussions. Blake and Walters (1987) noted that the oil embargo and price increases imposed by oil-producing states during 1973 and 1974 are dramatic examples of how interconnections between substantive economic issues transmit shocks throughout the global political economy. These actions produced an energy shortage and staggering import bills that curtailed general economic production in rich and poor states alike.

They also simultaneously produced a fertilizer shortage that aggravated an already precarious global food situation, huge balance-of-payments deficits in virtually all industrialized and developing countries, increased needs for foreign exchange by poor states in amounts that exceeded their total foreign aid receipts in 1973, a dramatic boost to an already unprecedented level of inflation plaguing the global economy, and a rapidly spreading economic downturn in many countries. All these phenomena are pointers to the interconnectedness of the global political economy. No single country is an island on its own. All countries are part and parcel of an interconnected global village.

GLOBAL INTERDEPENDENCE

Given the discussion of the concept of the village, the conceptualization of the village can be extended to cover the many habitats of humanity by assuming that certain conditions pertain. It is, however, crucial to note that the great depression of the 1930s, the war-torn world of the 1940s, the inflationary pressures of the 1950s, the economic slowdown of the 1960s, the energy crises of the 1970s, the problems of inflation and unemployment in the 1980s, the Gulf War, the escalating degradation of the environment, and the fear of a nuclear war outbreak in the 1990s reveal that growing global problems cannot be dealt with by any individual country single-handedly. As noted in Dolman (1976, 21–22):

Both the rich and poor worlds have pressing, unparalleled problems. They are not separate: they cannot be solved independently. Mankind's predicament is rooted in its past, in the economic and social structures that have emerged within and between nations. The present crisis, in the world economy and in the relations between nations, is a crisis of international structures. What both worlds must come to grips with is basically a sick system which cannot be healed by expeditious economic first aid. Marginal changes will not be sufficient. What is required are fundamental institutional reforms, based upon a recognition of a common interest and mutual concern, in an increasingly interdependent world. What is required is a New International Order in which all benefit from change.

In view of these observations, the realization that naturally and artificially created events in one nation can affect every facet of life in other countries creates the feeling that the many habitats of all humanity are fragments of a whole. Carrying this issue of interdependence a little further, Toffler (1980) observed the following:

Just as many problems are too small or localized for national government to handle effectively, new ones are fast arising that are too large for any nation to cope with. "The nation state, which regards itself as absolutely sovereign, is obviously too small to play a real role at the global level," writes the French political thinker, Denis de Rougement. "No one of our 28 European states can any longer by itself assure its military defense and its technological resources, the prevention of nuclear wars and the ecological catastrophes." Nor can the United States, the Soviet Union, or Japan.

This perception sets in motion an evolutionary process which leads to the development of various means of adaptation to the problems and concerns of humanity. It is shrinking the world's size in terms of time, space, and distance. A global village is being created.

There is a growing trend in the world that points to the fact that humanity is a well-knit and well-integrated society regardless of geographical location. That is, the whole world is much more than fragmented individual nation states living apart. As modernity advances, people of the world must stand as one whole unit and indirectly function as such. As humanity moves into the unknown future, the growing interdependencies among countries and their economies become more evident. Because of the distribution of resources by nature, it is highly noticeable that while certain areas of the world possess resources and raw materials that all people need and require, many other areas cannot boast of these resources. For example, only South Africa produces some vital minerals required in most advanced countries.

Since these resources are crucial for living, there is no other choice but to interact with other nations that have desired resources for improving living and welfare standards. For example, while some tropical countries can boast of large stocks of coffee, cocoa, cotton, and so on, temperate countries can boast of wheat, barley, oats, and the like. Since all people need these items, they have to depend on each other. Thus, the growing international interdependence is rendering the world into a huge global village. No individual country can exist by itself and be self-sufficient. In his book, *The Third Wave*, Toffler (1980) pointed out clearly that

"Tightened economic linkages between nations make it virtually impossible for any individual national government today to manage its own economy independently or to quarantine inflation. National politicians who claim their domestic policies can halt inflation or wipe out unemployment are either naive or lying, since most economic infections are now communicable across national boundaries. The Economic shell of the nation-state is now increasingly permeable."

What adds to this growing transformation of the world is the growing international specialization and division of labor which accelerate the transformation process (see Figure 7.1). Because of international comparative and competitive advantages, some nations have clear advantages in the production of certain products. For example, Gambia produces and exports peanuts. While the economies of Zaire and Chile depend solely on copper, those of Brazil, Rwanda, and Uganda produce and market coffee. In a similar way, while Australia and New Zealand produce dairy products and beef for export, Thailand and Cuba supply the rest of the world with huge quantities of rice and sugar, respectively. It is well-known that the Organization of Petroleum Exporting (OPEC) countries have become the chief suppliers of crude oil to the rest of the world for both domestic and industrial uses. The Organization for Economic Cooperation and Development (OECD) countries supply most of the world with their industrial products. Each of these categories of countries depends heavily on others for the materials or resources they need for their domestic and industrial programs.

It is well-known to almost everyone the strategic role oil plays in the industrialization process. This became more evident when the world experienced severe oil crises in the early 1970s and the 1980s. The Iranian revolution led to huge drops in their production of crude oil. This shortfall in the world's total oil supplies translated into higher prices, which in turn led to increased prices for both consumer items and producer goods and services. The final impact on the economies of all countries, developed and developing countries alike, led to a slowdown in industrial activities in the advanced countries. In general, inflation escalated and a great deal of unemployment followed. Because the rising oil prices posed difficulties for the developing countries, which were the major sources of relevant raw materials to the industrialized countries, they could not deliver all the raw materials required by the advanced countries for manufacturing purposes. The whole world was, therefore, affected by the oil crises created by the OPEC countries. Indeed, it is clear that the existing global interdependencies are so strong that when any minute point of these interdependencies breaks or suffers some damage, the whole economy of the world cannot be insulated against the resulting negative reverberations in the global village.

Countries specialize in the production of certain products and exchange them for other items they need. In addition, nations with abundant labor or capital resources tend to specialize in the production of items that can take advantage of the abundant resources (Heckscher and Ohlin 1933). Increasing specialization tends to increase global interdependencies among all countries. The growing specialization continually increases the rate of growth of the international division of labor, which in turn increases and encourages interdependencies among countries (refer to Figures 7.1 and 7.2). For example, Feketekuty noted,

In the old days, services had to be produced where they were consumed. In the new world, most of the information-based services can be produced anywhere in the world. As long as there is a telephone line. This has led to a new international division of labor, based on a traditional principle of comparative advantage and comparative costs. Engineers in India draw up blueprints that are reviewed by construction company managers in San Francisco and used by construction crews in Saudi Arabia. A credit card transaction in Spain is key punched in Jamaica, processed by computers in London and Arizona and the bill is sent to the card holder in another part of the world. A data processing center in Cleveland serves clients from New York to California during daylight hours, clients from Japan in the early evenings, then clients in Singapore, followed by Saudi Arabia and Europe in the early morning hours. (Quoted in Rosow 1988, 100)

Thus, the theory of the global village is an explanation of why the size of the whole world is apparently shrinking. In view of these observations, note that this global interdependence is just like a huge spider web, propped up by many concerns of all humanity. In the words of Lesourne (1986),

The spiders' webs of interdependence are many and varied: endless human migrations motivated by work, tourism, or fear; the flow of information transmitted through books, scientific journals, radio, television, newspapers; streams of oil, grain, or ore; shipments of shirts or machine tools; the transfer of money from one account to another; arms deliveries and the movements of aircraft carriers; groups of alliances, accords, and pacts; underground terrorist or intelligence networks; corps of diplomats flitting from one world conference to another; participation in all kinds of intergovernmental organizations. Interdependence is multidimensional: cultural, military, political, economic and social. There is no longer a single activity of human societies that escapes its net. How does it manifest itself? In the fixing of price, the increase of a flow, the creation of an institution, the change of a negotiating procedure, the strengthening of a military superiority.

It is indeed true in the modern world that there is little that can be done by nation states on their own without getting the whole world involved (see Paul Valery's "*Regads sur le monde actuel*," quoted in Lesourne 1986). Whatever one country or transnational company decides to do today depends on what others are doing or planning to do. Indeed, the policies and activities of one country or TNC will continue to affect others in the global village. For transnational companies, especially, the growing global interdependencies may force them to cooperate more on the global scene than to compete.

THE EMERGING GLOBAL ASSOCIATIONS

Toffler (1980, 339) noted that the whole world is experiencing significant increases in global trade and integration of nations (i.e., the European Community).

Figure 7.2
Some Implications of the Global Village

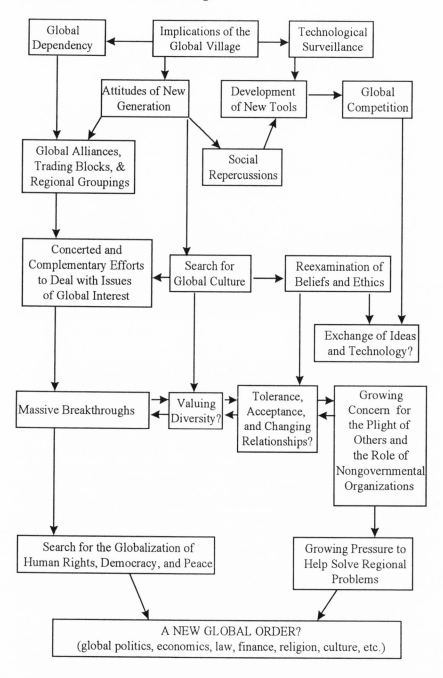

Most of these groups are usually formed to help deal effectively with specific world issues. In the last fifty years, hundreds of both international nongovernment organizations (INGOs) and international government organizations (IGOs) have mushroomed all over the world (see Toffler 1980). Both INGOs and IGOs are active in education, environment, health, nutrition, famine, human rights, discrimination, wildlife, global politics, nuclear issues, wars, exploitation, pollution, the operations of transnational companies, parenthood, democracy, multiculturalism, religious freedom, military activities, and so on. Specific IGOs include the International Atomic Energy Agency, OPEC, and the World Meteorological Organizations. Some of the major nongovernment organizations are International Students Ministries, Scripture Gift Mission, Greenpeace, YMCA, YWCA, Affiliation of Multicultural Services, International Defense and Aid Fund for Southern Africa, International Development Education Resources Association, Forestry for Africa Network, Global Health Project–Oxfam, and Hope International Development Agency. The key issues of concern for these groups include literacy, technical assistance and advice, financial support for urban and rural development projects, dissemination of information, environmental protection, afforestation programs, food for the hungry, and medical assistance to the poor (see Figure 7.2).

As they engage themselves in these activities, their message to the world is simple: Human beings, regardless of their geographical locations, are living in a global village. For this reason, it is critical to be aware that countries are not independent of each other. Humanity must always bear in mind that whatever it does, the results of all actions and activities are bound to impose economic, social, and political externalities on others. These externalities can either be positive or negative for others. Thus, these international organizations act to either help to increase the positive externalities of national (or individual) actions or to minimize their negative effects on life in the global village. They serve as conduits for the dissemination of information and hence raise global awareness of resulting externalities from human economic, business, political, and social activities.

THE GLOBALIZATION OF HUMAN RIGHTS

One other area where massive changes are taking place is the domain of human rights. For centuries, nation states defined their own statutes regarding how individual human beings must be treated. In these statutes, many countries had their own understanding of what should constitute inalienable human rights. The implication of this was that the treatment given to individuals in one country were hardly commented on by other countries. In cases where there were some concerns from other governments, they were accused of meddling in the internal affairs of other nations. Since many nation states thought they had complete sovereignty over their own land and people, they believed that whatever happened to people in their own nation states should not necessarily be spoken to by other nations or people. The days of this philosophy are almost gone. This is so because if people now feel that they are living in a global village, they feel obligated to do something about the treatment meted out to people of other countries (see Figure 7.2). The general feeling is that if everyone is a human being and has feelings, emotions, and so on, then whatever happens to them cannot be ignored. This development has led to new developments in the human rights issue. It is the beginning point of the globalization of human rights. Forsythe noted,

If we take a historical perspective, empirical evidence supports the argument of a growing acceptance across the globe of the basic idea of human rights. The idea is more important in public policy than ever before. There is a growing global agreement on what is meant by human rights, at least in a formal sense and in the sense of defining its outer parameters. That is, there is growing agreement that a list of treaties and declarations define human rights in contemporary times. At the same time, there is no denying that such agreements are subject to continuing attempts at revision or amendment, continuing debate over precise meaning, and continuing debate over choices in manner and priority in implementation. From roughly 1648 and the Peace of Westphalia endorsing supreme territorial authority, to 1945 and the UN era, human rights were regarded as mostly within the competence of the nation-state. This changed fundamentally in both legal theory and diplomatic practice starting in 1945 with the UN Charter and its provisions mandating all member states to promote observance of fundamental human rights without "distinction as to race, sex, language, or religion." (1991, 14–15)

The growing acceptance of the view that human rights issues are global issues is leading world leaders to come together to design and define what constitutes the proper delineation of global human rights. When this is successfully achieved, it will no longer be difficult to determine whether treatment meted out to people in one small corner of the world merits the status of global human rights violations or not. Jimmy Carter, while in office as the President of the United States, noted that all over the world the major goal of all human affairs and activities seems to be the desire for fundamental human rights (U.S. Department of State 1977, 3).

As a result of all these developments, any violations of the U.N. Charter on international human rights can easily lead to conflicts between nation states. In some cases, any such violations can lead to stringent diplomatic actions against countries or TNCs that are known or have been identified as violators of global human rights stipulations. What this means to TNCs is that they may no longer continue to operate in ways that are deemed by the international community to be either cruel to a group of people or unacceptable to the global community of nation states. As they seek more viable markets and locate their production plants all over the world, they also have to be aware that the global community watches their activities with keen interest. Any violations can cause tremendous difficulties for that TNC in terms of legal action. These interesting developments have led to the condemnation of human rights violations in Kenya, Sudan, Cuba, China, the former USSR, Togo, Haiti, Nicaragua, the Philippines, Mexico, the United States, Canada, Britain, Germany, Poland, and other countries.

COMMUNICATIONS, WEATHER, AND SPY SATELLITES

MacDonald (1968) observed that as humanity develops and uses communications, weather, and spy satellites, they solve old problems, but also create new ones. This is to say that new technological developments and advancements create both advantages and disadvantages for all humanity. In my view, it is the growing desire of all people all over the world to share the benefits of technological advancement and to corporately deal with the expected negative effects that are apparently drawing many nations together. As noted earlier, the heavy costs involved in these developments cannot be borne by single nation states. Thus, given that some of these developments would be of benefit to every nation, regardless of whether they contributed to the costs of financing the research and development of the new technology, the advanced countries cannot continue to exclude the poor nations from such developments.

For example, the development and use of effective communications satellites will definitely require the positioning of balloons and buoys in the airspace of other countries that are better located for such positioning and appropriate land stations for computer facilities that will have the capability to receive information from these space satellite stations and relay them to countries that participate in the whole program. These stations could be used to forecast the weather and climatic conditions in all countries involved in the program. Satellite sensor carriers can probe the atmosphere and relay any information about the weather to central computing facilities located at vantagepoints in every participating nation. However, as noted by MacDonald (1968),

Implementation of either of the above systems will require agreement among all nations participating on responsibility for the emplacement of sensors and for the operations of the communication systems. At present, discussions in international agencies such as the World Meteorological Organization are under way to develop a long-range global atmospheric research program. Such a research program would be an essential first step in developing an operational program. . . . The desire of a nation state to maintain its privacy may in the long run hamper the development of such worldwide forecasting systems; yet global cooperation is essential if a system is to be effective.

Any meaningful successes achieved from these developments may help humanity to deal with certain natural disasters such as earthquakes, famines, and droughts effectively.

As space satellite spy stations conduct successful secret surveillance missions on other nations, many nation states will lose their privacy. This transparency being imposed on nation states by technological developments has the potential of encouraging and drawing nation states together. Thus, the fear of losing national sovereignty would serve as a primary motivation for every country in the world to agree to participate in dealing with global issues and development programs. There is, therefore, a great openness required of every nation in the world. In view of this issue, MacDonald (1968) suggested the following:

The opportunity for a completely open world provided by technology raises the issue of the dependence of international stability on a degree of national privacy. Is the most stable situation one in which nations essentially possess no secrets? Or would international relations be so upset by widely available information that instability would result? Is there an optimum amount of information that all nations should share? National response to the development of a technology that can effectively violate national privacy may take one of several forms. There may be a gradual abandonment of the concept of sovereignty with the formation of federations of contiguous states. Such a move would receive impetus from the future development of global technologies such as weather modification and control. An alternative response might be the abandonment of open, large-scale warfare as a means of securing national advantage and the adoption of methods for secret or covert wars. There can be no doubt that technology, developing on a global scale, will profoundly alter the classical concepts of the nation-state system.

Thus, people must not only appreciate the usefulness of these developments today (depicted in Figure 7.1), but also their future repercussions on the evolving global village (illustrated in Figure 7.2).

Indeed, the implications of the evolving global village cannot be described easily in a few words or pages. The changes taking place in the world today will transform it by tomorrow. As is revealed in Figure 7.2, all humanity must expect both positive and negative results from the ensuing globalization process. The critical question, however, is whether or not the ongoing globalization process will lead to a new global order in which every aspect of human life and endeavor will be totally globalized. Though we may not be in the position to accurately answer this question to our satisfaction now, time will provide the best answers. Looking through our imperfect human lenses, we cannot predict with a high degree of certainty all the major implications of the globalization process. Note from Figure 7.2 that, as discussed earlier in this chapter, people from all over the world will continue to engage themselves in programs and activities aimed at looking for effective solutions to the SEPE problems. The existing SEPE problems and other natural phenomena (i.e., floods, earthquakes, tornadoes, famine) have the tendency to bring many nations together to deal with the observed problems. Yet it is also true that ongoing antagonism among nations can pull them apart and lead to many other SEPE problems and wars. In the final analysis, whether a new global political economy and social order would evolve under one global leadership is a matter for further research. In view of this, it can be argued that regardless of the main direction of the evolution process, a significant proportion of the actual and full impact of the globalization process on human life will primarily be determined by the state of the human factor in all countries in the global village.

CONCLUSION

Many changes are currently taking place in the world. The technological explosion is having a tremendous impact on all humanity. Yet regardless of these impressive changes, men and women have yet to develop a workable social order and an efficient political economy of development which could be used to conquer the scarcity problem. Above all, the significant technological advancement being made has not yet brought humanity to the point where it can boast of experiencing and living in peace, tranquility, and harmony. In view of these observations, it can be argued that there is a missing factor that needs to be deciphered and brought into the picture to help change the current direction of the human plight. Continuing academic theorizing, fanciful model building, and a myriad of scholarly conferences, seminars, and roundtable discussions seem to be missing the mark. In a similar way, existing historical evidence and stylized data do not seem to be suggesting that humanity is anywhere closer to successfully dealing with its many SEPE problems, despite the huge sums of money being poured into different types of research and development. There is a long way to go. In the next chapter, our focus will be on the human plight and predicament.

NOTE

1. The gong-gong is a funnel-shaped metallic musical instrument. Its primary function is to provide rhythm. It is, however, used by town criers in many African societies to catch peoples' attention in cases when new information has to be disseminated to all sections of the community.

CHAPTER EIGHT

THE HUMAN PLIGHT AND PREDICAMENT
Needs and Crises That Linger

The processes of development in the global political economy are not static. For centuries the conditions prevailing in the global political economy changed from one state into another. The history of humanity on planet earth is filled with events of progress, continuing disasters, and declines. Finding itself in harsh environments and conditions, humanity is continuously devising techniques to deal successfully with the many problems and hindrances to desired progress. To clearly perceive what is happening in the global political economy of present times, it is important to have a good understanding of what has happened in the past. This is only possible through the possession of adequate knowledge about the impacts of social engineering on human life on planet earth. As such, the primary objective of this chapter is to present a detailed analytical review of certain key global events and then discuss the pressing needs and crises that never go away. Their impacts on the global political economy, the human plight, and life are also presented. The continuing failure of all humanity to successfully deal with its ongoing problems is also presented and discussed. Indeed, as observed by Freud,

The communists believe that they have found the path to deliverance from our evils. According to them, man is wholly good and is well-disposed to his neighbor; but the institution of private property has corrupted his nature. The ownership of private wealth gives the individual power, and with it the temptation to ill-treat his neighbor; while the man who is excluded from possession is bound to rebel in hostility against his oppressor. If private property were abolished, all wealth held in common, and everyone allowed to share in the enjoyment of it, ill-will and hostility would disappear among men. Since everyone's needs would be satisfied, no one would have any reason to regard another as his enemy; all would willingly undertake the work that was necessary. (Quoted in McCullough 1989, 7)

Ingersoll and Matthews (1991, 9) also observed that most people have come to believe that the ideologies they hold are better than those held by others. These people usually believe that they are the sole agents of good rather than evil. Viewed in this light, it can be argued that Marx, Lenin, Madison, Jefferson, Mussolini, Hitler, and many others were all convinced that their ideologies and systems were the best among all others for their people. It is this type of belief that leads many people to work and sustain their personal vision.

THE EVOLUTION OF SYSTEMS AND ORGANIZATIONS

The evolutionary view of society, organizations, institutions, and the various species of living things seems to suggest that as humanity moves through time its genre will improve continuously on all fronts. Yet when viewed under the microscope of evolutionary theory, the current state of the human condition and modern organizations presents a myriad of puzzles and intricate questions and doubts that need to be discussed and analyzed. Social, economic, political, and educational conditions of the world today do not seem to be validating the view that society will ascend toward higher forms of civilization.[1] In view of this, the basic question is, "Why is the human condition deteriorating as the centuries pass by?" Recall that the various programs and projects of social engineering discussed in Chapter 6 are failing to achieve their intended goals. This failure leaves all humanity in a critical state of desperation. This phenomenon has created an environment in which men and women are continuously searching for workable solutions.

As human interaction becomes more complex and technological innovations and inventions continue to mingle in an ongoing state of flux, intricate SEPE problems are surfacing everyday. It seems, therefore, that society has reached a stage of development where it is failing to understand the underlying fundamental reasons for its SEPE problems. The inability to perceive what the exact causes of its problems are seems to be denying society the opportunity to gain a detailed insight into existing problems and the ability to come out with powerfully effective policies to deal with them successfully. In what follows, I present some evidence to both illustrate and substantiate the magnitude of the human plight and its predicament. In addition to this evidence, the needs and crises that linger are also discussed.

With this in view, I present the following arguments to explicate the view that it is the degeneration of excessive self-interest into human greed that leads not only to avarice, but also to the visible decay in personality characteristics and hence the continuing failure of social, economic, political, and educational institutions.

CRISES THROUGHOUT THE CENTURIES

Since the beginning of humanity, there has scarcely ever been any lasting tranquillity from crises or problem situations. On the natural front, events like floods, famine, disease epidemics, earthquakes, tornadoes, and many others have caused continuing wrack and ruin in the four corners of the globe. On the social front, there are ongoing waves of crime against all humanity, hatred, and the destruction of human life. Politically, many societies have never fared well, in that leadership in these countries has made life a living hell for many citizens. Economically, things have never been that great for most people over the world. Economic problems seem to be escalating throughout the centuries. Cameron (1993, 3) observed that due to unequal economic development in many countries, the people have experienced revolutions and *coups d'etat.* In these countries, totalitarian leaders and military dictators have defrauded their citizens of political liberty and personal freedom. Many people have died through starvation, malnutrition, and disease. Cameron (1993, 74) noted further that:

In 1348 an epidemic of bubonic plague, the infamous Black Death, reached Europe from Asia. Spreading rapidly along the main commercial routes, taking its greatest toll in cities and towns, for two years it ravaged the whole of Europe, from Sicily and Portugal to Norway, from Muscovy to Iceland. In some cities more than half the population succumbed. For Europe as a whole the population was probably reduced by at least one-third. Moreover, the plague became endemic, with new outbursts every ten or fifteen years for the remainder of the century. Adding to the misery engendered by the plague, warfare, both civil and international, reached a new peak of intensity and violence in the fourteenth and fifteenth centuries.

The Hundred Years War (1338–1453) fought between England and France caused huge devastation and loss of lives (Cameron 1993, 74). Episodes of crop failure and continuing famine have been frequent in the history of the world. The Great Famine of 1315–1317 affected the whole northern part of Europe and destroyed many lives. Throughout the years, wars have never ceased. In addition to the various sectional wars in Africa, Asia, Europe, and several other places, the whole world was at war twice—the first (1914–1918) and second (1939–1945) World Wars.

THE IMPACTS OF THE FIRST AND SECOND WORLD WARS

World War I was a terrible war. It caused significant levels of destruction through large-scale raids and bombardments. Famine, disease, death, and human suffering escalated during the war. Transportation facilities, industrial plants and equipment, communications instruments and channels, and many other relevant items were destroyed during the war. Ocean shipping suffered a severe blow due to submarine war (Cameron 1993, 348).

Relatively scarce resources were devoted to the production of war gear. As such, there was a massive loss of productivity. Many people were killed and others stayed without any gainful employment. There were also severe labor shortages. Raw materials were hard to come by. To put it succinctly, the whole global political economy was devastated and lost its ability to promote and sustain life to its full capacities.

The continuing antagonism between nations led to the destruction of foreign investment. As noted earlier, the destruction of the productive capacities of nations led to ongoing shortages and hence continuing inflation. This brought along with it continuing price-control policies. Economic nationalism reached its peak after the war. Most nations were much more engrossed in economic progress at home than abroad. Yet at this point in time the existing global financial and monetary systems (i.e., the gold standard) were severely incapacitated and later collapsed. Nations experienced terrible financial shortages and attendant problems. Cameron (1993, 352) pointed out that most Western countries resorted to many different forms of restrictions on international trade. They tried to promote exports, however, ignoring imports (see details on mercantilism in Chapter 3). This era in the history of humanity was full of inward-looking attitudes on the part of nations. Policies developed and implemented were aimed at domestic progress. To fulfill its intended reconstruction purposes, the United States raised tariffs significantly. For example, through its Emergency Tariff Act passed in 1921, a complete embargo was placed on the importation of German dyestuffs (Cameron 1993, 352). The many acts of this nature imposed by the United States against other nations led to continuing retaliatory behavior. Of all the acts, it was the passing of the Smoot–Hawley Tariff Act of 1930 that forced other nations to react promptly. Nations increased their tariffs against American commodities.

The devastating result of these beggar-my-neighbor policies led to a total collapse of the volume of global trade and economic activities. The global political economy suffered severely from the various peace treaties signed after World War I. The Germans experienced a terrible hyperinflation in the early 1920s. When the French and Belgian troops invaded and occupied the Ruhr in January 1923, they seized and controlled coal mines and railroads. Their main objective was to pressure German miners to deliver coal to their nations. At this point in time, the Germans responded by printing paper money to pay off some of the compensations they were required to make to the Ruhr workers and employers. This phenomenon led to a continuing wave of inflation in Germany (Cameron 1993, 353–354). When the existing waves of inflation were finally transformed into an ongoing hyperinflation, the German mark was rendered worthless. The primary problem, however, was that the German hyperinflation was not confined to Germany alone, but also spread to many other countries, such as Bulgaria, Greece, Poland, and France.

Britain lost many of her foreign investments and global markets. The immediate time period after the war was full of huge magnitudes of unemployment in many countries. The coal industry suffered greatly. There was a severe collapse of SEPE institutions and programs. As noted by Rider (1995, 491), the period immediately after World War I was marked by continuing failures in attempts to create a new world order. "Attempts to manage problems raised by the war only led to crises, partly because the balance of military and economic power had been dramatically altered by the events leading up to the war itself. There was a failure to recognize the nature of these changes, and attempted remedies were both unrealistic and based on poor economic theory. Short-term solutions were unable to solve long-term problems and they contributed to the total collapse of the international system."

Thus, the world has experienced severe problems and difficulties. Human engineering in the areas of international social, economic, and political systems was not in any position to bring continuing positive changes. It was as if all humanity was doomed to a gloomy future of unavoidable failure. From the 1930s throughout the 1990s, human problems have never abated. They have always escalated. This period has seen wars, famine, inflation, unemployment, depression, environmental degradation, racial discrimination, totalitarianism, hate crimes, illegal drug activities, human degradation, and so on. There were many severe consequences.

GOALS AND PRESSING NEEDS OF ALL HUMANITY

As noted earlier, economic and business activities permeate every sphere of human lives. In our daily activities, we are always trying to achieve certain goals and meet certain needs and expectations. People engage in economic activities for many reasons. For example, an individual's needs include (generally) the desire for self-actualization, self-esteem, belongingness, safety, and the ability to house, clothe, and feed him- or herself (see Figure 1.2). It is the fervent desire to meet these needs that moves people to engage in business and economic activities to make money. The amount of money made is spent to attain these pressing needs. For this reason, it is clear that self-interested behavior is, indeed, a significant motivator of human economic behavior (see details in Chapter 3). With this in view, the basic question is whether these activities should be pursued solely for their own sake or for the individual's own self-actualization and glorification.

Most attempts made at social engineering and global development have not led to any significant successes in dealing with the pertinent problems of all humanity. Social institutions, regardless of their ongoing efforts and activities, seem to be failing in achieving their intended goals. The immensity of the problems of all humanity is revealed in the symptoms listed in Figure 8.1. A detailed study of the material presented in Figure 8.1 reveals that what most people have come to view as problems are instead symptoms of a bigger problem—HF decay or underdevelopment. These symptoms are classified into four categories as social, economic, political, and educational. Each symptom is not independent of the others. As shown by the direction of arrows in the center square on Figure 8.1, the intensity of each type of symptom is affected by the others. Observe from Figure 8.1 that the real source of the existing human predicament is HF decay or underdevelopment. Being the primary source of most human problems, HF decay or underdevelopment produces pools of SEPE symptoms. The continuing interactions among these symptoms lead to severe cultural problems. By failing to correctly diagnose the primary sources of these symptoms, societies have been unable to overcome the resulting problems. The visible effects of this failure are evidenced in the weaknesses of every social institution. The global political enemy is, therefore, locked in a terrible battle for survival. The resulting problems include unemployment, inflation, weak political will and structures, low productivity, escalating tort

Figure 8.1
The Human Plight and Predicament

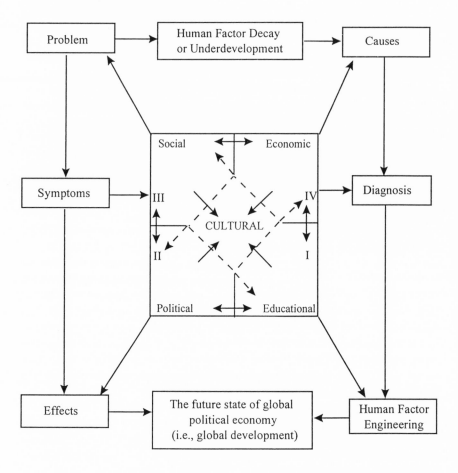

lawsuits, increasing abuses of human rights, global poverty, health problems, environmental degradation, rejection or resentment of legitimate authority, overpopulation, pollution, illegal drugs and criminal activities, racial atrocities, wars, human dishonesty, irresponsibility, and many others. In addition to these are the ongoing human tragedies of immense proportions. Top on the list are dictatorships, the development and use of nuclear weapons, Hitlerism in Germany, apartheid in South Africa, Stalinism in Russia, and so on.[2]

As shown in Figure 8.1, as long as human beings continue to fail to accurately diagnose the true sources of SEPE problems, their evolving cultures will not be successful in dealing with the observed symptoms. The ability to overcome most human problems requires true knowledge and programs aimed at HF engineering (see Chapters 9 and 10).

GETTING THE FACTS STRAIGHT: EVIDENCE OF HUMAN FAILURE

Scores of social scientists have applied the tools of quantitative analysis in their attempts to establish statistical relationships between social deviance and related variables (see Wootton 1959). The basic objective of this research agenda is to establish a high coefficient of determination between the dependent and independent variables. Since almost everybody believes in the scientific method, the conclusions of these quantitative analyses have filtered into many social, economic, political, and educational policies. This has been the trend for the past several decades and there is no indication that it will change in the near future. It is, however, encouraging to realize that scholars are beginning to look beyond the basic statistical results to find out whether there are any additional variables that have been missing in all their quantitative analyses.

Wootton (1959, 326) argued that many quantitative analyses have actually failed to provide necessary and sufficient evidence to substantiate the causal relationship between social problems and the variables that are deemed to bring them about. Most evidence and conclusions arrived at from using the scientific method in the social sciences have failed to produce any hopes for policy effectiveness. Unfortunately, society always tries to locate its problems in variables for which it will not necessarily have to blame existing failure on its own previous oversights. In addition, society is able to busy itself in attempting to solve problems by developing and implementing policies that attack symptoms rather than root causes (see Figure 8.1). Society fails to recognize that ineffectiveness in dealing with problems may lead to the escalation of further problems and crises. Suppose, for example, that an auto mechanic observes an oil leak in a car's engine and proceeds to wrap a plastic bag around it and tie it up tightly, believing that the problem is taken care of. He or she wakes up the next morning and observes that the plastic bag is heavily soaked with oil and dripping profusely. The nagging question is, "Did he or she actually solve the initial problem in the first place or did he or she just delay its time of intensification by band-aiding it?" Indeed, as is obvious, his or her band-aiding solution to the problem failed to accomplish the intended permanent solution.

As noted by Wootton (1959), what society usually claims to be the major sources of its problems are often not the case (see Figure 8.1). They are usually symptoms rather than causes. If only society will realize its past mistakes, it may stand up on its feet, reassess past diagnoses and policies, determine what the actual root causes are, and then proceed carefully to deal with them as may be necessary. Society is failing in this regard because leading social scientists have pursued scientism both excessively and sometimes wrongly to the total neglect or loss of the ability and desire for social thinking, philosophical analysis, and the conceptually creative evaluation of observable statistical facts and historical data. In addition, knowledge and information that cannot be easily quantified for the pursuit of the scientific method is usually either left out or treated as unimportant. Their research, observations, analysis, conclusions, and policy recommendations are therefore based on the so-called scientific methodology, which is usually unable to take into account all relevant information (i.e., both qualitative and quantitative data). The results of their research have, therefore, for many generations misled governments and SEPE institutions and hence cloud the policy horizon. It is therefore not surprising why those who operate social institutions fail to know how to react to and deal successfully with existing problems.

As a matter of fact, sociological and criminological studies have never established conclusively that both the death sentence and life imprisonment serve as good deterrents to murder and other types of criminal activities. *The Economist* (1994, 50) noted that incarceration rates increased by about 168 percent in the 1980s in the United States. While the minimum mandatory sentences have escalated, the rate of growth of prison services has been one of the fastest growing businesses in the United States. Heavy-duty criminal activities have mushroomed in many developed countries (Canada, Britain, France, and Germany, and also in many developing countries).

Table 8.1 lists the total estimated annual expenditure on crime prevention programs. Imagine how much impact these resources would have had on criminal activities if the funds were channeled into HF development (see Chapter 10). As revealed by the data presented in Table 8.1, humongous financial resources go into crime prevention in the United States every year. The situation is not too different for Canada and the other industrialized nations. Though a great deal of money is spent annually for crime prevention, little impact is being made on criminal statistics. As such, crime preventive measures may not always be as effective as expected.

Table 8.1
Estimated Annual Crime Cost in the United States, 1993

Type	Description	Cost (in billions)
Criminal justice	Spending on police, courts, and prisons	$90
Private protection	Spending on alarms, private guards, and security systems	65
Urban decay	Cost of lost jobs and fleeing residents	50
Property loss	Value of stolen goods	45
Medical care	Cost of treating crime victims	5
Shattered lives	Economic value of lost and broken lives	179
TOTAL		425

Source: Business Week, 13 December 1993, 72–79.

In today's world, treatises on the failure of social, economic, and political institutions and systems abound. The volumes that have been written and discussed on talkshows, radio programs, newspapers, and the like are overwhelming. Evidence abounds revealing the state of social, economic, and political conditions in society today. These conditions, problems, and setbacks are present in all societies. Developed as well as developing countries are struggling to deal with these problems.

Dow Corning, for example, manufactured and sold silicone breast implants that were later discovered to have caused auto-immune disease in the bodies of women who used them. Dow Corning and other defendants agreed to settle for 4.25 billion dollars. Other related cases of mass tort include agent orange, asbestos, and Dalcon Shield. Nocera (1995, 60) observed, "There aren't merely dozens of breast-implant lawsuits anymore, there are thousands of them—nay, tens of thousands. It has become one of the most fearsome waves of mass litigation ever to hit corporate America. Mithoff's first target, Dow Corning, has been laid waste by the litigation, driven into bankruptcy by the sheer impossibility of trying to defend itself against that many lawsuits. And its ordeal is not over. The plaintiffs' lawyers who pushed it into bankruptcy court are now trying to move in for the kill; they talk boldly about taking the company over completely." Indeed, whether people believe it or not, the primary reason underlying most of these litigations is ongoing HF decay or underdevelopment.

In recent years, the focus has been on values and how they are being eroded as the foundations of human behavior and activities. Those who believe in the usefulness of values continue to argue that their continuing erosion will lead to ongoing problems in society. That is, in the absence of values, people may revert to doing what they think to be right in their own eyes. *The Economist* (1994, 50) reported that "Asian countries are not immune to the social trends that trouble the West. However strong values may be, economic forces change. Development demands industrialization, which means luring young people to the cities." Thus, as wage employment lures people into urban areas, their values are severely challenged. Those who succumb to these challenges enter into criminal activities as means for survival in a socially and economically harsh environment.

The same issue of *The Economist* (1994, 31–32) noted further that in South Korea the divorce rate has jumped nearly threefold since 1970; in Singapore, Taiwan, and Hong Kong, twice as many couples are divorcing as in the early 1980s. In China the number of divorces has more than tripled in the past four years; engaged couples are drawing up pre-nuptial contracts, and even taking out insurance against splitting up.

Indeed, the rate at which many marriages are falling apart is alarming. Marriages that are founded on mere romance and infatuation usually go awry. In this case, divorce follows sooner or later. As will be discussed, the family is undergoing massive transformations and problems. Men and women who a while ago said to each other, "I do" and also added, "till death do us part," turn around a little later and say, "I hate you. See you in hell!" They then put each other away either for good or for a season, arguing that "We are incompatible and it is not working out anymore." Stark (1992, 288) observed, "Back when most couples had weak emotional ties at best, they seldom divorced; although couples marry for love, they often divorce in anger and disappointment. . . . Most people who get divorced report that their marriage ceased to provide adequate emotional satisfaction—that is, their relationship was no longer happy."

In view of this observation, the most common reason given for such separation or divorce is incompatibility. Husbands and wives are finding it increasingly difficult to keep their relationships ongoing. In many marriages there is little happiness and personal satisfaction. Many spouses abuse each other mentally, verbally, physically, spiritually, psychologically, and so on. Today, many young people are indeed afraid to get married and they therefore prefer to live together (common law) in many cases (see details in Chapter 9). In such relationships, there is actually no long-term commitment. Minor disagreements or other difficulties usually destroy such relationships. Both parties walk away from the informal quasimarriage contract, severely hurt and badly distraught; some for a little while and others for life. Recall, for example, when a man walked into a house in Vernon, British Columbia, Canada, on April 5, 1996 where his ex-wife, her parents, brothers, and sisters had gathered to prepare for her sister's wedding, scheduled for the next day. As soon as he entered into the room, he opened fire and killed almost everybody who was present. The bride was also killed. He later turned the gun on himself. Indeed, this was not an isolated incident. It is commonplace in most societies today. No wonder people are beginning to buy marital insurance, in case such traumatic marital experiences cross their path.

The institution of the family and its set-up are being challenged by new developments in society today (see also Stark 1992, 373–403). Social groups that view the traditional institution of the family as being too restrictive of human lifestyle have challenged its relevance to modern life. As such, the family set-up is struggling to survive. Issues such as single-parenting, gender, sexual orientation, the pro-life and pro-choice debate, all forms of abuse, and many others are continuing to threaten the survival of the traditional family institution. The negative impact of certain Hollywood celebrities on the status of the family is extremely damaging. Thus, in many societies, because of these issues, the accompanying problems of the family seem to be its inability to perform its SEPE functions effectively. Challenges to the traditional family structure and set-up are coming from gay and lesbian movements too. For example, in a letter to the editor of *The Wall Street Journal*, Evan Wolfson (1996, A13) wrote,

Up until 1967, the laws (again justified by religious–political extremists and even judges with quotes from the *Bible*) continually prosecuted people who married someone of the "wrong" race; we changed that. At one time, women getting married became the legal property of their husbands; we changed that. In the past, civil marriage legally bound people for life; we changed that (even though some religions haven't). Clearly, there is no single definition of marriage that has been around for even 200 years, let alone 6,000. Most important, repeating such anti-gay rhetorical fallacies obscures the main point: There is no good reason to prevent gay and lesbian couples from taking on the commitment of civil marriage, with the responsibilities, support, and protection that marriage offers to families.

Though all these new developments do not prove that the family is not a good institution, they are weakening its effectiveness in modern society. In some cases, certain government regulations have also militated against the efficient organization and operation of the family as a social institution. For example, to qualify for certain social assistance programs in both Canada and the United States, one has to be either single or a single parent. The cases in point are Medicare assistance for AIDS patients and hemophiliacs. Certain children with chronic illnesses may not easily receive government social assistance as long as both parents are still legally married and living together under one roof. The magnitude of the benefits paid out to divorced single parents and alimonies have tended to discourage the traditional family. A husband accused by his wife of being abusive in every regard may lose the right of visitation to see his wife and children on a regular basis, even if he desires to go through counseling to have the problem resolved. A husband and wife who have both been accused of having molested their child may end up losing the child to the state, even without proper investigation of the allegations. These phenomena continue whether the allegations are true or not. In some cases, there is neither validity nor evidence to the accusation. Families that experience these difficulties are usually torn apart permanently. Thus, as a social institution, the family in the modern world seems to be failing in performing its social functions of nurturing through education and training due to continuing stress and strain being imposed on it by members of society.

The contributions of businesses toward the breakdown of the family are tremendous. Clinard and Yeager (1982, 81) recalled that a job advertisement placed in *The Wall Street Journal* by the President of the Stolfan Corporation categorically stated, "The job of personnel director at our company is not for everyone. I know because this year I have already had two men in this position. It wasn't for them. *If your family or your 'lifestyle' or your kid's boy scout experience is more important to you than your job, then this isn't for you*" (emphasis mine).

Child Merchandise

The continuing pressures of technological progress and industrialization have created severe problems for many families all over the world. In some cases, parents either merchandise their children for token money or other material items, as was the case in Romania a few years ago. Several Romanian children were sold to Americans under the pretense of adoption. In the Romanian case, some parents sold their children for a few dollars, which were subsequently used to purchase such consumer items as television sets, stereo systems, and radios. In the United States, newborn babies are sometimes either suffocated, wrapped up in polythene bags and dumped in garbage cans, or just abandoned in shopping malls, bus or train stations, airports, and the like. For example, in 1995, in Seattle, passersby heard the cries of an infant from a garbage can into which it was dumped. They called the police, who came and rescued a healthy newborn baby. A similar example was the recent case of a baby found in the Vancouver International Airport.

In October 1994, an American mother strapped her two little boys into the seats of the family car, drove them into a lake, walked away, and left them to die. She later lied to the police and other family members that her children were abducted by a black man at gunpoint. Evidence later revealed that she was either emotionally out of it or insane. It could be argued, however, that she was a victim of social decay—a symptom of severe HF decay or underdevelopment.

Undesirable Baby Girls

In China as well as India, parents literally kill their newborn baby girls.[3] Cultural norms dictate that baby girls be either aborted or killed since boys are preferred to girls in these cultures. While the rearing of girls is still viewed today as watering plants in another family's garden, boys are perceived as sources of wealth and future security for their parents. Girls grow, marry, and carry away the family wealth in the form of the huge dowries their parents have to pay to the man they are married to. As such, parents who do not see anything wrong with the practice of terminating the lives of baby girls do so without any guilt. To many who do so, the practice is an accepted way of alleviating the family's problems of poverty. These examples are limitless. In China, for example, children are not only neglected in orphanages, but also maltreated and mutilated in many different ways, including starving, beating, and the like.

Ongoing Fraud in Society

Prime-Time Live, an American television news program, is in the habit of uncovering various scams in the United States. In one of the programs it recently aired, it revealed how there is a great proliferation of fake medical clinics in the United States. The most prominent location of these clinics was Miami. The operators of these clinics duped the U.S. government by creating phony medical programs that recruited senior citizens, performed fictitious medical tests and examinations on them, and then billed the health-care program. In some cases, the owners of these clinics paid those individuals who were lured to participate in the scam (either knowingly or unknowingly). Lies were fabricated and told about the medical conditions of participants and relevant tests performed by employees (who were usually not even qualified) at each fraudulent clinic on the participants. The medical system was then billed. In most cases, by the time the Medicare authorities were alerted, the clinics were closed and the owners moved to other locations to resume their clandestine activities. *Prime-Time Live* noted that these unnecessary diagnostic tests and procedures cost the taxpayer approximately 2 billion dollars each year.

On January 5, 1995, *Prime-Time Live* aired yet another program on certain suspicious relationships between young women and older men or young men and older women. When these relationships are struck, some quickly solidify into marriages. The younger spouses then have their names added to the assets (including bank accounts, personal wills, etc.) of the older ones. Over time, the older people are killed so that their younger spouses or "special friends" can claim the assets, other financial resources, and the contents of wills left behind by the deceased.

Welfare fraud is common in many countries. For example, in Canada, especially in the province of British Columbia, it has been uncovered recently (1994–1995) that some welfare recipients have been duping the welfare system by collecting several welfare checks at the same time by lying to the authorities. That is, individual welfare recipients either signed up at several places and then proceeded to collect checks from each of these places, or, after having received a welfare check, some individuals fabricated lies to prove that their checks were truly lost. New checks were therefore issued to them. They then proceeded to cash all checks made out in their names.

Serial Killers, Bombers, and Gunmen

Serial killers have caused continuing havoc and killed hundreds of people in different parts of the world. The fact that they were able to kill many people without being apprehended is indicative of either the weaknesses in or the failure of the police and other security agents. Ted Bundy and the Green River Killer, for example, together killed no less than eighty women (both young and old). Other violent serial killers of note include Charles Manson, the Boston Strangler, and Albert Henry DeSalvo. The so-called Unabomber eluded even the famous and most well-equipped intelligence unit in the whole world—the FBI—for almost two decades. In England in 1995, it was discovered that a serial killer had killed many women and buried their remains in the backyard of his house. He also was not caught until the damage had already been done. Many people (both young and old) disappeared, either because they ran away from home or were abducted and carried away. While some were found and rescued, others were not. A man walked into an elementary school classroom and killed sixteen children in addition to their teacher in March 1996 in Scotland. He later turned the gun on himself. Similar phenomena have occurred in many other countries, where gunmen jumped into classrooms, workplaces, restaurants, political rally grounds, abortion clinics, and many other places and opened fire at random, either killing or wounding many people. The story of how many child molesters sexually abused and then dismembered the bodies of little boys and girls is commonplace. Even those who have moved away from cities into rural areas or small towns, hoping to escape from city problems and violence, are now realizing they have brought these criminal activities along with them (see a detailed discussion on this issue in Chapter 9). These occurrences have diminished people's confidence in the effectiveness of individual safety and security systems. It leaves many people gasping for breath and asking themselves in excessive fear, "Who is next?"

Failing Education Systems and Training Programs

In the area of education, one may ask the question, "Where and how is society failing to educate the young people to have them become responsible men and women in society?" In the 1960s, when students began to rebel against authority in the advanced nations (i.e., Canada, the United States, the United Kingdom, Germany, France, etc.), students argued and fought for education systems and training programs that had no examination schemes attached to them. Today, many businesses are complaining that existing education systems and training programs are failing to produce the caliber of employees they want. They complain that many graduates coming from today's universities and colleges do not possess the knowledge and the skills necessary for effective performance on the job. A recent Canadian survey of employers in relation to the relevant skills employers look for revealed that employers hardly find in prospective graduates the requisite skills they look for during their hiring processes. To deal with these disappointments, most organizations are beginning to establish their own management training programs to help them prepare their employees for the positions for which they have been hired. This, indeed, is a continuing frustration for most businesses.

A similar experience is that involving children who receive little benefit from the existing school system. Many go through the school system and neither learn to read nor write nor think properly. For example, in British Columbia, some parents have recently become so disillusioned and frustrated with the province's educational system that they have begun a new move called *Back to the Basics*, a system of schooling that places emphasis on discipline, good behavior, principles, values, and so on. This program began in Surrey, British Columbia, in the fall of 1994. Other municipalities are watching the experiment very closely and hope to adopt it, given its results.

Teenagers and Violent Criminal Activities

Putting this evidence together, it can be conclusively argued that educational institutions and programs are failing to achieve their stipulated and intended goals. Lineberry (1994), an urban crime historian, speaking on the Texan teen rapists and killers, observed, "I think they [the teenagers] are more or less oblivious. From their point of view, life is of little value. Our logic toward the criminal-justice system is people are rational, but I think you're dealing with a crowd of people who are not rational by the standards of the criminal justice system. In the past, teenagers tended to at worst knock off the 7-Eleven store. These days, teenagers knock off the store and murder the manager at the same time. That was almost unheard of 20 or 30 or 50 years ago."

Street crime is common everywhere. Cities such as New York, Los Angeles, Boston, Washington D.C., Seattle, Tokyo, London, Berlin, Vancouver, Toronto, Montreal, Paris, Lagos, and many others all over the world are reeling under extensive criminal activities. Rape, murder, mugging, gang activities, drive-by shooting, terrorism, and many other crimes happen around us every day (Corelli 1994, 15).

In reality, the sources of teenage deviant behavior can be located in both the ongoing failure of the school system and the sordid state of the family. For example,

Clinard and Yeager (1982, 86) recalled that a Harvard Business School professor, in teaching a course on business decision making, taught students that the falsification of information for business negotiations and contracting is not really wrong. During the course of the semester, students perceived that one could obtain better payoffs by obscuring relevant information and cheating. Lying and getting away with it helped some to even obtain better grades in the course. The sad part of the whole story is that most of these students probably ended up becoming leaders in the business world. The problems of the modern educational, training, and mentoring systems also come partly as results of certain government rules and regulations, usually based on unproved educational research conclusions regarding how children learn.

The Judicial System, Lawyers, and Law Enforcement Agencies

The contribution of legal practitioners to the continuing failure of social institutions and systems is horrendous and pervasive. As such, many people all over the world have become continually dissatisfied with legal systems in their own countries and those of others. To some, the legal system is there to protect the interests of offenders rather than victims. For example, in many documented cases, those whose rights have been severely violated sometimes end up experiencing a mistrial. Worst of all, when it comes to trying criminals, the idea of jury nullification is now threatening to destroy the effectiveness and honesty of both the legal and jury deliberation processes. In the event jury nullification occurs, the court may let a guilty criminal go free. Usually, this happens on the basis of race, gender, creed, and so on. Members of a jury will acquit the guilty individual who is also a member of their own race, gender, or creed. This may occur even when the individual is proven beyond all reasonable doubts to be guilty. Jury nullification is not only devastating, but also destroys people's confidence in the legal system.

It seems, therefore, that the legal system in many countries is either driven by the desire to acquire personal wealth or the system has been infiltrated by individuals who are staunch members of societies that engage in criminal activities. In the former Soviet Union, for example, the police are in league with the crooks. In Hong Kong and the Philippines, certain members of law-enforcement agencies (i.e., the police, lawyers, and other high-ranking public officials) work hand in hand with well-known criminals. In Nigeria, Ghana, Kenya, Uganda, and many other countries, they work together. This is also true for Canada, the United States, the United Kingdom, Germany, Italy, France, and many other countries (Sutherland 1982; Hobbs 1995). Some lawyers would do everything possible to block any proposed legal reforms that threaten to reduce their personal financial gains from clients. An article entitled "Lawyer Lies," in *The Wall Street Journal*, 22 March 1996, revealed that some trial lawyers in the United States began to fight to protect their ill-gotten wealth, knowing very well that Propositions 201 and 202 would impose restrictions on their legal earnings. Elliot (1994, 40) noted,

Thailand is the classic example. Prostitution is formally illegal there. But thousands of brothels, massage palors and go-go bars simply put a cop on the payroll, slapping him $120 to $600 monthly; a recent study . . . estimates that the city's 1,000 entertainment houses pay bribes of $600,000 monthly to the local police. That keeps Thailand's police secure in their suburban villas and BMWs; a retired police colonel was recently found to have $920,000 in his bank account. The truth is that he could not have saved that much given the magnitude of income he receives from his regular job and/or duty.

Business Tycoons and Criminal Activities

Businesses are not excluded from ongoing suspicious financial deals and scandals. Sutherland (1982, 54–55), for example, pointed out that "Businessmen [and women] characteristically believe that the least government is the best, and in many cases regard the enactment of a law rather than the violation of the law as the crime. The businessman's [and woman's] contempt for law, like that of the professional thief, grows out of the fact that the law impedes his behavior. . . . Businessmen [and women] are organized formally, also, for the control of legislation, selection of administrators, and restriction of appropriations for the enforcement of laws which may affect themselves."

Millions of crooked deals and fraudulent behavior have been documented and discussed by Blumberg (1989), Domanick (1989), Ekman (1989), Ellul (1990), Keating (1991), Kohn (1986), Lindskoog (1993), Noel and Watterson (1992), and Parenti (1986). Sutherland (1982, 58–59) observed further,

With the objective of maintaining status and a conception of themselves as non-criminal, the corporations employ experts in law, public relations, and advertising. These agencies are the corporate equivalent of the professional thief's "mouthpiece." The "mouthpiece" of the professional thief has as his principal function the defense of his client against specific charges. The function of the "mouthpiece" of the white collar criminal is much more inclusive. He has the function of influencing the enactment and administration of the law as it applies to his clients, of advising his clients in advance as to the methods which may be used with relative impunity, as well as defending his client before the courts and before the public when specific charges are made against them.

Sutherland (1982, 53) noted that business corporations always commit crimes against consumers, competitors, stockholders, states, inventors, employees, and many others. They cheat on their taxes and offer huge sums of money in bribes to state officials in order to get away with crooked business deals and constant violations of government regulations and standards.[4] These crimes are not discreet and inadvertent violations of technical regulations. Corporate crime in Canada, the United States, the United Kingdom, Japan, Germany, the Philippines, Haiti, China, Russia, Kenya, Nigeria, Zaire, and many other places is horrendous. Though the laws and relevant institutions are put in place to discourage these types of behavior, they are usually ineffectual because those who are placed in charge are involved in the crooked deals themselves.

In cases like these, the law is often twisted to favor the members of a clique or group. True justice, therefore, usually eludes those to whom it is due. As such, those who operate the legal system and all other law-enforcement agencies fail those who need their services. This is where jury nullification causes severe heartache and pain for victims and their relatives and friends. This is one of the primary reasons why, though a society may have a well-organized criminal justice system, that system may not achieve its intended goals when it is manipulated in this manner. The rule of law will be violated and miscarriage of justice will prevail on a continuing basis. A pertinent question, however, is, "Does this failure imply that the system has failed?" We will return to this question in Chapter 9.

Politicians and Their Self-Interest

The contributions of politicians to the continuing failure of SEPE institutions and systems cannot be ignored. For centuries, politicians, the leadership of political parties and government representatives, have been deeply involved in messy and horrendous financial, sexual, conflict of interest, and related scandals. Politicians usually use their positions to gain personal advantages. By so doing, they become less efficient in performing their roles and duties as public servants. As such, many social institutions fail to achieve their intended goals because of the life, attitudes, and behavior of politicians. Top on the list of political scandals are Watergate, global arms deals, cases of overseas bribery and corruption (i.e., the cases of Lockheed, Gulf Oil, Northrup, pharmaceutical companies, etc.), securities fraud and abuses, antitrust enforcement, and various kinds of political swindling (for a detailed discussion of each of these issues, refer to Sobel 1977).

The Failure of Correctional Systems

Professor John Donohue observed that the flawed theory of incapacitation is usually used to support the bid for locking up criminals. This theory suggests that by locking up a criminal, he or she is prevented from committing certain crimes he or she could have committed without having been incarcerated. Professor Donohue pointed out that this view is wrong because once a criminal is arrested and imprisoned, others, probably more energetic and vicious, take his or her place (see *The Economist* 1994, 26). Yet threatening to lock up drug dealers and criminals for life has little effect in discouraging criminal behavior. Jerome Skolnick argued that people who trade dope are already making a living in a world that is more dangerous than mere threats of imprisonment or a death sentence.

Policies based on the views of the great economists (i.e., those who view criminal activity as a utility-maximizing behavior) do not seem to be achieving their intended goals. *Business Week* (1993, 75) noted, "Now the law of diminishing returns is setting in. Building and staffing prisons is extremely expensive, especially as sentences get longer and older inmates require increased medical care. Imprisoning a 25-year-old for life costs a total of $600,000 to $1 million. So putting someone in prison for life puts a huge financial burden on the next generation—just as a big budget deficit does."

The Impact of Highly Monetized Economic Activities and Principles

Where family values are being gobbled down by varying and divergent personal views and other value systems, HF decay is either terribly bad or is on ascendancy. In many cases, the high priority accorded to individual participation in the global marketplace or economy preoccupies all participants to such an extent that the authority of universal principles either fades away into the background or is surrendered to the goddess of self-interest and wealth acquisition in highly monetized economies. Thousands of illustrative examples exist across the globe. For example, in the recent past, newspapers, radios, television, and other forms of media documented and reported cases where a friend, a spouse, or a child killed others for financial gain or advantage. The most frequently observed example is the killing of a spouse or parents or grandparents in order to receive the expected insurance benefits. The traditional view is that people who behave in this manner are either suffering from some kind of mental illness or psychological trauma. Such people plead not guilty by reason of insanity.[5]

Indeed, from the HF theoretical perspective, the traditional view obscures a great deal. Taking the lives of others in order to gain personal advantage and wealth is not necessarily because of insanity or psychological problems. Crimes committed against humanity, as evidenced in Hitler's Nazi Germany, Verwoerd's apartheid South Africa, Charles Taylor's Liberia, Bosnia, Rwanda, international aggression and terrorism, the continuing pursuit of political dissidents, and so on are all human tragedies that continue to haunt all humanity today.

The fruits of HF decay or underdevelopment can be seen in all types of discrimination, fraudulent behavior, low productivity, painfully sour and abusive relationships, and so on.[6] Blacks have suffered racial discrimination all over the world, especially in the United States, South Africa, Germany, France, Britain, and so on. The Jews suffered the worst plight in Nazi Germany. The Japanese, the Chinese, and Native North American Indians have also suffered similar plights. The civil rights movement that took off in the 1960s in the United States was an attempt to end discrimination against Blacks. The leader of the movement, Dr. Martin Luther King, Jr., was brutally assassinated, probably for his outspoken views on and advocacy for equal civil rights for all Americans, regardless of race, gender, or creed. *The Economist* (1994, 15), for example, observed,

Oliver Brown brought his lawsuit because he and his daughter wished to choose where she went to school; because of her race, she could not. The desegregation ruling allowed her, and all blacks, to choose their schools in the future. But it was not quite as simple as that. Many school boards tried to comply with Brown merely by saying that, of course, blacks could go where they liked. But the courts knew that long-standing patterns of segregation did not allow true freedom from choice. They ordered active steps—numerical quotas and forced busing of both blacks and whites—to integrate the schools. In short, to achieve what they assumed would be the results of freedom of choice, they took some freedom of choice away.

The evidence presented in this chapter is a mere scratch on the surface of the primary causes of and reasons for the failure or inefficiency of SEPE institutions. The trend will continue to escalate into the twenty-first century and beyond. As such, until the true sources of the failure are discovered and dealt with appropriately, society will make little progress in its attempts to improve the performance and efficiency of SEPE institutions so as to successfully contend with the scarcity problem.

CONCLUSION

Every society or country has its own ways and means for dealing with the scarcity problem. Social, economic, and political activities, as practiced throughout all human history, have been solely concerned with efficient and effective use of resources in order to obtain the greatest benefits from their use to all people in society. In their continuing efforts to develop, improve, and, if possible, perfect every aspect of human life, men and women have continuously failed to perceive that one of the greatest aspects of civilization, and in fact, the most important, is human development (see detailed discussions in Chapters 9 through 11). This oversight has led to an ongoing focus on the development of social, economic, and political institutions and techniques that are necessary but not sufficient for enhancing humanity's mastery over nature (see details in Chapters 6 through 8). Though significant technological inventions and innovations have been made since the beginning of time, men and women are still very far away from annihilating the pertinent problems that plague their civilizations. Scarcity, the basic economizing problem, is still yet to be conquered and, if possible, permanently tamed. In the remainder of this book, the emphasis will be placed on the role of the HF in creating and also solving the pertinent SEPE problems.

NOTES

1. It is quite possible that men and women will continue to make significant advances in the area of technological invention and innovation. However, as things stand today, it is becoming increasingly difficult to believe that the human quality will improve if nothing is done specifically to develop it.

2. Auschwitz, a product of Hitlerism, still remains as one of the greatest reminders of human failure.

3. An East Indian pediatrician who performs ultrasound for pregnant Indian women, advises them on the sex of the fetus and proceeds with abortion if the ultrasound reveals that the fetus will turn out to be a baby girl. This medical doctor believes that his practice of aborting the fetuses of baby girls is invaluable to India because the country is overpopulated. He is also convinced beyond all reasonable doubt that there is no one in India who

can stop him from continuing on with his practice. When asked what he would do when law-enforcement agents come after him, he maintained that since most members of the law-enforcement agencies are his avowed clients and believe in his service to India, there is no way any of these individuals can either arrest or terminate his practice and service to his society. As is obvious from this example, it can hardly be denied that a people's culture can either liberate or imprison them, thus preventing them from achieving the greatest level of progress for themselves. Above all, the passionate desire for money and all kinds of pleasure determines the bulk of human behavior. These, in many cases, subdue the application of and adherence to universal principles of life.

4. For detailed discussion on business fraud, political espionage, and other forms of bribery and corruption, see Sobel (1977).

5. Court cases and legal arguments are full of examples.

6. *Newsweek*, 2 January 1989, 44–48; *Newsweek*, 10 April 1989, 49; *Time*, 10 April 1989, 26; *Time*, 13 March 1989, 17–32; *Time*, 26 February 1989, 40–45; *Time*, 18 December 1989, 44–50.

HUMAN FACTOR PERSPECTIVES

HUMAN FACTOR PERSPECTIVES ON FAILING SOCIAL INSTITUTIONS AND SYSTEMS

An orderly, peaceful, and economically stable society is what people prefer to dwell in. Such a society cannot be legislated into being permanently. Bottomore (1987, 144) observed that "political institutions are concerned with the distribution of power in society. Max Weber defined the state as 'a human community which successfully claims the monopoly of the legitimate use of physical force within a given territory.' Thus the state is one of the [most] important agencies of social control whose functions are carried out by means of law, backed ultimately by physical force." The various activities, programs, rules, systems, and institutions that are aimed at development, when taken together, form the sum total of a people's way of taming their environment and surviving in it. In light of this, it can be argued that a people's culture is the amalgamation of all rules, regulations, beliefs, values, principles, practices, and procedures developed for solving problems and for dealing with issues concerning human interaction and coordination in production, distribution, exchange, and consumption (Adjibolosoo 1995a). These processes, technologies, well-developed procedures, principles, institutions, theories, and so on provide the foundation pillars that guide and promote life, work, and play in their particular environment.

Since every group of people is uniquely different from others in the way they live and act, the rules, regulations, techniques, and procedures they evolve or arrive at are usually different and unique to their specific society. This is the case because of the varying levels of perception, insight, tradition, values, theories, principles, and belief systems they have. Due to the fact that each society is always being faced with continuing problems in its environment, which are usually different from those prevailing in other societies, the evolutionary process that leads to the creation of theories, principles, plans, policies, programs, projects, methodologies, and procedures for dealing with ongoing problems is both varied and dynamic. Lack of understanding may mislead people to try to solve their problems using the wrong procedures. When this happens, failure is the ultimate outcome.

For centuries, humanity has toiled continuously to develop social, economic, political, and educational institutions and other systems to be used to encourage and promote the development and efficient operation of societies (see details in Chapters 1 through 8). As societies move from technologically primitive states into more technologically advanced stages, they continue to create different types of SEPE institutions, systems, and technologies whose primary objective is to facilitate the effective organization, administration, and development of societies. The rules, regulations, procedures, and techniques developed by those who organize and operate the SEPE institutions usually serve as guideposts to individuals in society regarding how they must relate to each other and live in harmony together. Thus, whether a society runs smoothly and succeeds in its endeavors is dependent on the ability of its members to live, work, and play together in love, peace, and harmony (see details in Chapter 10). The direct outcomes are social, economic, political, and intellectual liberty, equity, and justice for all. In recent years, continuing escalation of SEPE problems is forcing people all over the world to call for the reinstatement of capital punishment in some countries, the tightening of young offenders' acts, increasing jail terms for criminals, and many other solutions. Many people have come to believe that SEPE problems can be solved by either promulgating new laws or tightening and strictly enforcing existing laws or both.

In view of these observations, the primary objective of this chapter is to discuss and explain in detail the continuing failure of SEPE institutions and systems in societies, using social deviance or the continuing prevalence of crime as the main illustration. The chapter argues that deviance in society is major empirical evidence of the failure of SEPE institutions and that this failure is a complete reflection of HF decay or underdevelopment. This chapter argues, therefore, that, contrary to popularly held opinion, unless societies concentrate on the development of relevant HF characteristics, every type of SEPE program, though it may achieve short-term successes, will not produce any long-term positive results in the presence of continuing HF decay or underdevelopment. I will discuss and analyze in detail the varying problems that plague all humanity and also provide a HF perspective on the primary source of SEPE problems in society. To begin, I present a brief review of existing traditional arguments usually put forward to either explain or rationalize the continuing failure of SEPE institutions in the modern world. A more detailed HF perspective on this failure is provided in subsequent sections.

HUMAN FAILURE: CONVENTIONAL EXPLANATIONS

In Chapter 8, a detailed discussion was presented on the human plight and predicament. The evidence presented in Chapter 8 revealed that humanity not only has many unsatisfied needs, but is also in crisis. Today, people of all walks of life are still struggling to comprehend the underlying reasons for the ongoing SEPE problems and to find solutions for them. Scull (1988, 667) noted that the early twentieth-century writers on deviance and social control viewed social control as implying all social arrangements and practices employed in society to maintain the existing social order and conformity (see also Borgatta and Meyer 1959; Ross 1901; Park and Burgess 1921; Cohen 1966). "For these early theorists, social control was seen as those processes that operated to produce an emerging consensus on social goals, a 'consensus' whose character and existence were presumed to emerge essentially spontaneously through mechanisms that remained almost wholly opaque and unscrutinized" (Scull 1988, 669).

For many years, orthodox scholars have viewed social controls as the forces of an invisible hand that restored social order and conformity whenever it entered some sort of social disequilibrium (see Janowitz 1978; Cooley 1918; Thomas and Znaniecki 1927). Social controls are aimed at dealing with social problems—violations of mores and ideals of society (Lemert 1951; Mills 1943). Society expects and hopes that all its institutions will deal efficiently with any imbalances and quickly restore social equilibrium, thus silencing all negative forces that try to jeopardize human well-being. While Janowitz viewed social control as the ability of society to regulate itself, Park and Burgess (1921) viewed social problems as direct results of social control. This was the same view held and propagated by the Chicago School of Sociology (see Matza 1969; Scull 1988; Wirth 1964).

Raab and Selznick (1964, 4) observed that "A social problem exists when organized society's ability to order relationships among people seems to be failing; when its institutions are faltering, its laws are being flaunted, the framework of expectations is being shaken" (quoted in Bottomore 1987, 310). Durkheim (1951, 248) argued that moral deregulation is destructive to the social order. There are hundreds of scholarly works discussing the basic reasons for social deviance and the problems of society. As such, social policy uses the conclusions of these studies to determine programs it deems appropriate to use to deal with the setbacks society experiences.[1]

Humanity has accomplished a great deal in terms of its attempts to help people overcome their ongoing problems. Unfortunately, all these achievements have not yet been translated into successful social engineering. Though humanity has made significant progress in the area of technological advancement, it is losing on the attainment of efficient and effective social engineering. It seems, therefore, that though we are learning to be more efficient in the use of available resources and facilities we are not really achieving effectiveness. That is, the direction toward which all humanity seems to be heading is not necessarily where most people really want to go. Though the attempts to crack open the many puzzling causes of human problems are numerous, the growing desire for and attempts at social engineering do not seem to be making any significant headway. This observation brings four critical questions to mind: (1) Why do most human attempts at social engineering for continuing development seem to be failing? (2) Why are the SEPE institutions and systems failing to accomplish their intended goals? (3) Have they outlived their usefulness? (4) Why is it that some of these systems seem to have functioned much better in the past than they do today, being unable to stand up successfully to the challenges of the day?

THE HUMAN FACTOR PERSPECTIVE ON THE FAILURE OF SOCIAL ENGINEERING PROGRAMS

When men and women fail to pursue effective and efficient social engineering programs based on human factor principles, the primary outcome is usually continuing HF decay or underdevelopment. In the long term, this will lead to the failure of SEPE institutions. This failure will finally lead to the decline or demise of a society or civilization. As is obvious from Figure 8.1, failing to create and utilize effective SEPE institutions causes SEPE problems to escalate. When this occurs, people's adherence to the existing social contract will stagger. More complicated problems therefore arise. Individualism and self-interest will be carried to higher degrees of selfishness and cupidity. When human greed finally takes over, the ongoing SEPE problems and failure will lead further to HF decay or underdevelopment. In the final analysis, if these trends are not reversed quickly, these problems will escalate into crises of higher proportions which will finally destroy the society or civilization. The problems and difficulties that ensue will afflict all people in society. The intensity of these problems is such that if nothing positive and concrete is done to deal with them, the demise will come very quickly.

SEPE institutions and their corresponding plans, policies, programs, and projects are experiencing tough rides on the boisterous waves of SEPE oceans as they struggle to help society to successfully deal with its pertinent problems. This observation brings to light another series of questions: Why are things not getting better and better for all humanity? Is society on a threshold, where it has lost knowledge of what it will take to deliver the good and happy life to all humanity? Why is there escalating socially deviant behavior among both the youth and adults in society? Why does the moral standing of societies today seem to be no better in certain regards than what it was several thousands of years ago? Where, how, and why is humanity failing to subdue the underlying causes of its problems? Are there any solutions to the problems being faced by the SEPE institutions? Can anything be done about the human condition to make the good life easily attainable to all people? In every society, many plans are made, policies implemented, and programs established to deal with poverty and other forms of SEPE problems. Many of these have failed to achieve their intended objectives.

From the HF perspective, each society's ability to accomplish relevant tasks lies in people who have been properly nurtured to live and uphold the higher moral and ethical principles that nurture, enhance, and promote human life. That is, the effectiveness of a society's institutions, institutional structures, technology, and so on is determined by the kinds of human factor traits possessed by its inhabitants. As such, the continuing failure being experienced by SEPE institutions in all societies today is a direct result of HF decay or underdevelopment. From the HF perspective, Janowitz (1978, 3) was correct when he noted that "In its classical conception social control does not imply coercion or the repression of the individual by societal institutions. Social control is, rather, the obverse of coercive control. Social control refers to the capacity of a social group, including a whole society, to regulate itself. Self regulation must imply a set of 'higher moral principles' beyond those of self-interest." Commenting on Janowitz's view, Scull (1988, 669) noted that we need to pay particular attention to moral bonds if it is our desire to coexist. In the absence of social controls, social disequilibrium will prevail. That is, society will be saturated with continuing criminal activity and escalating ineffectiveness of social institutions.

The view that social problems are the results of social control is partially true (Park and Burgess 1921; Cohen 1955; Cloward and Ohlin 1960; Becker 1963). This is so because HF decay or underdevelopment is not only the key primary cause of social problems, but also promotes them (see Figure 8.1). It is true that, when stringent social controls are instituted, those who are bent on pursuing careers in criminal activities will always look for alternative procedures whereby they can either flout or flaunt their ingenious evasions of formally imposed legal controls and sanctions. When necessary, they are ready to go into head-on collision with the law and its injunctions. The fact that, even when these controls are nonexistent, social problems still persist is indicative of the fact that the primary reason for the failure of social institutions is HF decay or underdevelopment. Viewed from this perspective, it can be argued that the view of the Chicago School of Sociology that deviance is the fruit of social disorganization and fragmentation is not only false, but also clouds the true picture. It fails to dig deeper into the root causes of social deviance. In this regard, it is, therefore, a severely misleading view. For example, one cannot successfully explain the practice of jury nullification (see details in Chapter 8) using social-deviance theory. In reality, the practice of jury nullification is a direct result of HF decay or underdevelopment. This is the case because such a practice not only ignores the universal principles on which human life is based, but also destroys people's confidence in existing legal systems.

Orthodox views regarding the problems and explanations for the failure of SEPE institutions and systems are extremely inadequate. They not only sweep the dirt under the rug, but also lead to the misuse of scarce public resources in pursuing irrelevant and ineffective public policy. This is a result of the failure of orthodoxy to locate the actual source of the SEPE problems. If any successes would be attained in dealing effectively with SEPE problems, the authorities have to accurately determine the variables that cause institutional or systems failure.

The institution of SEPE regulations and systems does not necessarily enhance the effectiveness of plans, policies, programs, and projects. Though their existence is necessary, they are not sufficient for the achievement of institutional efficiency and effectiveness. Societies that aim at continuing progress must help their people to acquire the necessary HF required for the attainment of the intended goals.

Human Factor Decay in Real Life

People who lack both spiritual and moral capital may not perform to their best ability (see details in Chapter 6 and also Adjibolosoo 1995a). They will find it too difficult to successfully deal with personal and interpersonal emotional, psychological, and other problems. They will usually get locked up in relational problems with either management or coworkers or both. These people's performance and effectiveness on the job are frequently unstable and unreliable. Since they normally do not see workable solutions to their problems, they may seek answers in alcohol, drugs, absenteeism, shirking, and so on. They are often evasive and usually lose or waste many work hours (see the list of selected behaviors and problems in Table 9.1). To perform, they will often require increased and continuing monitoring. The possession of aesthetic capital, human abilities, and human potentials is also an invaluable asset for employee effectiveness (see details in Chapter 6). HF engineering programs that fail to produce spiritual and moral capital in people are usually unsuccessful in encouraging and helping them to use their human abilities and potentials (see Chapter 11 and also Adjibolosoo 1995a, Chapter 3).

In many cases, those who perpetrate antisocial acts suffer from either the phenomenon of HF decay or its underdevelopment. Most orthodox attempts at social engineering do not achieve any significant results because they fail to promote HF development in societies. Historical records and stylized data reveal that many programs put in place in the past to deal with pervasive racial discrimination achieved little results. One would have thought that if all things went as expected, the Brown ruling should have solved the problems of segregation in the United States. Instead, it led people to develop other cunning procedures to go around the ruling (see details in Chapter 8). The behavior being addressed continued to be perpetrated, without necessarily violating the ruling. In a sense, the problem was accommodated rather than solved (Adjibolosoo 1995b). This is typical of most human attempts to deal with problems in society. Several decades have passed since the Brown ruling, and it still seems as if no such ruling had ever occurred on this matter in American social history. Clearly, since the Brown ruling did not lead to HF development, it only band-aided and left the problem permanently unsolved. It, however, led people to devise different techniques for perpetrating the same acts of violence and discriminative behavior. It must be clear, therefore, that when official government policy and legislation do not lead to HF development, the problems being addressed will not be dealt with successfully. They usually are left permanently unresolved.

This phenomenon substantiates the HF view that until societies develop their HF they will be putting the cart before the horse in enacting rules and regulations to deal with SEPE problems. (Testable hypotheses are presented later.) In this case, the tail will control the dog. Rules, regulations, and programs that fail to develop HF characteristics in people are not recommended by the HF model (Adjibolosoo 1995a). The success or failure of relationships between acquaintances, doctors and patients, lawyers and clients, businesses and customers, parents and children, teachers and students, husbands and wives, and so on depend on the state of each person's acquired HF characteristics. A well-developed HF produces people who are not only ready to perform to meet their own needs, but also possess a social mind and behave accordingly (see details in Chapter 11).

Efficient and effective human performance requires continuing development of every component of the HF (Adjibolosoo 1995a). Thus, unless the HF is developed and maintained on a continuing basis, SEPE institutions and systems will not work as efficiently as expected. Rules, regulations, and injunctions instituted to directly force people to do what is expected will not achieve their intended goals, except in cases where positive HF traits exist. The current state of human performance is a significant reflection of the magnitude of the resources society has devoted to HF development in the past.

From the HF perspective, though laws, regulations, and injunctions are necessary, they are not sufficient requirements for dealing successfully with human problems that militate against all forms of SEPE progress. This is one of the primary reasons why SEPE institutions and systems are failing worldwide and have been unable to cope with the growing pressures being placed on them in today's global political economy. Again, contrary to popular opinion, men and women can and do very often escape the law. That is, the long arms of the law become so crooked and twining that they hardly ever reach those who they should—the criminals. This phenomenon in itself is a typical HF decay or underdevelopment problem.

Nepotism and cronyism in their most extreme forms are indicative of both HF decay and underdevelopment. In societies where they are pervasive, SEPE and intellectual problems become endemic and systemwide (Adjibolosoo 1994a, 123–132). Human life, work, and play revolve around the existing state of a society's HF. Tribalism, ethnic rivalry, and the inability of a people to resolve conflicts successfully and peacefully are good indicators of either HF decay or underdevelopment or both. In such societies, intricately complicated networks exist among people of the same ethnicity, class, and associations. Influence peddling is a strong foundation on which one's performance of duty relies. The bonds among group members are extremely tight and are usually impervious to nonmembers. When placed in authority, positions of trust, leadership, management, and administration, both hiring and the conferring of honor on other members of society are not based on merit. While group members are usually favored and selected for positions of trust and influence, nonmembers are most frequently discriminated against.

Since this type of social organization is usually too difficult to dismantle, more policing, stringent crime bills, and the like are continually ineffective. This is indeed the case because in societies where such characteristics are prevalent due to HF decay or underdevelopment, state officials and civil servants, who are expected to uphold the law, are, in many cases, staunch members of groups that perpetrate unacceptable atrocities. Such groups often have as their members the best lawyers, judges, engineers, doctors, politicians, and businesspeople. This, in most cases, makes it extremely difficult for society to deal effectively with its pertinent problems. This is true in most societies—both developed and developing countries. The degree of intensity of the number of outlawed activities these groups engage themselves in in each country is a direct function of the state of its available HF traits.

HF decay and underdevelopment pose significant threats to peace and the continuing survival of the human race. Until society recognizes its plight and puts up relevant programs to halt HF decay, the continuing problems of humanity will not be solved. Humanity may continue to pull the rug over the dirt, as illustrated in the story presented in the next section. Unfortunately, we cannot have our living rooms cleaned in that manner. In this case, out of sight is not necessarily out of mind. The stench will perpetually remain, unless it has been dealt with appropriately.

Human Factor Decay, Problem Accommodation, and the Denial Syndrome

Those who try to live their lives and also act against the laws of nature will hardly ever make any substantial and permanent progress. The universe is not only ordered, but is also governed by universal laws (see details in Chapter 10). People need to know these natural laws and universal principles of life and then live by them. Failure to do so, according to the Physiocrats, will spell imminent disaster. Cherif (1996) observed that "We exist in a world controlled by the laws of nature and within a thin band of atmosphere. Hence, we are truly restricted in our freedom of conduct and choice. Trying to escape the laws of nature, rather than to live with them, indicates a dangerous failure to understand nature and our place in the natural world." This is the issue of problem accommodation discussed by Adjibolosoo (1995b, 1–35). This problem is illustrated vividly in the following story.

A man was expecting company for dinner on a Saturday, a great summer evening. He therefore got up early in the morning and began to prepare for the evening meal. After having cleaned his house and dusted all chairs, tables, speakers, and windows he opened the windows in all rooms and then left for the grocery store to pick up a few items. His trip to the store was very successful, because he was able to purchase everything he had planned and budgeted for. He then drove back home with a great deal of excitement. But this feeling of success and happiness did not last for long. No sooner had he entered into his house than he began to smell the scent of rotten eggs. As if he could neither believe nor trust his sense of smell, he went upstairs only to find that someone had thrown rotten eggs into all three bedrooms. The stench was so overwhelming and overpowering that if he did not deal with it immediately, it could ruin the evening dinner and fellowship with his invited guests. First, he thought of cleaning the three rooms and then applying a strong shampoo and deodorizer to the carpets. Yet, after having given further consideration to this idea, he abandoned it, thinking that it would take too much time to accomplish. As he thought further and more critically about quick-fix solutions, he decided to spray all three rooms with a powerful fragrance and pot-pourri. This idea was so appealing to him that he dashed out of the house into a nearby corner store to purchase the necessary items. He came back home and quickly sprayed each room—a task he repeated every now and then.

At five o'clock in the evening, the guests began to arrive. Everyone who entered the house perceived that there was a bad smell. Yet for the sake of courtesy, no one had the courage to say anything about it. Since everyone had already learned the brand new lessons of political correctness, it was put into practice. By five-thirty, the rest of the guests (a husband and wife) arrived with their five-year-old daughter, Annie. Unfortunately, Annie did not have any concepts of political correctness in her mind, nor had she learned about personal politeness. After having entered the house, five-year-old Annie looked at her mom and shrieked, "Mom, this house smells! I can't stand it! Let's go home!" Her mom quickly jumped and wrapped herself around her daughter, lifted her up in her arms, covered her mouth, and said, "Honey, that's not a nice thing to say when you are visiting someone. Could you please not say that again?" Little Annie nodded her head in acquiescence and said "OK, mom." To this, her mom and dad replied in unison, "That's the girl." Annie and her parents, therefore, went upstairs, where the host came to meet and welcome them. Everybody was busy and happily chatting away with a glass of wine in hand. By that point, some guests had already drunk themselves into apparently forgetting about their real-life problems. Though Annie had just been given a crash course on political correctness and problem accommodation and how to practice it, she has not yet learned and internalized the critical lessons on these subjects. Unexpectedly and unsuspectingly, Annie, with her childhood sincerity and innocence, blurted out loudly again, "Mom, this house smells a lot!" Her mother struggled to get to Annie in order to make her swallow the remainder of her sentence by covering her mouth immediately. However, it was too late. Annie had completed her sentence. Everyone, including the host, heard what little Annie blurted out. Annie's mom pulled Annie closer to herself, rushed her to one corner of the living room, and scolded her, saying, "You're a naughty little girl. Mom and Dad will deal with you as soon as we get back home, OK? From now on, you better behave yourself, or else you will be grounded for a very long time. You will also miss your most favorite dessert after dinner tomorrow and the opportunity to play with your well-cherished dolls. You know what they mean to you, don't you?" By this time she had completed nodding her head in agreement to the question her mom had just asked her. Annie's comments had woken up everyone who was seriously practicing his or her lessons on political correctness, being mute about the smell in the house. Indeed, Annie had somehow liberated all the guests and the host and drawn them out of their fool's paradise. Now everyone began to say that they also smelled some bad scent when they first entered the house.

Johnny, the host, could no longer hide the secret. His carefully thought out solution did not work for a little five-year-old girl. In tears, he broke the news about the scent in the room to the guests. Everyone stared into each other's eyes and shouted in unison, "Then little Annie has been right all this while and we are all wrong and too pretentious." It was during this time that someone mentioned to Johnny that the best solution was to recognize the magnitude of the problem, clean it up, and then shampoo each room afterward. With guilt and shame, Johnny said, "Indeed, you're correct. I just didn't think I could have accomplished that task today. Besides, there were no theories for me to fall back on. Please pardon me. Indeed, quick fixes usually don't work. In the final analysis, they create further problems, by initially accommodating them. They usually backfire on those who use them."

Like Johnny, humanity has become a captive of its own pretentious ignorance, imaginations, and denial syndrome and has, therefore, been experiencing wave upon wave of problems for centuries. While some of these problems are minor, others are major, even to the point of threatening the future existence of all humanity. In the past, nations waged wars against each other. Some of these wars lasted for several decades. In the same way, many groups of people were (and still are) confronted with severe disease epidemics, drought, and famine.

As I have discussed in Chapter 8 and elsewhere, regardless of the intensity of the human endeavor to achieve the "good life," very little is being accomplished because the focus has been placed on symptoms rather than on their root causes. Like Johnny, who could not successfully deal with the stench of rotten eggs in his house by merely accommodating it, humanity is also failing to master its problems. In terms of solving SEPE problems, all humanity seems to be channelling significant financial resources into plans, policies, programs, and projects and yet reaping little in positive results. These problems continue to escalate even in the presence of new knowledge and technologies. The human search for solutions to its pertinent problems seems to be going awry. This observation brings several additional questions to mind: Are key scholars in every academic discipline seeking diligently for solutions to all human problems? How successful have they been to date? If these intended human attempts are not solving all known problems, what are they missing? Can all humanity discover an effective social order and an efficient global political economy? Where is humanity today in terms of its attempts to overcome existing problems? If societies are failing to find the necessary solutions, does it mean that they are either looking in the wrong direction for solutions or investing their financial resources in activities that have little to do with their problems? Maybe all societies are thriving on the shores of illusion and ignorance. All humanity may be caught up in a denial syndrome, as illustrated in the story about Johnny and the stench of rotten eggs. If this is the case, then there is the need for a significant change in the ways we think, rationalize with the intent of accommodating problems, and respond to all phenomena that impact human progress and welfare.

Relating Johnny's experience to the human enterprise, humanity seems to be caught up in the trap of solution generation with the intent of accommodating pertinent problems. As noted in Chapter 6, the race for the development or creation of new solutions through the evolution of new programs and academic disciplines is escalating. Today, scholars are continuously coming out with new ideas and academic disciplines aimed at discovering workable solutions to human problems. Based on the study and conclusions arrived at through research in these disciplines, plans, policies, programs, and projects are designed and directed at complex SEPE problems. The meaning, scope, and objectives of each discipline are clear. The disciplines are mainly concerned about articulating and dealing with SEPE problems. The subject areas represented reveal their importance. Each subject focuses on a specific area of human endeavor. If these disciplines were dealing successfully with critical human problems, human life and welfare might improve. They are, however, always failing to accomplish their intended tasks because they rely on tunnel vision and poorly fragmented disciplinary thinking.

The primary questions, therefore, are the following: How could humanity integrate and use the knowledge gained from each of these academic disciplines to successfully deal with its pertinent problems? Is it possible to restructure the study of each academic discipline so that men and women can be thoroughly educated and trained to acquire the appropriate human factor traits required for dealing with SEPE problems in society? Societies that are willing to provide excellent answers to these questions need to recognize that the true intent of human life transcends mere wealth acquisition. Yet, since self-directed actions may lead to actual material-wealth acquisition, most individuals are always tempted to believe and act in deceptive or demeaning ways to increase their personal wealth. When people fail to recognize that the sources of their own prosperity and wealth are not necessarily what they have actually done of and by themselves alone, false pride and a presumed sense of security overtake them. This, in turn, opens the door for the spell of selfishness to overpower them, because they think that the reasons behind their present successes are their own strengths and self-directed actions. No wonder some people find it rather difficult to extend their arms of love, care, and concern to others. As such, it becomes "everybody for himself or herself and God for us all." The avid pursuit of self-interest usually degenerates into personal passion for selfishness and narrow-minded greed as people experience HF decay or underdevelopment. Thus, in societies where these phenomena occur and continuously replicate themselves, SEPE institutions always fail to achieve their intended objectives.

In general, human character tends toward self-seeking behavior that may sometimes negatively affect productivity and quality. This will be unacceptable to management because the firm's future market share and global competitiveness may be in balance. National development programs will also suffer severe blows. As such, they may fail to achieve the intended objectives of national reconstruction. Some of the problems due to either HF decay or poorly developed HF traits or both include the following:

- Bribery and corruption on the job
- Organized criminal activities
- Continuing absenteeism

- Shirking and misuse of official work hours
- Professional indecency and incompetence
- Crooked litigation
- Employee unruliness
- Flippant employee behavior
- Employee inactivity
- Lack of integrity, responsibility, accountability, and commitment

In what follows, we will assess the performance effectiveness of the SEPE institutions.

ASSESSING THE EFFECTIVENESS OF SEPE INSTITUTIONS

In view of the discussion so far, the following testable propositions are relevant. The propositions presented and discussed refer to the significance of human qualities in relation to the effectiveness of human performance and its impact on the running of all human programs and social institutions. These propositions make varying assertions about the various problems being experienced in society today. The basic thrust of all eight propositions is the primary source of most problems in modern society and how people think each of these problems can be dealt with.

Proposition 1: The creation and institutionalization of affirmative action programs, employment quotas, sexual harassment regulations or clauses, gun control laws, and so on are inefficient and ineffective procedures for dealing with pertinent social problems because they do not address the root causes of the problems.

This proposition focuses on the efficiency and effectiveness of government programs. It tries to find out whether government plans, policies, programs, and projects continue to fail because they do not successfully tackle the root causes of the ongoing failure being experienced by those who develop and implement government programs. Specifically, the statement maintains that the development of regulations or laws and their implementation are usually ineffective in dealing with pertinent SEPE problems.

Proposition 2: The vigor with which affirmative action clauses, employment equity regulations, gun control laws, and revisions to the young offenders' act are made, institutionalized, and legally enforced reveals the degree to which such relevant human qualities as honesty, integrity, accountability, understanding, and tolerance are declining in society.

Proposition 2 claims that when the rate of development and implementation of certain programs like affirmative action, employment equity, gun control regulations, revisions to the young offenders' act, and so on grows at an increasing rate, it implies that the HF is either decaying or is being neglected or underdeveloped continuously. It means, therefore, that if those programs fail to reverse the trend of HF decay or underdevelopment, they will not be potent in dealing with SEPE problems in society. When the rate of HF decay or underdevelopment increases in society, there is the tendency for government, using its programs and law-enforcement agencies, to pursue heavy-handed programs in an attempt to deal with pertinent problems. Yet, since these plans, policies, programs, and projects do not actually focus on the root causes of the problems, they end up being ineffective. It can be argued, therefore, that failure to create and implement effective HF development programs will perpetuate a culture of human neglect of critical duty, which finally will create a fertile environment for pertinent problems to mushroom and blossom in the long term. Indeed, those who develop and implement affirmative action programs know that they will not work. Yet, since they sound politically correct, governments continue to promote and finance them.

Thus, from the HF perspective, whenever people begin to call for the toughening of the young offenders' act and the prosecution of businesses and organizations that violate affirmative action regulations and employment equity rules, it implies that either HF decay is escalating or HF underdevelopment is on the rise, or both.[2]

Proposition 3: A society's ability to recognize its social, economic, political, and intellectual problems, to articulate them clearly and accurately, and to create workable solutions depends primarily on the existence of such positive human qualities as integrity, accountability, responsibility, knowledge, understanding, wisdom, tolerance, and so on.

This proposition affirms that when one observes a society that is unable to recognize, articulate, and create workable solutions to its SEPE problems, that society is suffering from severe HF decay or underdevelopment. Indeed, without well-developed HF traits, people may not successfully deal with their pertinent problems. This is the case because they not only fail to recognize what the problems and their exact causes are, but also fail to develop effective solutions to them.

Proposition 4: Social, economic, and political institutions are not only ineffective at achieving their intended goals and objectives, but also at keeping with changing attitudes, new trends, deviant behavior, and so on.

Proposition 4 postulates the view that one of the primary reasons why social, economic, political, and educational institutions seem to be failing is that they are finding it excessively difficult to appropriately respond to continuing global changes in values and attitudes. Most people in society are beginning to realize that huge and complicated government bureaucracy encourages continuing sluggishness and inefficiency. As such, SEPE institutions usually fail to keep up and deal successfully with trends, even when they accurately identify them. The implication of this observation is that continuing resistance to change renders these institutions powerless and ineffective. They become severely handicapped in carrying out their intended objectives and functions.

Proposition 5:   The greatest problems facing social, economic, political, and educational institutions and organizations include the inability to find managers or leaders who possess such qualities as responsibility, accountability, integrity, honesty, and dedication, and who are free from avarice and selfishness.

Proposition 5 argues that the primary problem of SEPE institutions is HF decay or underdevelopment. In a sense, Proposition 5 suggests that these institutions lack both good leadership and effective or efficient employees. Indeed, no SEPE institutions can discharge their duties and obligations successfully without having people who have acquired the HF. As such, failure to use men and women who possess the relevant HF traits will also lead to continuing failure to comprehend and deal effectively with changing trends, attitudes, and deviant behavior.

Proposition 6:   Even if society can enact and enforce more stringent regulations, tighten the young offenders' acts, create strong rewards and punishments schemes, and build more community parks, recreational facilities, and teenage hangouts, it will still be unsuccessful in dealing with social, economic, political, and educational problems—especially in the presence of ongoing human factor decay or underdevelopment.

Proposition 6 states that the development and implementation of stringent laws and the provision of recreational facilities for young people will not necessarily help society to successfully deal with its SEPE problems in the midst of severe HF decay. Proposition 6 is similar to Proposition 1. However, while Proposition 1 suggests that enacted laws and regulations are inefficient ways of solving society's problems, Proposition 6 suggests that the use of rewards and punishments will not affect people's defiance of the law.

In the past, societies created stringent rules, tightened regulations, and imposed severe penalties on wrongdoers. Yet people not only violated the law and got sentenced to prison, but also came out of prison and committed the same offense again (and probably in a much more violent fashion). Indeed, most repeat offenders neither worry about the strictness of punishment nor give critical consideration to continuing incarceration. It can be argued, therefore, that any attempts made by society to impose restrictive regulations on its people may backfire. This will be more severe in situations where HF decay or underdevelopment are extremely high. In a similar way, programs such as community parks, recreational facilities, teenage hangouts, and so on are nothing more than weak palliative or cosmetic measures. They do not solve existing problems because they fail to get at the established root causes. At best, they sweep the dirt under the rug. A situation of this nature may also, in the long term, lead to escalating HF decay or underdevelopment in society. If this happens, society's long-term problems will become significantly more complicated and compounded.

Proposition 7:   If society uses existing educational, training, and mentoring programs successfully to educate and produce people of integrity, accountability, and responsibility, it will facilitate and enhance the effectiveness of social, economic, political, and educational institutions.

Proposition 7 asserts that by improving the efficiency and effectiveness of existing educational, training, and mentoring programs, a society will be successful in developing the appropriate HF characteristics that are necessary for the attainment of institutional effectiveness. In a sense, while Proposition 6 seems to be stressing the ineffectiveness of the penal code as the solution to the problems of society, Proposition 7 suggests that improvements made in education, training, and mentoring programs will be the most effective means for dealing successfully with SEPE problems, as long as they focus on HF development. In general, existing educational, training, and mentoring programs are failing to achieve their intended objectives. Thus, any additional expenditure aimed at enhancing the effectiveness of the school, college, and university programs to develop the appropriate HF characteristics will lead to ongoing progress. When this is successfully accomplished, the effectiveness of SEPE institutions will be enhanced. Failure to do so will lead to further HF decay. The result will be ongoing poor performance in every sphere of human endeavor.

Proposition 8:   Most people prefer to live together (common law) rather than be committed to a marital relationship that may not work in the long run.

Proposition 8 maintains that most people are preferring common law relationships to the traditional marital relationship between a man and a woman because they are not only afraid of failing, but also apprehensive of committing themselves to a contract that may not only usher in pain and suffering in the long term to both people involved, but whose desolution may lead to other forms of personal trauma and nerve-wracking experiences. In order to not go through the emotional trauma and additional social stigma and economic difficulties associated with marriage breakups, some people feel that they may either avoid complete disaster or significantly minimize the severity of most of these negative impacts by not getting married. Thus, when the "loose" association breaks down, they can walk away from it, probably feeling infinitesimal loss. Little do they realize that it does not work out that easily every time.

Contrary to the popularly held belief in Western society that the traditional family set-up and the marriage institution are declining, it can be argued that this is not really the case. What is happening to the family in Western society today is a result of severe HF decay or underdevelopment. As such, as soon as Western societies overcome the problem of HF decay, the whole trend will reverse itself. The implication, therefore, is that there is hope for the traditional marriage and family structure.

Pooling the contents of these eight propositions, three consistent themes stand out conspicuously:

1. The failure of SEPE institutions is due essentially to continuing HF decay or underdevelopment.
2. SEPE problems will remain unsolved as long as societies fail to develop the appropriate HF traits.
3. The enactment, implementation, and enforcement of regulations will not deal successfully with SEPE problems in the midst of ongoing HF decay or underdevelopment.

In view of these observations, pertinent questions that face all societies today include the following: Who should change or improve the effectiveness of SEPE institutions? Can human beings change themselves first in order to pave the way for SEPE institutions to become effective? In other words, is personal transformation from the HF perspective a *sine qua non* to positive social transformation? Indeed, meaningful answers provided to these questions will go a long way toward helping all humanity to deal effectively with its pertinent SEPE problems.

FURTHER OBSERVATIONS AND IMPLICATIONS FOR PUBLIC POLICY

In general, the provision of more community facilities and enhancing education programs may provide some positive results in the short term. This may not, however, successfully counteract the effects of abuse at home. Today, society is too concerned with individual rights, yet continuously failing in promoting the concept of rights and responsibilities. If society will make any positive and lasting progress in dealing with its problems, then rights, privileges, and responsibilities have to be balanced always.

There is usually an inherent confusion in people's mind when they talk about values, human philosophies, and universal principles of life. In view of this observation, the difference among these has to be clarified. In most cases, people's dishonesty is a result of HF decay or underdevelopment. As societies go through time, people are continuously denying the very philosophical views on which past civilizations built their societies. Today, men and women continue to make serious errors in both reasoning and judgment and then argue that, since values change, society too must change with them. Regardless of how true this view may be to many people, such human qualities as integrity, responsibility, accountability, and others like these are founded on universal principles rather than values. As such, since they do not change over time regardless of the diversity of human culture, they cannot be labeled as values. People should not be excessively ignorant of the fact that most humanly developed philosophies and worldviews that serve as primary foundations of human behavior are not only human creations, but also inanimate (Adjibolosoo 1995a). As such, though they either affect or determine the kinds of values that people in any society may hold, they do not necessarily determine the kinds of human qualities that are necessary for successful human performance in the SEPE arena. In reality, human qualities, insights, and revelation knowledge determine the kinds of social philosophy and worldviews subscribed and adhered to by members of a specific society (i.e., the architects of the American Constitution, the leaders of the Russian revolution, Hitler and his followers, etc.).

The mistake many scholars make is to turn certain critical issues head over heels and then continue to think and argue that human philosophies and worldviews give credence to universal principles of life. Unfortunately, this type of thinking is only true in terms of human values that continue to change and shift over time depending on the stream of philosophies and worldviews that reigns in society in any specific period of time. Universal principles of life, however, predate all human philosophies or worldviews. This being the case, any society that desires to successfully deal with its pertinent problems cannot achieve its objectives by establishing SEPE programs on fickle human values or philosophies. If it does and either a shift or change in existing values or philosophies occurs, its SEPE institutions will fail continuously.[3] However, by discovering and using universal principles of life as the primary basis for the operation of these institutions, the requisite HF would be developed and used to create and support a workable social contract.

Therefore, contrary to what one may think, human qualities such as accountability, responsibility, integrity, commitment, trustworthiness, and the like are not the fruit of some base reality, philosophy, or belief. This type of warped thinking has contributed, in significant ways, to the current plight of all humanity. Unfortunately, though human values are supposed to be human extrapolations or abstractions of universal laws and principles, they are no more than approximate conceptualizations of what people think must necessarily make society work through its culture, social contracts, and engineering programs. This result is also an offspring of HF decay or underdevelopment.

Most human beings continue to forget or fail to perceive that the finiteness of the human mind does not allow men and women to discover all existing truth at one time. Even when some discover certain universal truths, others reject them in arrogance because they feel that they do not meet with the stipulations of the so-called scientific method. By so doing, we continue to discard and dispose of knowledge that we cannot easily prove in test tubes in scientific laboratories. Some people hide their ignorance by classifying such knowledge as being religious, subjective, and unsubstantiated. They are then classified and filed away, never to be looked at again. No wonder most people try to escape the problems of the city by buying property in rural areas, only to realize sooner or later they are not immune to the crimes of the city. The problems hunt them down because the problems' roosting and nesting places are in the human mind, heart, and psyche. It is probably time to keep a more open mind and seek diligently for solutions to all human problems through the use of an integrated knowledge based on true wisdom.

In view of the discussions presented in this chapter, the future of humanity looks bleak indeed because of the current deplorable state of the HF in most countries. If, in fact, societies continue to fail in developing relevant and efficient HF engineering programs to motivate their citizens to acquire the appropriate HF traits, institutional and technological failure may one day lead to the total annihilation of the human race. Even those who would be successful in relocating themselves to the moon or other planets, if possible and easily practicable, will never escape the severity of the problems that arise from HF decay and underdevelopment. This is so because those who have the resources to take them to other parts of the world or new planets will carry along the current levels of their own acquired HF traits. In this case, the same problems that forced them out of their current locations would also prevail in their new lands or planets of adoption because their acquired HF traits could not have been left behind. The probability that every person who relocates will have a serial killer or pedophile as a neighbor is still excessively high. The moral to this observation is that men and women cannot run away from their inherent problems to safer havens.

Society's problems are rooted in the personality characteristics and psyches of its inhabitants. Indeed, if we have had the tendency to decimate our earthly resources in addition to overpolluting the earth, the likelihood of repeating the same behavior on any new planets we would find is as high as 100 percent. Men and women will always act and behave in a manner that mirrors their acquired personality characteristics, regardless of where they find themselves.[4] This is why problem accommodation is no solution at all (see details in Adjibolosoo 1995b). As such, like human shadows, ongoing human problems would travel every inch with people who move to new locations hoping to gain reprieve from SEPE problems. Human problems, like shadows or culture, travel with people just as fleas do with domestic animals. The only way to get rid of them is to willingly face and deal with them effectively.

This being an indisputable fact, if men and women sincerely desire to be free from certain pertinent problems that prevail in society today, there is the need for all humanity to sit down in workable groups, reflect upon the problems critically, and then take effective and efficient steps to deal with the real root causes of these problems. Neither problem accommodation nor band-aiding approaches will work. Sweeping the problems under the rug will not make them go away either. Running away to other locations, either on earth or other planets yet to be discovered will also not work (recall the story about Johnny's plight). There can never be any successful running away from any human problems. It does not work.[5] What will work, however, is for all human beings to rethink what they have done right or wrong in the past and try to find out whether they have been sincere with themselves. It is important to revisit other available solutions that have been ignorantly rejected without either giving them due consideration or trying them. Having done so, it is important to find out whether it will be productive to adopt continuing openmindedness in the search for solutions to the continuing failure of SEPE institutions.

Whatever our personal answers to these questions are, the implications of this chapter are obvious. Indeed, humanity has succeeded in changing and achieving many things. We have changed our lifestyles in terms of eating, sleeping, drinking, working, traveling, and much else. We have triumphed in space and are still continuing to make significant advances in both space and the undersea world. We have gained significant mastery over nature, using our acquired knowledge through science and technology. Even the way we do business across the globe changes almost every second. We pride ourselves on every success we achieve due to our increasing knowledge in science and its method. We have not only increased our longevity, but have also developed fertility drugs in addition to techniques for manufacturing babies. Today, because of advances in technology, we manufacture babies when we want and in the quantities we want, not forgetting about our ability to even select the gender and the intelligence of the offspring to be birthed through genetic engineering. In all our endeavors, our technological inventions and innovations have become smarter over the years. Our knowledge about the universe is growing. Indeed, we have achieved a great deal. Yet still, there is a lot to be discovered about our own common humanity. Even in cases where some of this knowledge exists, we refuse to use it to guide all our endeavors. We are always engaging ourselves in more and more research and development programs. Yet the more knowledge we generate, the less we know about how to live our lives to the betterment of all humanity. We know a great deal about this universe and how it functions. Our scholars and academicians are quick to provide academically and politically correct yet ineffective answers to observed SEPE problems and phenomena.

Unfortunately, it is both sad and extremely disheartening to reflect on the fact that we are continuously failing to learn to live a life of peaceful coexistence with other people who are either of the same stock as we are or completely different from us. Many people have little concept of the sanctity and beauty of every individual life. As such, these people continue to deny their common humanity. Often, they are at loggerheads with those people who look differently, see differently, hear and speak differently, believe differently, and act differently from them.

In view of all these observations, what is to be done? From the HF perspective, the answer to this question is very simple: Develop the HF (see Chapters 10 and 11). Gleaning from the discussions presented in this chapter, it is obvious that the creation of HF-based educational, training, and mentoring approaches for dealing with problems of institutional failure will achieve more concrete results than the use of the existing rewards and punishments approach. It is more likely that a judicious balance of both approaches may lead to more effective results. Education, training, and mentoring programs should not revert to mere schooling, in that they will focus primarily on academic exercises of knowledge or skill (i.e., human capital) acquisition, but on the total development of the appropriate HF traits. Educational, training, and mentoring programs in the institutions of HF development must be prescriptive as far as human quality development is concerned. There must be room for descriptive standards, too. None of these should be sacrificed for the other. Whether this task is going to be easy or not cannot be easily deciphered until we begin the program. In view of this, the critical question is, "How do we go about developing the HF?" To answer this question successfully, people need to comprehend the concept of global development and the critical universal principles that serve as its cornerstone. It is this comprehension that will lead them to relentlessly search for SEPE programs that will promote HF development and, hence, human-centered development. These issues are, therefore, taken up and discussed in detail in Chapters 10 and 11.

CONCLUSION

The fact that existing SEPE institutions are doing their best to help society to deal with its ongoing SEPE problems cannot be denied. While humanly created systems encourage some degree of individual freedom in some countries, they stifle it in others. These systems sometimes provide incentives to some people to act in ways that would lead to the betterment of their own economic conditions, but they deny to grant social and economic freedom and political liberty to others—the severely handicapped and the powerless. The continuing operation of these systems sometimes leads to results that are not socially desirable. When this happens, Adam Smith's invisible hand leads astray when economic agents lack the appropriate HF characteristics. Thus, as rational individuals, the critics of existing systems continue to argue that it is necessary to search for solutions to the many hindrances to those systems' effectiveness and efficiency. There is no pretense in their arguments.

If we all believe that the malfunctioning of humanly created systems sometimes makes life unbearable for those who suffer losses after certain SEPE changes have occurred, then there is the need to develop the HF in people who would also devise and operate institutional structures to correct the existing maladies. Since blind and extreme fanaticism could rob us of the ability to observe the problems of the system and therefore be detrimental to all humanity, we need to learn to call a spade a spade, and, above all, be willing to join forces with the search party in order to find solutions to the problems of the system.

It is rather unfortunate that most people would prefer to close their eyes to certain adverse impacts of the inherent problems that result from the ongoing functioning of various economic systems and paradigms. These systems and paradigms have driven many to commit all forms of felony or suicide, to experience increased feelings of personal worthlessness, and to go crazy. Ongoing HF decay and underdevelopment leads these systems to fail. This, in turn, destroys the lives of many. People who do not wish to be viewed and treated as failures may be forced to lower their moral standards (if they have any at all) and change their value and belief systems in order to be "successful" like others. This phenomenon sometimes leads to extreme and unacceptable human behavior. Values cherished in an economic system (whether good or bad) usually affect people's behavior and character formation.

Yet, in today's world, the primary problem is that while almost every country aspires to pursue national development plans, policies, programs, and projects in order to attain economic progress, little do they know that without helping people to hone their personality characteristics (i.e., the HF traits), these attempts will not by themselves provide the necessary engine that drives the development process. In the same way, these countries usually fail to understand that one of the most important ingredients of national development plans, policies, programs, and projects is the HF. Since most countries fail to perceive that the success of any national development program rests primarily on the state of a nation's HF, they continue to wrongly focus on issues relating to nuts and bolts, forgetting that one also needs wrenches and screwdrivers to put the nuts and bolts in their right places. What this means, therefore, is that many countries continue to fail in all their endeavors to develop because they are always placing the cart before the horse. Every development plan, policy, program, and project that ignores HF development at its inception will have a hard time in accomplishing its intended objectives.

HF development is what all SEPE plans, policies, programs, and projects must strive to achieve as their primary noncompromising goal. Everything else, I believe, will fall in its own proper place later.

NOTES

1. In the case of economic growth theory, refer to Chapter 3 for the various policy recommendations. These are results of orthodox thinking and theorizing.

2. "People" here may refer to all citizens of a particular country or just the members of one specific locality or community.

3. Note, however, that it is possible that any new changes that bring society closer to adhering to principles or philosophies that mimic the universal principles discussed in Chapter 10 will lead to better performance of SEPE institutions.

4. We can successfully design and implement what it will take to transform the personality characteristics of people so that they can live their lives based on universal principles of life (see Chapter 10 for details).

5. Exceptions to this view may relate to moving away from areas of natural disasters or calamities. Even in these cases, successful evacuation and flights into new areas of residence may engender new problems.

CHAPTER TEN

THE HUMAN FACTOR CONCEPT OF GLOBAL DEVELOPMENT

In the preparation of people for work, life, and duty to all humanity, there are no known existing shortcuts. The view that there are no quick-fixes in dealing with society's problems needs continuing evaluation, analysis, and reaffirmation. Those who pursue shortcuts that are not necessarily relevant are like people who band-aid a sore without having cleaned and properly disinfected it first. This solution will not work in the long term. In the short run, there may be some temporary relief for the afflicted. In the long run, however, the conditions of the sore may worsen and therefore lead to possible amputation (see Adjibolosoo 1995a). Wilkins (1989, 2, 10) observed that books like *Theory Z* (1981), *In Search of Excellence* (1982), and *A Passion for Excellence* (1985) turned out to be best sellers because of the following:

They promised, by implication, that if the bulk of America's companies would initiate the practices of certain successful firms, they too would be much more successful. Some managers intentionally attempted to initiate these practices while others have employed alternative models. Whatever the ideal was, many businesses have failed to change as much as they wanted, and they often encountered significant problems as they engaged in dramatic organizational transitions. In their rush to become more competitive, they often destroyed some intangibles that are the essence of what makes an organization competitive in the long run. . . . Distinctive organizational performance is mostly the result of deeply ingrained repertoires developed over time. Adopting a program or practice from another firm is likely to require more than just an understanding of procedures or a particular technology. . . . A myth among many executives is that they can implement the practices of successful companies and reap their success. Sustainable competitive advantage, however, comes only from developing unique social conventions, skills, and orientations within the firm.

From the HF perspective, therefore, the belief that society only needs to make many more stiff laws, set aside more financial resources for community policing and upholding the rule of law, the institution of extensive affirmative action programs, human rights regulations, sexual harassment laws, more censorship in the area of reading materials, television, and radio programs, the regulation of the Internet, and so on is a lame duck (see a detailed discussion on this issue in Chapter 9). These are band-aiding procedures and will yield few long-term results in societies.

For every human being to function effectively and efficiently, there has to be continuing human factor development and improvement (see detailed discussions in Chapter 11). Yet, unfortunately, though human beings are the most primary requisite for societal progress, they have been the least developed in terms of HF acquisition. Over the years, most people have learned that physical fitness, eating healthy, and the development and acquisition of skills are critical to human life, longevity, personal well-being, sustained fitness, and technological advancement. Yet the continuing focus on these issues has led to the gross neglect of total HF development, a necessary ingredient for global development. Those who oversee and provide leadership for the operations of the human enterprise seem to focus solely on issues that have little to do with the creation of the right conditions for global development. Thus, the plans, policies, programs, and projects they pursue are not usually slanted toward the development of HF characteristics. The ongoing nurturing of people to acquire a favorable mix of the ingredients of the HF must not only supersede what society focuses on when it talks about, makes, and implements plans, policies, and programs to help people to acquire human capital (i.e., knowledge, skills, physical fitness, healthy lifestyles, etc.), but also serve as the central focus of the development program. It is society's inability to develop the whole person that leads to the poor preparation of people for a life of service, productivity, and success. Throughout the centuries, the human being has been one of the most neglected, least developed, and least maintained objects among all known sources of civilization and wealth creation.

In most societies today, people are always interested in and solely concerned with the development of institutions, technologies, techniques, methodologies, and all kinds of structures they believe will help them to solve existing problems. But the unfortunate thing that happens as societies focus on creating and perfecting these cooperant factors is that they forget that the primary key to all human achievements and progress is HF development. They forget that technology can never happen without human beings. They forget that systems will not work without well-groomed people. They also forget that every institutional structure requires people who are well-educated, well-trained, and have acquired the critical HF to make them operational in all areas of human endeavor. Most of all, humanity has been under the illusion that if people can develop good systems and design good technology, good institutions, and so on, societies will achieve great successes. As such, development plans, policies, programs, and projects are aimed at facilitating ongoing advancement in these areas. Viewing these items as prerequisites to progress, nations spend their scarce resources on specialized R&D activities or programs aimed at more technological advancement. Though investment in advanced technology R&D is not wrong, overemphasis on technological advancement programs that will not change the human condition for the better is tantamount to gross misuse of scarce resources. From the HF perspective, the current views and beliefs held by well-known academicians, business leaders, and politicians are usually untrue, misleading, and excessively unproductive. Indeed, without human beings who possess the appropriate HF characteristics, little progress will be accomplished.

The HF research I have been involved in over the last couple of years has now clearly revealed that people who have indeed acquired the requisite HF traits make global development happen. As such, without people who possess positive HF characteristics, very little will be achieved in society. If all humanity is really interested in solving existing social, economic, political, and educational problems, men and women have to look deep down inside the core of their inner personalities in order to discover what it is that they have done wrong to themselves to bring their societies into face-to-face contact with currently prevailing problems. From the HF perspective, it can be conclusively argued that the critical problems we all face in the world today are due mostly to HF decay or underdevelopment (see Adjibolosoo 1993a, 1994a, 1994b, 1994c, 1995a, 1996a, 1996b). That is, problems relating to SEPE issues are inherent in society because human beings have continuously failed to develop themselves in the ways they should have.

The continuing problems of society throughout the ages are signs of either HF decay or HF underdevelopment or both (see details in Figure 10.1). Leaders and followers will be able to successfully deal with society's problems by combining their acquired HF characteristics. If the acquired levels of HF traits are significantly high for both groups, society will find itself in quadrant IV.[1] If, however, it is low for both leaders and followers, society will be operating in quadrant II. It is, however, possible that while the leadership possesses higher levels of HF development, the followers might not (see details in quadrant III). The exact opposite of this case is presented in quadrant I. The corresponding results are shown in Figure 10.2. Indeed, the HF is key to the national development agenda.

True and lasting solutions to SEPE problems can only be found in HF development and hence the ongoing appreciation of the human quality (see details in Figure 10.2). There are no human institutions that are capable of bringing about true racial and ethnic tolerance, peaceful human coexistence, understanding, and the promotion of the dignity of labor and the sanctity of life except if these institutions have people who possess positive HF characteristics to lead, organize, plan, manage, and direct them. In the absence of properly developed HF traits, rules and regulations imposed on people from outside their own sense of responsibility, accountability, integrity, commitment, and devotion to duty will not necessarily lead to the expected behavior. It is, however, the case that those who have properly developed their HF traits, all things being equal, will do their best to live a life based on relevant universal principles of life.

Figure 10.1
The Leadership and Followership Performance Interaction Matrix

Leadership (Rulers)

Leadership / Followership		Levels of Human Factor Development	
		High	Low
Levels of Human Factor Development	High	Whole Human Factor Development IV	Varying magnitudes of Human Factor Development (followers and/or subjects have acquired greater levels of human factor traits than their leaders.) III
	Low	Varying levels of Human Factor Development (leaders have acquired higher levels of human factor characteristics than followers.) I	Total Human Factor Decay II

Followership (Citizens)

THE HUMAN FACTOR CONCEPT OF GLOBAL DEVELOPMENT

In view of these facts and observations, the real political economy of global development and social order must necessarily direct and lead individual passions and emotions in order to arrive at the best welfare results for society as a whole. They must create the business and economic environment within which proper *oikonomikos* will ensue. Indeed, it is obvious that since all humanity wears a selfish nature, there will always be some levels of human misconduct on the part of certain agents in the existing social, economic, and political systems. From the HF perspective, programs of the global political economy of development must lead

Figure 10.2
Labor Force Heterogeneity and Its Impact on Productivity

Leaders and Rulers

		Productivity-Augmenting Human Factor Characteristics	Productivity-Diminishing Human Factor Characteristics
		High	**Low**
Followers and Subjects	Productivity-Augmenting Human Factor Characteristics — **High**	1. Exceptional levels of personal integrity, responsibility, accountability, commitment, trustworthiness, courage, wisdom, etc. 2. Both rulers/leaders and followers will complement each other's performance in an orderly and consistent manner. This will lead to higher levels of productivity. 3. Sustained growth and development. 4. Higher levels of human performance and productivity. 5. Ongoing progress. IV	1. Higher magnitudes of leadership incompetence, inefficiency, ineffectiveness, manipulation, and abusive use of authority and power. 2. The behavior of leaders and/or rulers frustrates followers. 3. Followers look for procedures to deal with a disturbing situation. 4. Enmity between leaders and rulers. 5. Difficulties regarding human performance. 6. Escalating SEPE problems. III
	Productivity-Diminishing Human Factor Characteristics — **Low**	1. Increasing levels of followership incompetence, ineffectiveness, inefficiency, etc. 2. High-powered leadership performance. 3. Leadership frustrations and/or exhaustion. 4. Plans, policies, programs, and projects stagger. 5. Significant problems of performance and productivity. 6. Ongoing SEPE problems. I	1. Growing levels of human factor decay and/or underdevelopment. 2. System-wide inefficiency and ineffectiveness. 3. Perpetually low human performance and/or productivity. 4. Economic decline and/or underdevelopment. 5. Deteriorating institutional effectiveness and human welfare. 6. Severe social injustice, economic inequity, social unrest, etc. II

to ongoing improvements in the outcomes of the existing SEPE institutions and systems, which have been driven by passionate and ruthless self-interest for centuries. No other system could ever achieve the best for society than an economic system based on the universal principles of love and respect for God and the love for fellow men and women. To these two universal principles, all human beings have to completely subject their self-interested behavior.

Indeed, every human being desires and also deserves the best for him- or herself. This is the sole reason why human behavior and motives must not always be controlled by self-interest. Behavior based solely on individual self-interest sometimes leads to economic and social sub-optimality. Yet modern economic and business activities, by concentrating on and emphasizing increased productivity and economic and technological efficiency, eliminate the ultimate (intangible) goals of what proper economic and business life must aggressively pursue. By so doing, a culture that places too much emphasis on the tangible ends of life to the neglect of the invaluable intangible values of life is created. The result of this phenomenon is the creation of a culture or society within which universal principles are thrown out and buried deeply under the waters of the vast ocean of human greed and self-aggrandizement (Niebuhr 1953, 453).

As a matter of fact, proper economic activities or pursuits must be based on the key and relevant universal principles to be discussed later in this chapter. In this way, a better society for men and women will result because many agents will choose to die rather than either compromise or renege on their cherished universal principles on which the real essence of their lives depends.

In the view of Socrates, an unexamined life is not worth living. Indeed, those who go through life with no purpose usually do not succeed in making the best out of life. This is why it is usually the case that individuals who aimlessly roam the streets and alleys of cities, towns, and villages end up as society's nonproductive human resources. Instead of having these able-bodied people contribute to the total factor productivity and welfare of society, they end up miserably hopeless and helpless dependents on society.

These individuals have lived unexamined lifestyles. In the final analysis, the way they lived their lives when they were young catches up with them. They become like warriors who have been severely defeated and beaten to submission by an ill-equipped enemy force on a battlefield of life located in the greenish fields that grow in their own impressionable minds. The vagaries of life heap heavy loads of emotional and/or psychiatric burdens on their psyches and shackle their minds, wrists, necks, knees, and ankles with the chains of discouragement. They walk through life terribly bent forward, with their tongues drooping, heavily gasping for breath, struggling under the pains and afflictions of their own guilt and total human abuse. Indeed, it is usually true that in the lives of these people there have been few calculated plans regarding their hopes and expectations and what to do to attain them. Even if they did have well-calculated plans for their lives, they lost them through the cracks of life and human disappointments.

Yet, in real life, most successful people prefer to plan and then organize their lives around these paths. They do so because they are able to focus on the goals and objectives of their lives after having outlined them. In cases where people fail to describe or define what their life's objectives are, they may get into severe difficulties in that they will always find it too difficult to decipher what their individual priorities are. In fact, it can be argued that if one does not know the direction to which one is heading, how can one perceive it when one has arrived there? Indeed, knowing where one is heading is a necessary condition for ongoing success in life, because this knowledge alone will lead one to search for, locate, and utilize the relevant information required to achieve one's intended objectives.

In view of these observations, the HF concept of development relates to knowing what society needs and pursuing its attainment through programs that focus primarily on HF development at the initial stages of the global development program. This is why it is important for every society in the global village to understand and then define what it views as constituting sustained human-centered development. Though each society can receive help from others in its attempt to define its own conceptualization of development, it need not step aside and leave such a critical function of domestic development to foreigners. To be in position to articulate what, to them, sustained human-centered development implies, the people will do well by studying what has been happening in other societies and learning from them. Adjibolosoo (1995a, 13) noted the following:

The primary objective of any national economic development program must be the development of the human factor (HF). Countries must be in a position to create fertile economic environments in which jobs can be fashioned for their people; provide adequate and affordable health services for everyone; develop and offer relevant education, training and mentoring programs for the entire population; and, above all, achieve and sustain national economic self-sufficiency. . . . The acid test for successful economic development policies and programs is the effectiveness of society, not only in telling the poor and the severely disadvantaged about the various practical ways through which they can get over their predicament, but also in creating the environment within which every citizen is able to feed, clothe and shelter himself or herself and, above all, feel strongly that he or she belongs to a humane society. Increasing success in healing individual broken heartedness in society; continuously rescuing those who are under perpetual lure of idleness and self-destruction; lessening human ignorance and aimlessness; recognizing and correcting follies of past policies and programs; changing, minimizing and transforming the society's cultural beliefs, habits and customs of the heart that mitigate against the economic development process in order to promote positive adaptation; and the growing capacity to feed, clothe and house all people in society are therefore to be viewed as the major objects of economic development. . . . The often forgotten dimension of development, belongingness, must be fostered.

In view of these observations, one can argue that programs aimed at human-centered development must transcend mere concerns about the changes in national economic growth-rate indicators and structural changes in the national economy. Whatever changes that come as results of global development plans, policies, programs, and projects must lead to the betterment of all people. As long as this does not happen, a society cannot claim to have achieved any significant progress. Global development is about altering people's existing attitudes (see *Fortune* 1994, 30–35) to take a detailed look at the critical universal principles of life which would improve human welfare and quality of life.[2] It implies helping people in well-informed and civilized ways to get together in peace, regardless of race, color, creed, and gender, to discuss differences among people and working relentlessly to discover permanent solutions to the key hindrances to ongoing human success. Global development is not about organizing, arranging, and putting up international conferences, conventions, seminars, and the like to discuss which new laws and regulations to make, conventions to sign, and how to enforce them.[3] Instead, it involves calculated and ongoing attempts to discover and use, both efficiently and effectively, the true map of the city of sustained human-centered development, without which no development planners and policy makers can successfully navigate the wild and deep oceans of underdevelopment. Until this map is either located or newly created to help facilitate development planning and policy development, it will be impossible for national leaders to successfully navigate through the huge pile of hindrances to economic growth and development.

Indeed, from the HF perspective of global development, a society's development program must be primarily and purposefully aimed at intensive HF development activities. When these programs are built on the universal principles of life (i.e., the necessary and sufficient map of the city of sustained human-centered development), they will lead to the rejuvenation of the human spirit and encourage it to rise up and relentlessly work for the progress and welfare of all humanity. At the heart of the HF concept of global development is citizenship development for building and establishing civil society, as determined by the universal principles of life.[4] In the global development program, both character building and skill development must be seen as being complementary rather than substitutes. That is, to achieve and sustain national productivity growth, any investments that society makes in people's lives must simultaneously focus on both character formation and skill acquisition. In essence, global development must of necessity begin with HF development.

From the HF perspective, therefore, global development programs must not focus on the solicitation for bilateral or multilateral foreign aid (in its many forms) and technical assistance, modernization of administrative procedures and techniques, development administration, economic stabilization policies, structural adjustment programs, the maintenance of systems and institutions, extensive technology transfer, community development programs, the building of health clinics and other primary health facilities, and so on. Though these are necessary, they are not sufficient in themselves for the attainment of sustained global development. Each of these must be viewed as a natural outflow of intensive HF development programs that focus on the development of HF characteristics. The successful creation and operation of each of these programs and activities depends on the level of HF development in society. The meeting of national leaders to discuss and create international rules, regulations, and clauses regarding human rights is a serious waste of scarce resources if these activities fail to focus first on how to improve the human quality. Indeed, human quality development, from the HF perspective, is a prerequisite for sustained human-centered global development because it leads to the discovery of the necessary map of the development process. No such proceedings of international conventions can be successfully implemented and adhered to by people if their HF traits are not developed. A well-conceptualized, effectively organized, and meticulously implemented global development program must do the following:

1. Foster continuing nurturing of HF traits that will promote human effectiveness and efficiency in all endeavors.
2. Promote and uphold both individual and group human rights, privileges, and responsibilities.
3. Give respect and honor to all people regardless of race, gender, and creed.
4. Defend and protect the property and all other interests of all people.
5. Build walls of personal security and insulate them with materials of peace and tranquillity. That is, there must evolve a global HF fence of protection for all people.
6. Create the spirit of domestic and global sharing that promotes, nurtures, and cares and provides for others, regardless of who they are and their location in the global village.
7. Nurture and encourage others to devote their lives to searching for the most effective and efficient procedures for the promotion of human progress.
8. Build and develop in the minds and hearts of men and women internal personal beacons of ongoing enlightenment for self-monitoring to establish duty consciousness and service to all humanity as is in line with universal principles of human life.

It must be noted, however, that these objectives will never be achieved in the presence of severe HF decay or underdevelopment.

Most advanced countries, such as Canada, the United States, the United Kingdom, France, Germany, and many others continue to pride themselves on their technological prowess and progress and point to them as achievements being made (see Chapters 5 through 7). The problems and difficulties of the severely disadvantaged and the prevailing conditions of hopeless and helpless people are usually buried deep in order to pursue ongoing technological advancement. Stylized data and historical evidence not only abound, but also reveal that, in all advanced countries, there are large numbers of children, teenagers, middle-aged men and women, and seniors who go about collecting soda cans and empty bottles to be traded for money for food.[5] While some starve, others make daily trips to garbage cans where they collect their daily sustenance. In the winter months in these countries, some poor and street people freeze to death. While this phenomenon is ongoing, there are huge volumes of food items that are dumped into garbage cans and dumps by huge grocery stores and restaurants at the close of every business day. Many people have sold themselves to deadly drugs. They lose their bearings because they have few clues about the real map of personal development. Their lives are being destroyed gradually. If, in the midst of all these happenings, we can still view ourselves as having achieved significant progress and brag about our intelligence and greatness, then there is something extremely wrong with our individual and group perception and concept of what actually constitutes sustained human-centered global development. To avoid this failure, it is important to return to the foundational universal principles of life that will serve as guidance—the true blueprint for concrete progress.

RECOMMENDATIONS FOR A GLOBAL DEVELOPMENT STRATEGY

The creation and development of viably productive enterprises and the building and growing of nations are more continuing processes than steady-state phenomena. In the course of these processes, many problems and difficulties will be encountered. Societies that are unable to develop the critical HF traits necessary for accomplishing the tasks of business and economic development will likely fail to achieve the long-term goals of development plans and nation-building programs, regardless of how much effort they put into other relevant activities. In Figure 10.2, a matrix of labor-force heterogeneity and productivity is presented. As discussed in Adjibolosoo (1995a), a nation's labor force is heterogeneous in that, while a section of the labor force possesses productivity augmenting human factor characteristics, the rest contains people who most of the time exhibit productivity diminishing human factor traits. Thus, in cases where the leadership possesses productivity-augmenting HF characteristics, they will achieve significant results when their followers possess similar qualities (see quadrant IV in Figure 10.2). In this case, society will be in an excellent position to accomplish the objectives of its global development program. Alternatively, if society finds itself in quadrant II, continuing failure of its SEPE institutions will prevail. As a result, economic underdevelopment will plague that country. In quadrants I and III, both leaders and followers will experience significant problems in their attempt to make progress happen in their society. To avoid future disappointments, societies need to allocate considerable financial resources to HF engineering. Deliberate attempts must be made to create the environment within which every person can develop the various components of the HF (see Chapter 11 for detailed discussion).

By merely concentrating on human-capital development alone, a society will produce people who may possess knowledge, intelligence, and different types of skills and yet be inadequate in performing the tasks necessary for the achievement of higher productivity and better quality of life for all. When this occurs, businesses will fail. The grand design and desire for achieving greater employee productivity and enhanced quality will melt away into nothingness like a late-spring snow. This failure will affect total factor productivity negatively. In the long term, economic underdevelopment will be the outcome. This, however, will not be the case when the whole HF is developed.

Indeed, the major problem that faces most HF development programs today is that while there are effective programs for the development and acquisition of human capital and aesthetic capital, there are hardly any programs for the nurturing of both the spiritual and moral capital within public educational and training institutions. Based on this observation, one might conclude the following:

1. Most societies have come to believe—wrongly—that both spiritual and moral capital are not crucial for the attainment of higher worker productivity and improved quality of goods and services.

2. National leaders and prospective employers assume that people acquire both spiritual and moral capital privately. In view of this, it is not deemed important to justify the expenditure of huge public or company financial resources to create programs aimed at deliberately planned activities for the acquisition of both spiritual and moral capital by private individuals.

3. Most political and business leaders today do not really understand the roles spiritual and moral capital have to play in the development process; some of these leaders are not even aware of the inner ingredients of the HF and what actually constitutes a successful program for its development.

To overcome this mentality, each society must commit adequate resources to research, education, and training for the exploration of these areas to excavate their relevance to the attainment of continuing business success and human progress. This will pave the way for humanity to rediscover the proper place for each component of the HF in long-lasting business success, economic growth, and national development. The achievement of this goal will help each nation, society, and business organization to successfully accomplish its intended objectives. That is, as specified in Figure 10.3, people who have acquired the appropriate HF will foster effective interaction between plans and policies on one hand and projects and programs on the other. The continuing interaction will lead to ongoing evolution and performance of institutions, infrastructure, technology, and systems. By supporting the operation of each of these areas with continuing HF engineering programs, the direct results will be productivity and economic growth, as shown in Figure 10.3. Any failures experienced in the area of HF engineering will lead to economic stagnation and decay.

CRITICAL FOUNDATION PRINCIPLES OF GLOBAL DEVELOPMENT

In what follows, I present a HF perspective on the global political economy of development and social order, discussing the key universal principles that must underlie all social, economic, political, and educational activities.[6] To begin with, it is important to note that a properly developed HF perspective on the global political economy and social order cannot exclude normative economics. This is so because by failing to include normative economics as an integral part of the global political economy of development and social order, people will not be able to boldly speak to pertinent issues or human behavior from the perspective of universal principles of life. Since every economic activity involves dealings with other people, it is important to stipulate relevant and workable rules of conduct regarding such activities and contractual arrangements. These stipulations have to speak to and deal with self-interested human behavior. That is, in this economic system, individual economic agents must learn to subject their personal self-interests to the general and continuing welfare of all humanity. By so doing, economic agents will learn to engage themselves in activities with the view of not necessarily

Figure 10.3
The Human Factor and Productivity Growth

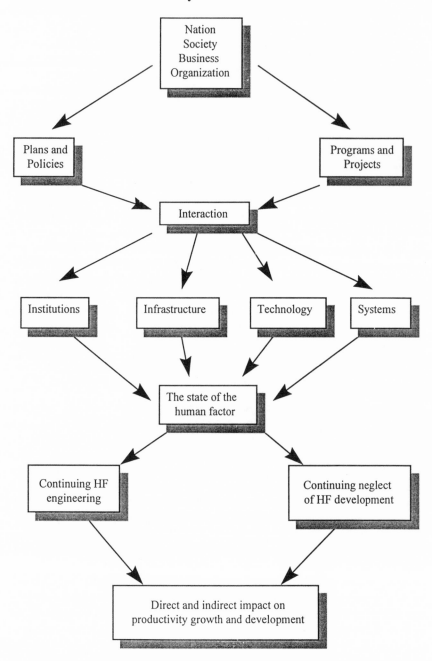

promoting their own interests alone at the expense of the welfare of others, but also recognize they are stewards of the resources they either earn or acquire. That is, they must learn to manage these resources prudently.

In a true global political economy and a just social order, producers and consumers will not only be profit and utility maximizers alone, but will also uphold the pertinent universal principles that underlie life, work, and human behavior. For example, the global political economic system and social order must be designed and operated to assist individual economic agents to uphold and promote enhanced welfare for all people. As such, the welfare of the downtrodden, helpless, hopeless, poor, hungry, afflicted, sick, terminally ill, oppressed, and grossly abused must be advanced on a continuing basis. Selflessness and the willingness to seek and promote the welfare of all humanity must be upheld always. Based on these observations, the real global political economic system and social order must function on the basis of universal principles of life. In what follows, I present two key foundational principles and then discuss how adhering to them simultaneously could promote other cherished ideals of all humanity. By helping and educating people to perceive their relevance to the success of the human enterprise, a workable global political economy and social order will be established to cater to the needs of all humanity in the global village.

The First Principle: Love for God and God-Centeredness

An economic system based on universal principles of life must promote and also encourage people to let the love of God lead and direct them in everything they do. The pertinent principles and theories of the global political economy and social order must make individuals become aware that they are not only responsible to themselves and society for their economic and business activities, but also to God ultimately. God's role and place in the life of humanity must be lauded in every social order and global political economy.

The Second Principle: Love for Fellow Men and Women

The social order and global political economy of development must adhere to and also promote personal love for one's neighbors as well as oneself. Basically, as a foundation principle for an effective and efficient global economic system, the goal of this second principle is not only to promote self-interested pursuits (behavior), but also to lead everyone to hold in high esteem love for fellow human beings. These two principles must serve as eternal elements of the personal moral compass to guide the economic and business activities of individuals toward the true economic north pole. When one loves others, one will scarcely inflict harm on them. Any contracts one participates in, one must always ensure that the stipulations of these contractual arrangements and agreements are carefully thought out to not only be useful to them alone, but also to be in consonance with the perceived and acknowledged universal principles. When this principle is adhered to closely, the global political economic system and its attendant social order will automatically promote and foster social, economic, political, and educational activities that will minimize greed and extortion, overemphasis on self-enriching pursuits of material things to the detriment of the welfare of others, unjust economic relationships and contractual arrangements and agreements, and intentional swindling of the means of sustenance that belong to others. It must be borne in mind that adherence to this principle will facilitate continuing development of HF characteristics. It will lead to the creation of a pleasant social order and an efficient global political economic system. Indeed, Paul the Apostle (I Corinthians 13:1–13) once pointed out the following:

> If I speak in tongues of mortals and angels, but do not have love, I am a noisy gong or a clanging cymbal. And if I have prophetic powers, and understand all mysteries and all knowledge, and if I have all faith, so as to remove mountains, but do not have love, I am nothing. If I give away all my possessions, and if I hand over my body so that I may boast, but do not have love, I gain nothing. Love is patient; love is kind; love is not envious or boastful or arrogant or rude. It does not insist on its own way; it is not irritable or resentful; it does not rejoice in wrongdoing, but rejoices in the truth. It bears all things, believes all things, hopes all things, endures all things. Love never ends. But as for prophecies, they will come to an end; as for tongues, they will cease; as for knowledge, it will come to an end. For we know only in part, and we prophesy only in part; but when the complete comes, the partial will come to an end. When I was a child, I spoke like a child, I thought like a child, I reasoned like a child; when I became an adult, I put an end to childish ways. For now we see in a mirror, dimly, but then we will see face to face. Now I know only in part; then I will know fully, even as I have been fully known. And now faith, hope, and love abide, these three; and the greatest of these is love.

If people continuously fail to acquire this human quality, racial discrimination, gender bias, class oppression, ethnic strife, and so on can never be dealt with successfully. By instituting, upholding, and defending these critical principles in every human society, the numerous benefits to all people will be countless and will include but not be limited to the following.

Individual Freedom and Justice.   In the global political economic system and social order, the pursuit of equity, justice, and fairness will prevail when people learn to live by the primary universal principles of life. Every individual will be given what is due to him or her. The pursuit of true and lasting justice will not be compromised. In addition, the extreme levels of inequity and injustice that previously prevailed in the political economic system and social order will be dealt with successfully. If the global political economic system and its accompanying social order fail to encourage (and also lead) agents to pursue human freedom, equity, and justice, humanity may be faced with huge problems that it can never solve.

Personal Stewardship and Service.   The global political economic system and the social order that operate on the basis of the two primary universal principles of life will facilitate personal stewardship and service. Every social, economic, political, and educational activity will be directed to the service of all humanity.

Most people will learn to view themselves as designated stewards of all resources that come into their possession. The way and manner in which people use these resources will therefore promote continuing human progress. Anything that falls short of this objective has to be reevaluated and, if need be, dealt with accordingly.

Honor and Respect.   Many things in this world could be used more effectively by people as complements rather than being viewed as substitutes or rivalrous items. For example, men and women are meant to complement each other. Racial diversity is more of a strength to humanity than a hindrance to its progress. Both the identity of the individual and his or her life are sanctified. Men and women who sincerely uphold the two key universal principles of life will not only learn the importance of honoring others, but also giving the right kind of respect due to others. Again, this will also be extended to the property of other men and women. Violence against property and the person (i.e., verbal, physical, spiritual, mental, and psychological abuse) will diminish significantly. People will come to comprehend the usefulness and meaningfulness of honoring and respecting others. Few human beings will actually respect and uphold the rights of others (especially the right to self-determination and coexistence) if the leaders in society do not help them to understand and live by the foundation principles of human life.

Individual Rights and Responsibilities.   Though oppression and slavery are demeaning, humanity has experienced them and still does today in many devastating ways. However, by establishing the foundational principles and inculcating them in ourselves, people will learn to treat others with respect and dignity. Whatever social, economic, political, and educational activities people find themselves pursuing, they will most often make sure that they do not engage in any of these at the expense of the rights of others by denying their responsibilities. In a democratic environment, people will be prepared to give careful and reasonable consideration to the thoughts, activities, and functions of others, if indeed they have acquired the appropriate HF characteristics. In this way, the global political economic system and social order will be nurtured to promote respect for both individual and group rights and responsibilities. This will foster the assignment and protection of individual private property ownership rights and responsibilities. Social, economic, political, educational, and religious programs and activities that oppress, kill, and perpetrate the dehumanization of others will be minimized. Where any of these atrocities exist, they will be punished according to the legal precepts of each society if most people pursue and uphold the universal principles of life.

Right and Wrong.   On December 18, 1996, a group of business associates put together an informal Christmas party. At the gathering, there were several different activities for people to engage themselves in at will. I chose to play pool, a game I had played just once before, several years ago. While we played, my partner and I were losing the game against a father-and-son team. When our opponents realized that we were losing the game due to the very little knowledge and skill I had to play pool, they decided to teach me by providing me with the necessary basic knowledge and proper skills to play the game better. In that instance, they taught me how to hold the cue and position my whole body and its weight behind the ball, how much force I needed to apply while hitting a ball, and the direction and angle toward which I must hit each ball in order to sink it and many others simultaneously and successfully into the various nets positioned at the four corners of the pool table.

As the night wore on and we continued to play many more games together, the real eye-opener for me that evening was that when I listened to my on-the-spot pool instructors, learned the lessons taught informally, and did exactly what they instructed me to do regarding how to get the balls into the nets, I was very successful in sinking as many balls as possible. However, any time I either forgot or intentionally ignored the basic concepts I was taught and tried to sink the balls in my own way, everything else went wrong again. On these occasions, I always failed to sink the balls. Indeed, I learned very quickly and clearly that evening that, in many cases, there is always the best or right way to accomplish tasks. Though many people think that there are many different ways for performing certain tasks, there is certainly one best (i.e., most effective and efficient) way to be successful at each task to be accomplished. In view of this observation, I learned that evening that people who desire to achieve higher levels of success in any chosen activities, professions, and so on must of necessity locate and utilize any successfully proven existing system. Those who fail to do so will flounder or wander for a very long time without being able to achieve their intended goals. In the end, they will lose their golden chances for success. To avoid this failure, it is important to decipher the critical differences between the right and the wrong ways of doing things.

In view of this experience and many other similar real-life observations, it can be argued that, whether people agree or not, there are both right and wrong ways of accomplishing tasks. To stretch this concept further, just as gravity exists whether people believe in the concept or not, so also do right and wrong exist, no matter what human beings think and feel. That is, whether people believe it or not, there is truth and this truth will always stand in all circumstances, no matter how much it is being suppressed. Indeed, it is easier to acknowledge the difference between right and wrong when a society operates on the primary universal principles of life. Principles regarding right and wrong need to be identified, explored further, and lived by all people in society. In view of this concept, the desire of many people to create, live by, and do things by their own, individually created rules and understanding is an excellent recipe for imminent chaos and disaster in any society where this sentiment becomes established in its people. Even societies that have attained significant levels of social, economic, political, and educational development (i.e., the advanced countries) currently run the risk of experiencing continuing decline in their welfare because of their continuing failure to recognize and admit that the view of certain influential scholars that truth is relative is an extremely destructive hoax. The dangers such a view poses to the effective and efficient operation of the global political economy and social order transcend that which can be unleashed on all humanity by the most powerful and deadly nuclear bomb. Such societies will go through significant SEPE problems as their existing HF continues to undergo severe decay and underdevelopment.

Failure to recognize and differentiate between right or wrong will create significant problems for society. It will not only lead to the loss of the moral compass of society, but will also jeopardize the right to life, work, own property, and be both accountable and responsible. In societies where people have come to believe that truth is relative, and that its universality is a myth, people will face ongoing problems regarding the definition of what is right and wrong. In most cases, the fine line drawn by the universal principles of life between right and wrong becomes excessively blurred because of poor and short-sighted academic theorizing by certain scholars and national leaders to promote their own personal whims and caprices. In recent years, various American television talk-show programs have compounded this problem, because these shows draw on peoples' feelings, emotions, and so on. To the producers, everything goes. Such a society will suffer from ongoing HF decay or underdevelopment. Where this is the case, it will be extremely difficult to implement and promote people's adherence to established rules and regulations based on the principles of life and designed to guide human behavior, action, and life, including the Nuremberg Principles originating from Nazi war-crimes trials (1945), the Universal Declaration of Human Rights (1948), the Convention on the Prevention and Punishment of Crime of Genocide (1948), the International Convention on the Elimination of All Forms of Racial Discrimination (1965), the International Covenant on Economic, Social and Cultural Rights (1966), the International Covenant on Civil and Political Rights (1966), and others like these.

Gurtov (1985, 44) observed that "These values carry with them a set of *positive assumptions about the nature of humankind* and optimism about the prospects for human change" (emphasis original). Indeed, Gurtov's observation is accurate in that these international documents are prepared to be implemented by nation states. The usual assumption made is that people are inherently good and will want to implement, operate, and pay due allegiance to the contents of these international conventions. Yet this assumption is only valid if a society has already been able to establish and live by the two primary universal principles of life regarding one's love for God and other people. It is indeed naïve to think that these declarations would be adhered to and successfully implemented in an era when most people have come to believe in the relativity of truth. How can these declarations hold for all peoples of the world when each people's group is convinced that truth is relative? Truly, this phenomenon is an oxymoron.

From the HF perspective, however, these declarations and many others like them are useless when all humanity refuses to live according to the two critical universal principles of life. In their absence, HF decay and underdevelopment are the results (see extended discussion in Chapter 11). For people all over the world to agree to adhere to these documents, they must have first developed a fair amount of their HF traits. Human behavior cannot be legislated and expected to act itself out in the absence of the authority of the primary universal principles of life. Instead, it requires long-term investment in human quality development through ongoing adherence to the observed universal principles of life. These kinds of investments in human factor development will produce men and women who will wield significant personal powers to exercise self-control and the ability to receive, understand, and abide by the laws of the land. In this way, men and women, political animals (à la Aristotle and Aquinas), will be thoroughly prepared to achieve their greatest potential. This is what will make it possible to achieve and even soar high above the currently attained heights in all human actions and endeavors.

Human Welfare Promotion and Distributional Equity. If whatever people do is aimed at making the good life possible, then people need to cautiously pursue their individual economic goals in order to promote the welfare of all. While businesses should not indulge in activities to the detriment of the individual consumer, government policies must be designed, pursued, and implemented with meticulous care so they do not hurt people. If government leaders lose track of the fact that policies are made for the welfare of citizens, they will run into horrendous problems. In the modern social engineering process (see details in Chapter 6), plans, policies, programs, and projects are usually developed without necessarily having the needs of all people in mind. For example, governments may put policies in place to maximize their votes in future elections, even when it hurts a section of the society. The global political economic system and social order must avoid these pitfalls. Welfare payments or gifts must be made available to those who deserve them. Where chances of potential abuse exist, these avenues must be minimized (and, when possible, eliminated completely).

In many cases, scarcity can be due to the inability to efficiently distribute those goods and services that have already been produced. In this case, while people in certain areas of the globe will have abundance, others will suffer from severe lacks. It is also the case that distributional problems can lead to severe inequities in the distribution of the world total production. If this problem is not dealt with effectively, many people will continue to suffer from severe food shortages and other problems (see details in Chapter 1).

Though this discussion is not necessarily exhaustive, the continuing pursuit of what has been discussed in this chapter will lead to improvements in human welfare for all people. The two primary universal principles of life will not be operational until humanity pays attention to the significance of the HF and goes ahead to develop it. If the HF is not developed, all the good intentions of all humanity will never be realized to their full optimality. As such, certain needs and crises that have lingered on for generations will continue to plague us all forever. For positive changes, one may wish that a significant proportion of all humanity will learn to act and live as suggested several centuries ago by Saint Francis of Assisi, who once wrote and sincerely prayed the following words: "LORD, make me an instrument of thy peace; where there is hatred, let me sow love; where there is injury, pardon; where there is doubt, faith; where there is despair, hope; where there is darkness, light; and where there is sadness, joy. . . . Divine Master, grant that I may not so much seek to be consoled as to console; to be understood as to understand; to be loved as to love; for it is in giving that we receive; it is in pardoning that we are pardoned; and it is in dying that we are born to eternal life."

Indeed, there is a dire need for us to reeducate and retrain ourselves. This kind of reeducation and retraining must be aimed at programs that will lead to improvements in the ongoing attainment of positive changes in the human quality. This is what the HF perspective of global development is all about. This is the primary reason why the development and implementation of HF development programs are critical to the global development program. In the light of these observations, any successes achieved in this regard will lead to sustained human-centered development—a desirable process that can be attained and propelled through the course of human history by way of continuing HF development programs. The issue of HF engineering is presented, analyzed, and discussed in detail in Chapter 11.

CONCLUSION

Nations that have developed the HF in the past and now ignore its continuing development and sustainability and continuously depreciate its magnitude and quality may lose all the gains achieved in the past. The enjoyment of continuing high standards of living and improvements in the human condition, therefore, require that HF development be made an ongoing priority in every society. The HF must be installed as the primary integrating core of the social order and global political economy. When public education programs fail to develop the requisite HF traits in the labor force, private educational, training, and mentoring programs must be designed and effectively and efficiently operated by concerned citizens to engineer the relevant HF characteristics in all citizens.

One of the main concerns of every country must be the successful implementation of economic development programs and policies that will improve living conditions. If living standards are to be raised, the average labor productivity must also be increased. Attempts to achieve this objective, however, have not been very successful in the past due to the neglect of HF development. If all societies are to improve their average labor productivity, they must groom, manage, and motivate their citizens to comprehend and learn to uphold and live by the primary universal principles of life. Indeed, the social order and the global political economy need the HF characteristics to buttress them up. National and global leaders from all walks of life cannot do the job by themselves without having first acquired the relevant HF traits. If people fail to develop their HF characteristics, they cannot hope to attain and sustain the desirable human-centered development. In view of this, both an efficient global political economy of development and a workable social order will be unattainable.

NOTES

1. The presentations in Figures 10.1 and 10.2 are not intended to illustrate that, at any given time, while leaders may possess productivity-augmenting HF traits, all followers may at the same time possess either productivity-augmenting or productivity-enhancing HF characteristics. This dichotomy will not necessarily exist in real life. A more practical

scenario is the case discussed in Adjibolosoo (1995a), where the labor force is divided into two groups—those that possess productivity-augmenting HF characteristics and the others who have acquired productivity-diminishing HF traits. In each category, there may be found both leaders and followers. People in leadership positions who fall into the productivity-diminishing category must be replaced as soon as the discovery is made before they cause permanent damage to the nation's development program.

2. The motto of the Langley Meadows Elementary School, in Langley, British Columbia, is quite illuminating. It says, "My attitude, not my aptitude, determines my altitude." Indeed, if teachers and educators in every society can successfully educate, train, and mentor every child that comes to them to grasp and learn to live his or her life by this basic motto, a wonderful generation of future leaders would be produced. Children would, indeed, have learned very easily in the infant years of their pilgrimage of life that a person's frame of mind not only affects his or her attitudes, but also produces corresponding actions. This chain will repeat itself in an ongoing cycle. This is why a wise thing to do is to create a fertile educational environment within which future generations can be educated, trained, nurtured, and mentored into becoming leaders with high levels of integrity, responsibility, accountability, trustworthiness, commitment, and devotion.

3. These, unfortunately, have been the objectives of most international conferences and conventions sponsored by the United Nations and other groups that are interested in making rules and regulations to bind human behavior in all countries (e.g., the recent population conference in Egypt and also the U.N. conference on women held in China). If we will achieve any progress, we must have the necessary courage to change course and begin to pay more attention to HF development rather than writing and discussing international conventions.

4. Civil society, in my understanding, is one in which citizens adhere to the rules and regulations on which that society is built. Indeed, it is a society in which men and women live their lives as commensurate with the two critical universal principles discussed in this chapter. In these societies, people learn and practice courtesy toward one another. They give thoughtful considerations to their fellow men and women. Such societies usually experience higher degrees and magnitudes of civility.

5. While this is neither illegal nor a bad economic activity to be engaged in, it is an extremely inefficient use of scarce human talents and abilities. People could be used much more productively than this.

6. These principles form the basis of human life. I am convinced that humanity's failure to acknowledge the sovereignty of God is at the center of all the social, economic, political, educational, and environmental problems the world is currently going through.

CHAPTER ELEVEN

ACHIEVING GLOBAL DEVELOPMENT THROUGH HUMAN FACTOR ENGINEERING

Throughout civilizations, men and women have always done what they perceived to be fitting in order to come out with ideas, techniques, and methodologies that were relevant to the attainment of progress (see details in Chapters 1 through 7). In view of this, many societies try to pursue programs geared toward national and global development. In the past, many countries have put up plans, policies, programs, and projects aimed at the attainment of the goals and objectives of national development. Because of the high levels of successes achieved in recent years in the developed countries, many developing countries have also been encouraged to pursue similar national development programs. Yet, no matter what is currently being done by most countries, very little is being achieved. As was discussed in Chapters 8 and 9, the primary reason for this failure is the varying magnitudes of ongoing HF decay and underdevelopment being experienced by all countries. Thus, if humanity will make any significant and lasting progress in its global development programs, it has to pay continuing attention to HF development. In this chapter, the emphasis is placed on both the HF requirements for the development of the global political economy and programs aimed at its development. It is, therefore, critical to begin with a discussion on issues relating to the required HF engineering process.

THE HUMAN FACTOR ENGINEERING PROCESS

If we establish the fact that the major objectives of countries and business enterprises are nation building through citizenship development and ardent pursuit of profits, respectively, it follows that all relevant activities must be directed toward the fulfillment of these goals. It is, however, true that the attainment of maximum human welfare and social, economic, political, and educational progress requires the whole HF development. Every effort made by both society and the business community to achieve viable economic activities and successful business programs must focus primarily on HF development. The development of each component of the HF is a challenge to each society. To be successful, therefore, every development program requires strong underlying HF development education, training, and mentoring programs. This implies that every society needs to develop and institutionalize relevant programs to cultivate every dimension of the HF in all citizens or employees.

HF engineering will create continuing progress, provided society has the will to pursue it relentlessly. Humanity has often avoided this route to progress because its fruitful gestation period is usually long. What society wants and delights in are quick-fixes. This is why those who run governments devote their energies and the whole term of office to the pursuit of mere cosmetic changes. This is the case because citizens are most frequently in the habit of continuously delighting themselves in perceiving the government leaders of the day as making attempts to deal with social, economic, political, and educational problems.[1] Whether these programs will be successful in achieving their intended goals in the long term is not really an issue of concern to many.

HF development programs must, therefore, be aimed at educating people and preparing employees to effectively participate in the productivity and quality enhancement revolution to foster both domestic and global development. The HF engineering process must include a carefully articulated vision for helping to reform those who have already fallen prey to low productivity syndrome, continuing absenteeism, and shirking of duty. Whenever possible, the process must also prevent other employees from falling into this same trap. HF engineering programs must focus on the discovery of the truth about employee effectiveness and how to stand for it, since the possession of true knowledge about this is necessary for progress and peak performance. Those who are trained and educated in this manner may successfully live by and defend the timeless principles of life and work discussed in Chapter 10.

When business schools, professional business institutes, universities, colleges, business companies, and many others fail to educate and train prospective employees to become morally responsible and continually committed to their work life, company goals, principles of life and work, the desire to achieve continuing higher levels of productivity, excellent quality goods and services, and increased gross domestic product may not be attainable goals. On the basis of these arguments, it becomes clear that HF engineering must be made the primary foundation of every human program aimed at progress and global development. Societies, countries, business organizations, and institutions will fail to attain national goals if the people are not educated to acquire the HF traits necessary for the achievement of intended goals. In terms of the productivity and quality-enhancement revolution, a more permanent gain will be made by companies that put sufficient resources into HF engineering programs. HF engineering is, therefore, the primary core of the productivity and quality-enhancement process. Thus, just as a solidly established foundation is to the life of a building, so also is HF engineering to the development program. There can, therefore, be no successes in the continuing pursuit of progress without intensive and effective HF engineering plans, policies, and programs. In view of the presentation so far, it is true that environmental conditions play their role, too (see details in Chapter 7). Since, in most cases, the system is unable to deal with most of its problems, it is important that we devise other techniques and rules for dealing with inherent abnormalities.

Those who go through the national educational institutions must acquire knowledge, skills, and human qualities that are necessary for effective and efficient human performance. The products of educational institutions must satisfy both societal and business needs. If both businesses and the rest of society are extremely unhappy about the products being turned out by national elementary schools, universities, and colleges, the educational systems would have failed in achieving their primary mandate. Indeed, if a society desires to experience positive changes in all spheres of life, then it needs to alter the existing curricula of all educational institutions from first grade right up to the university level. The new curriculum must focus on HF development rather than mere human-capital acquisition. Any society whose educational institutions neglect continuous HF development will face serious social, economic, and political problems. The mere pursuit of higher degrees and advanced knowledge in ideologies through further disciplinary study of principles, theories, and so on will not produce expected results. The hope is that by the time students graduate, they would not only have been furnished with a huge tool box of information, knowledge, and skills into which they can dig their hands to pick up relevant tools to be used to solve day-to-day problems, but they also must have acquired the critical HF characteristics. Otherwise, they would graduate with higher degrees and yet become social misfits. This will be the case because, sooner or later, most graduates will learn that the actual tools they need to cope with every social, economic, political, and educational problem transcend the mere acquisition of academic tools of knowledge and skills.

I am strongly convinced that a society's educational institutions must never cripple its own common future by running students through hodgepodge educational systems and training programs that have little to do with the preparation of people for life. I must also add that I am not talking about education as it relates to mere knowledge acquisition. Instead, I am talking about education, training, and mentoring programs as they relate to continuing HF development in primary, secondary, college, and university students. It is critical that educational programs and their accompanying activities must transcend mere schooling and focus intensively on people development. There is no better way of achieving HF development successfully than by revisiting existing education systems and training programs and altering them in the manner that will meet the current needs of society. Creating new educational institutions to focus on information technology, technical education, knowledge acquisition, computer literacy, economic literacy, and the like will not necessarily solve the social, economic, political, and educational problems being experienced in many societies today. If humanity, at the present moment, focuses on these programs and channels huge financial resources into them, it will realize later, to its utter dismay, that these programs do not have what it takes to produce civilized and disciplined citizens who will form the core of the national labor force. As such, within ten to fifteen years, societies will begin to perceive once again that their cherished ideals and dreams may not be realized. The glorious ideas they might have had ten or fifteen years earlier will fizzle away quickly. These programs will crumble on them. They will not be relevant anymore. This will be the case because society has failed to develop the relevant HF characteristics in the people who went through them.

The HF perspective maintains that since institutions, systems, technology, and the like are inanimate, they cannot achieve their optimal performance without having people who have acquired the relevant HF traits to manage and operate them (Adjibolosoo 1995a). As such, if societies desire to experience continuing success in the operations of their social, economic, political, and educational institutions, they must of necessity develop and implement a curriculum that will provide opportunities for vigorous programs through which the HF traits can be developed in students. As all humanity enters into the twenty-first century and beyond, any national schools, colleges, and universities that fail to implement a curriculum that is aimed at HF development will become irrelevant to the future of their own society. Such institutions deserve to be either closed down or receive diminished funding.

It is now time to focus on HF development. Every professional or academic program developed and run in elementary schools, high schools, colleges, and universities must have continuing HF engineering as its primary objective. All subject areas, from archaeology to zoology, must be treated as such. Failure to do so will jeopardize the collective future of all humanity. That is, by allowing the existing HF to decay and refusing to develop it in the youth, human beings will be nursing a future of excessive disappointments, pain, and suffering.

THE HUMAN FACTOR REQUIREMENTS FOR GLOBAL DEVELOPMENT

The HF development process requires that at the commencement of any development plans, policies, programs, and projects the people in charge need to determine first the caliber of citizens required for the implementation of the program. Second, they must proceed to evaluate and ascertain for themselves the nature and state of the nation's existing HF. That is, leaders who function in all walks of life must find out whether the existing labor force possesses the HF traits necessary for the successful implementation of the national development program. In terms of the quality of the people required for the national development program, Adjibolosoo

(1995a, 84–85) observed that to be able to successfully carry out its objectives of development, every nation requires people who fit the following characteristics:

1. Have the ambition and the imagination to search for clues; have the intent always to perform and are of one mind; have the willingness to search for and insist on discovering solutions to existing national problems.

2. Are determined to search for and acquire understanding about current problems, existing levels of available skills, and the additional abilities required for the enhancement of productivity, and have knowledge about what must be done and how and the wisdom to use acquired knowledge to solve problems. These people will facilitate the rate at which solutions are found for overcoming hindrances to the economic development process.

3. Have the zeal and the willingness to liberally give their best in contributing to the national economic development program. The industry brought to the reconstruction process by each person must grow out of individual free will and commitment to self-interest insofar as it is consonant with national economic development goals.

4. Provide the required leadership that is apt to facilitate the process of providing the opportunities for every citizen to contribute freely to the success of the national program for economic progress.

5. Have the assurance that courage, resourcefulness, and hard work will not only increase the wealth of their society, but will also lead to the continuing enjoyment of the fruits of their munificence.

6. Possess a sense of purpose, insight, vision, and direction; are skillful in wisdom and scientific knowledge; are steadfast in commitment to risk taking; and are dedicated to personal integrity. These are the people who possess relevant human qualities and know what is good and required for human progress (i.e., effective and efficient maintenance of law and order, respect for the rule of law and property rights, the promotion of hard work and social welfare, and an unrelenting respect for the sanctity of human life and the dignity of labor).

When the labor force possesses the necessary HF traits, it will be in the right position to make development happen in the nation in the long run because it will be fully equipped to fashion workable development plans, policies, programs, and projects, and the relevant institutions, institutional structures, methodologies, and techniques that will be necessary for the successful working of national development plans and policies (Adjibolosoo 1995a, 83–85).

It is the continuing failure of countries to undergo proper and relevant preparations that makes them fail. Because they are usually unable to successfully discern the exact requisites of the development process, they always put the wrong foot forward and badly screw up the whole national development program. In the long run, the haste to develop through the implementation of quick-fix programs leads to continuing failure. To avoid this problem of continuing failure, the HF model of development must be pursued in place of every existing ideological model of development. To be successful in the human search for a workable global political economy of development and an excellent social order, people in all societies must learn commitment, responsibility, integrity, loyalty, trustworthiness, and so on. In what follows, I present a detailed discussion on the implementation of the HF agenda of development.

IMPLEMENTING THE HUMAN FACTOR DEVELOPMENT AGENDA

In what follows, I present a series of propositions regarding how the HF agenda can be used to accomplish the intended tasks of social, economic, political, and educational progress. The HF is extremely important to everything we do as human beings (see details in Figures 10.1, 10.2, and 10.3). For many years, people have continued to reject any ideas that relate to the total development of the individual. From the HF perspective, HF development holds the key to effective and efficient human performance. This being the case, one critical question that one must always ask is as follows: "If the HF is that important, how then can a society or an institution or organization or nation or country go about developing it?"[2] Elsewhere (Adjibolosoo 1993a, 1994a, 1994b, 1994c, 1995a, 1996b) I have argued extensively how developing countries can achieve progress through the HF development agenda. In this chapter, I am proposing a further program of activities regarding how nations or societies or businesses or professional organizations can evolve the HF way. To accomplish these tasks, it is important to recognize that students need to be nurtured in an academic environment that will provide them with the opportunity to reflect, review, and, if need be, reform their acquired personality characteristics.

The measuring rod for this activity of reflexivity is the nationwide composition of principles and standards that are set in the academic environment within which students operate. Indeed, students must be encouraged to evaluate their acquired HF characteristics and then work assiduously to develop in areas in which they find themselves to be lacking in certain HF traits. The next step will be to look for help to improve the areas of lack. In the view of Heath (1994, 297), it is important that the educational and training curriculum clearly identifies the various competencies, norms, and values that students need to possess by the time of graduation. If students are assisted to acquire these successfully, they will be better prepared for a life of service to all humanity. "Schools should also build into their curriculum the opportunity for teachers to keep educating themselves about their own interests and expanding their talents with their students without sacrificing one iota of their academic integrity" (Heath 1994, 298). Just as intellectual development is essential, so also is character formation through the ongoing development of personality characteristics. These must be developed concurrently. In view of these observations, the following procedures should be in place.

The Identification of Principles

It is critical to identify universal principles or natural laws which must be used to serve as the foundation pillars on which subsequent programs can be based (refer to the two critical universal principles discussed in Chapter 10). In terms of universal principles, a society may need to think about the role of love in active human behavior. A society may also want to think about stewardship (i.e., people serving or helping others in life and all human endeavors). It is also important that a society must agree to and honor the view that human life is both sacred and sanctified. This is important because when a people can convince themselves and believe strongly that life is both sacred and sanctified, then they will do everything possible to preserve it. In addition, it is useful to realize that any society that fails to promote both personal and group freedom, liberty, equity, and fairness will find it too difficult to successfully deal with every inherent SEPE problem. It is also important to give regard to the continuing development of the spiritual dimension of every human being. The act of nurturing the spiritual dynamism of the human being has been neglected by many people in most societies. Societies that are serious about overcoming their SEPE malaise cannot do so by continuously ignoring the spiritual development of people. The HF agenda requires that there be a strong interest in both the spirituality and morality of people. Otherwise, the task of solving SEPE problems will become too difficult to accomplish.

At the starting point of the HF agenda, it is important for every society to highlight, discuss, select, and promote the relevant universal principles or natural laws on which to base programs and activities (see Chapter 10). Once these principles are discovered, critically evaluated, accepted, and then established to be the standards by which human life, activity, and behavior are based or measured against, people must be nurtured and guided to live as stipulated by these principles.

Providing the Relevant Training and Education

At the starting point of the HF agenda of development, it is essential to educate people to evaluate, understand, and then accept the fact that a personal life of service to others, loving and forgiving others and being loved and forgiven, and human life are not only priceless, but also that the true worth and value of these cannot be measured accurately. The magnitude of the long-term benefits to be derived from the acceptance and adherence to these three concepts far exceeds all temporal or instant human gratification to be derived from a life of activities that ignores them.

Indeed, all human behavior based on all forms of selfish perversions, avid greed, overeating, and dirty pride (i.e., in terms of one's material possessions) will abort the success of the development program in the long term. True human pride must necessarily be based on the beauty of the inner person as brought about by spiritual maturity and moral sensitivity—adherence to universal principles of life. These issues are so critical that if a people's education, training, and mentoring systems ignore them, people who are educated and trained in these institutions will not acquire the necessary HF traits to make their societies work as effectively and efficiently as they may desire. As such, any society that desires to experience the good life must be prepared to base its education and training systems on the identified universal principles of life. These education systems and training programs must be carefully crafted and articulated so that they can inculcate these ideals and principles in their people. As is often said, prevention is better than cure. Children who are lost to the streets and left on their own may not be transformed that easily for the better. Indeed, an apple tree that had always borne apples cannot, all of a sudden, produce grapes in its old age.

The New Human Factor Curriculum

Develop the new HF curriculum, discuss it, and debate its contents across the nation. For instance, look at the contents and make sure that the elements of the curriculum stress intellectual, moral, spiritual, and physical development; the acquisition of love and the ability to forgive others; the promotion of the principles that relate to the sacredness and sanctity of life; the respect for human rights and human distinctiveness; the inculcation of the skills and qualities that facilitate the peaceful resolution of conflicts and all forms of disagreements; the understanding of how to make choices through personal evaluation of the associated opportunity costs to oneself and to the rest of society; and so on. These issues are vital and must therefore not be bypassed. It will be suicidal to delete this step in the development process if a society is pursuing the HF development agenda.

When the curriculum is approved by parliament or the highest decision-making body in the country, the HF development agenda must begin with intensive teacher training and adult education programs. Since teachers will be given the mantle of education, training, and mentoring, they should be educated and trained first. For the HF education and training agenda to work, there must be a large number of trained and educated teachers in addition to other personnel who will be ready to make the system work as effectively as possible.

The social, economic, political, and educational machinery must utilize the existing agencies of education and training to promote citizens' acquisition of the following:

1. Self-confidence.

2. Sense of right and wrong.

3. Curiosity and intellectual inquisitiveness.

4. Respect for the rule of law and the sanctity of human life.

5. Interpersonal strengths such as curiosity, sensitivity, and tolerance (see Heath 1994, 125–147).

6. Motivational strengths such as curiosity and openness to challenges and change (see Heath 1994, 125–147).

7. Ethical values and a strong moral sense with regard to integrity, trustworthiness, honesty, loyalty, and so on.

8. Self-directing qualities such as motivation, commitment, perseverance, and so on.

9. Conflict resolving and negotiating skills.

10. Personal adaptability and communications skills.

11. Interpersonal attitudes such as tolerance, cooperative spirit, sensitivity to others, compassion, mercy, forgiving, love, and so on.

12. Concept of self as an individual, a member of a family, and part of society.

13. Ability to identify, articulate, and solve problems.

14. Personal independence, interdependence, and creativity.

15. Knowledge, understanding, and wisdom.

When all these have been successfully completed, the national educational curriculum must be phased in gradually. In this case, it is important to develop and empower the following people:

1. Family (i.e., parents, as understood by and constituted in each society)

2. People who work in the education system, training programs, and mentoring arrangements

3. Government employees and politicians operating in the system

4. Defense lawyers, soldiers, police officers, and all other people who are involved in the defense sector of the nation to promote HF development in society

Religious groups must also be brought into the picture and held accountable for their programs and actions. In this case, the government is not necessarily expected to regulate what religious organizations should or should not do, but there must be a meaningful dialogue in regard to what is expected of them and what they must be doing as their religions allow—and this must be commensurate with the identified universal principles of human life and action, making sure that they contribute to the development of personality characteristics that are necessary for promoting an efficient global political economy and a just social order. Any religious groups that work contrary to the key universal principles and the corresponding HF development agenda can either be challenged by other citizens or be made to lose any financial assistance they receive from taxpayers.

Putting Teeth to the Program

What I mean by "putting teeth to the program" is devising several mechanisms to be operated and organized by people who have acquired the desirable HF traits to make sure that those who are in responsible positions carry out their responsibilities with a great deal of commitment, integrity, accountability, loyalty, trustworthiness, and so on. What their job should be is making sure that deviant behavior is dealt with immediately and appropriately. Parents could be made responsible for the behavior of their children both at home and outside the home. Teachers should be made responsible for the behavior of their students both at school and outside school premises.[3]

Other associations or organizations, political parties, and groups can also be made responsible for the conduct of their members. This also goes for all professional associations. Those who either violate the law or deny others their basic human rights and privileges or engage themselves in corrupt practices that cause harm to other people as well as jeopardize the success of the global development program must be made to lose their professional licenses or their practice or be suspended from practicing for a period of time (see Adjibolosoo 1996b, Chapter 11). Anything that could be done to serve as a significant deterrent to unacceptable professional and business behavior must be promoted to enhance the effectiveness of the HF agenda.[4]

For example, the licenses or memberships of professional people may be revoked. In addition, they could be ostracized for a season. A document, which must be published either monthly or annually, containing the names of all professional people from all walks of life who have been found to be either corrupt or ineffective or unethical in their practices should be made available to all people (i.e., customers and clients alike) so that they can use the information in deciding on whether to continue visiting them. If any clients read this information and yet still decide to go to people who have been classified as crooks, they must take responsibility for their own actions. Privileges that these people have had in the past can also be withdrawn for having engaged in professional misconduct. These people should not only be fined for professional misdemeanor. If they are ever fined, some of them may have enough money to quickly get themselves back to where they were. Thus, a mere fine might not be a big deal for many of them. If they should be fined at all, the fines should be large enough that most professionals and businesspeople would be greatly deterred from engaging in either corrupt or unethical practices. The fine should be so large that it will hit them hard where it hurts.[5] In cases of severe offenses and professional misconduct, the license to practice should either be revoked or suspended for a selected number of years. When these penal measures are carried out appropriately and effectively, many professional people will be more careful about how they go about doing their daily practices.

Indeed, had society been doing this effectively in the past, a lot of recent lawsuits filed against many businesses and other organizations by customers who feel victimized in the advanced countries would not have happened—at least not to the extent we hear about in the United States. These problems exist because of HF decay and underdevelopment. If every society were to deal with the HF effectively, many of these horrendous problems will diminish. From this point on it will always be beneficial to society to allocate additional financial resources to start on the right footing. Though the HF can be engineered, the process is not easy to accomplish. It may take a whole generation for a nation that is currently experiencing severe HF decay or underdevelopment to overcome its SEPE problems if it pursues the HF development agenda. Indeed, it is true that if societies do not look at themselves and think about reeducating and retraining people to acquire the HF, almost everything they engage themselves in will fail. The human pride in going to the moon, the excitement in devising excellent technology for genetic engineering, the confidence in computerization, the hope and pride in all other things developed by all humanity will lose their potency, meaning, and, hence, lead to nothingness. In this case, what will be the point of developing technology and systems if people are unable to enjoy their full benefits? Societies that refuse to invest huge sums of money in the development of HF characteristics in its citizens will experience continuing HF decay or underdevelopment until their demise finally comes (see details in Figures 10.1 and 10.2).

Heath (1994, 128) noted that interpersonal strengths are the core of human adaptability. Indeed, the following can be argued:

1. Education for citizenship, community leadership, and development must focus on helping people to acquire the necessary human qualities (Adjibolosoo 1995a, 1996b).
2. Intellectual curiosity, self-direction, and self-reflection are necessary strengths required to be a successful manager (Heath 1994, 130; see also the original work on this issue in Evangelauf 1990).
3. Academic and athletic excellence must also be given top priority in the educational and training institutions (Heath 1994, 131).

Both historical evidence and existing stylized data are revealing that the pursuit of personal virtue in today's society is almost an endangered species. When these virtues finally suffer the same plight as did the dinosaurs, humanity will face an imminent collapse. Societies that are interested in optimizing the human potential must always remember that long-lasting human excellence in every regard is impossible without total personal commitment to a life of virtuousness (see Heath 1994, 132). Heath observed that scientific evidence exists to substantiate the claim of religion that virtue "is indispensable to human excellence." Men and women who live their lives based on the cardinal virtues are usually healthier, happier, and more successful than those who do not (Heath 1994). They exhibit greater magnitudes of personal professional maturity. A good human character is a *sine qua non* to personal well-being. Heath (1994, 138–139) could not have been any more accurate when he noted the following:

To live and work with others with minimal strain and strife frees energies and talents for adaptive purposes. The maturing person becomes progressively more integrated and acts with integrity. . . . Learning how to develop adaptive habits enhances efficiency, frees awareness and energy for new learning, and provides resiliency to recover from temporary disorganization. The maturing person develops a more stable identity, centered in predictable values and purposes, as well as more enduring individual and community relationship and commitments. . . . As we become more well-grounded, our growth moves toward increased self-discipline, self-regulation, and self-education, thereby bringing our potential strengths under our own control.

Schools that fail to promote fertile academic environments to facilitate the development and nurturing of positive attitudes, habits, and human qualities in their students cannot birth excellence in personal performance (see Heath 1994, 241). Heath also pointed out that society should not view its schools as being made up of beautiful, huge, and well-furnished classrooms, gymnasiums, libraries, swimming pools, and so on. Instead, a school consists of human beings who gather in one place to learn. The value of a school is not reflected in the number of faculty that holds higher degrees, or the magnificence of its teaching resources, library materials, and so on. An excellent school produces men and women who are educated to develop and have control over their own mind, character, spirit, and actions. These people grow up learning and preferring to live their lives as determined by the two critical universal principles of life.

Indeed, an effective school must necessarily provide a fertile and productive environment in which its students can be nurtured to grow and mature spiritually, morally, intellectually, culturally, physically, and so on. Students must learn, know, remember, and be able to apply knowledge gained to dealing successfully with everyday problems (Heath 1994, 287). In every regard, therefore, effective liberal arts education must go beyond mere knowledge acquisition in academic disciplines. It must, in fact, pay keen attention to the development of students' personality characteristics and capabilities, which, in the long term, affect their thought processes, deed, and action. Whatever schooling, educational, training, and mentoring programs are put in place, every student must be assisted to develop his or her full potential. Those students who bring pleasant personalities along with them to school from home should be assisted to develop them further. Alternatively, those students who lack these human qualities at the commencement of their educational career must be assisted and encouraged in nonthreatening ways to not only appreciate the beauty of desirable personality characteristics (i.e., the HF), but also covet them.

Maria Montesorri (1912, 1949) clearly showed that education must be carefully carried out to help children develop their individual personalities in addition to the development of their mind. This will help them to learn to adapt easily. To Montesorri, the natural laws (i.e., the critical universal principles) that underlie our common humanity should be exploited when developing the education curriculum (see also Erikson 1950; Heath 1994, 292). Keen and genuine self-interest generated in people will lead to the birth of long-lasting personal motivation to be involved in activities or programs that will produce positive and significant benefits for all people.

ENHANCING HUMAN POTENTIAL AND PERFORMANCE

One of the most difficult things to do in the world today is to get people who believe in, accept, and live by the principles of liberalism to agree on how to pursue human development. This is a difficult problem because it denies all humanity the ability to deal with its pertinent problems. What these people fail to do, however, is to realize that every human right or privilege carries along with it responsibilities that must neither be forsaken nor taken for granted. For it is in forsaking of these responsibilities that we experience severe SEPE problems (see details in Chapters 8 and 9).

It is now time for all humanity to take every social institution to task and request that it engages itself in HF development. This objective must be made a priority because when these institutions fail to accomplish the task of HF development, society will be permanently mortgaging its future. Education, training, and mentoring programs pursued by social institutions must guarantee a secure future for everyone. This is, however, only achievable if each social institution is able to assist each citizen to acquire and support him- or herself with intrinsic human qualities that contribute to an ongoing appreciation in personal well-being.[6] As an integral part of their ongoing mandate, SEPE institutions must, therefore, do the following:

1. Teach and encourage people to seek truth and universal principles that bring about personal fulfillment in life in terms of love, peace, forgiveness, and tranquillity. Those who discover these principles and agree to live by them will develop and live by personal ideals that place emphasis on the sacredness, sanctity, and net worth of human life and its many stages.

2. Pursue knowledge acquisition, clear understanding, and wisdom. These three are vital to the enhancement of personal life and duty to oneself, one's family, and all humanity. Those who acquire these will perceive that their lives will be anchored on foundation pillars that cannot be mowed down by SEPE circumstances.

3. Help people to learn the value of self-control (i.e., continence) and also strive to attain it relentlessly. Self-control is a rich human virtue whose acquisition and use usually lead to the appreciation of personal net worth in society. As one's bank account of self-control grows in magnitude, one's significance to society will shoot up and glitter like gold. Those who continuously deposit into their bank account of self-control usually gain the capability to help society to successfully deal with its conflicts. The continuing drawing down or depreciation of this account in many societies over the years has birthed painful SEPE problems. Vivid examples include spousal and child abuse, wars, broken engagements, unemployment, sexual harassment, and political corruption, scandals, and so on. Lack of self-control usually transforms a known serene individual into a vicious barracuda in the long term.

4. Encourage people to learn and practice accountability, loyalty, integrity, responsibility, commitment, and personal endurance. Like self-control, people who lack the ability to commit and endure will quit making good on their word when they feel like it. People who act and live their lives in this manner can hardly ever accomplish tasks of significant importance. They will not necessarily care about the prevailing problems in society. All they will always wish for is seeing the problems disappear on their own. A society will experience a barrage of problems when its citizens lack commitment and endurance. If this happens, many things can go wrong very easily. Those who lack commitment and personal endurance are not veteran problem solvers. Every society will do well to facilitate the development of personal and group commitment and endurance in its people by engaging in programs and activities that deracinate personal slothfulness.

Cherish and promote love in all people. Social psychological research has shown that short-term attraction and love is affected by physical attractiveness, competence, interests, attitudes, values, beliefs, and so on (Singer 1984; Byrne 1969, 1971; Kerschoff and David 1962; Levinger, Senn, and Jorgenson 1970; Walster 1970; Walster et al. 1966; Zajonc 1968). This type of love does not, however, build cohesive societies. At best, in many cases, it serves only as a weak basis for shallow relationships among members of a community. It breaks down when the conditions on which it is built vanish. The love that transcends all conditions and barriers, (i.e., unconditional love) is the true love brought about in the presence of positive HF. Real love is a crown. It is a permanent foundation to human behavior and action. True love guides and determines personal interaction with people and reaction to circumstances and events. The absence of true and sincere love among men and women in society can lead to ugly situations. In society today, many social evils, economic problems, and political difficulties are brought about by people who fail to acquire and live a life of love. Love is not an uncontrolled sensual personal feeling. It is truth. It has sensitivity, insight, power, and authority. Its true circle of influence guides, nurtures, and establishes personal commitment, integrity, responsibility, accountability, loyalty, and trustworthiness (see details in Chapter 10). It is the best ruler a nation and its people can ever elect and enthrone to reign. It breathes confidence, peace, and serenity. It is intelligent, forgiving, caring, and reassuring. A society whose members acquire and practice an unadulterated love and forgiveness will enjoy the greatest level of human well-being. In this society, the nature of SEPE problems will be contingent on the true strength of the magnitude of the quality of personal love exhibited by all people. In this way, this society will achieve sustainable human-centered development. Global development the human factor way will be a natural outflow.

CRITICAL STEPS IN THE IMPLEMENTATION OF THE HF MODEL

It requires unflinching efforts from everyone to develop and maintain every dimension of the human being. This process can be likened to the tuning up of a motor vehicle. At the garage, the mechanic uses the appropriate gadgets to check different parts of the vehicle to find out whether they are in good shape. The brakes, gearboxes, muffler, spark plugs, and many other parts are frequently evaluated. When any faults are detected, they are corrected immediately. Frequent tune-ups are critical to efficient vehicle performance. Vehicles that are poorly maintained run the risk of either breaking down often or causing accidents or both. In a similar way, for more effective and efficient performance, every human being requires the garage experience, metaphorically speaking.[7] People require the education and training that will enhance the development of the six major dimensions of the HF: spiritual, moral, aesthetic, human capital, human abilities, and human potential (Adjibolosoo 1995a; see also Chapter 6 in this book). The development and continued nurturing of each of these component parts of every human being are not only hard work, but also take considerable time to achieve. Thus, people who are fond of quick-fixes and ad hoc programs will find these to be difficult tasks to engage in. The six aspects of the HF need to be developed and maintained simultaneously on an ongoing basis to guarantee the best performance of people. It will be an unfortunate mistake to focus on the development of the human intellect, physique, or other parts of the physical body to the glaring neglect of continuing investment in the development of both spiritual and moral capital. Sad to say, however, this is the plight of all humanity today.

Any society that finds itself in this situation will experience HF decay or underdevelopment. Often, as noted, many scholars and government officials have come to wrongly believe that principle- and value-free education is sufficient in preparing men and women for a life of meaning and success in society. That is, various societies are currently in the habit of pumping huge financial resources into human-capital development, community policing, incarceration, the reformation of the criminal code, and severely punishing deviant behavior in society (see details in Chapter 9). These wrong approaches to problem solving have to change immediately. Based on the HF view of development, the following activities are relevant.

First, start with a nationwide awareness development program through seminars, conferences, lectures, and any other relevant programs aimed at informing and educating all citizens about the goals of nation building and the tasks at hand. Increase the effectiveness of these programs through personal and group morale building, using television, radio, newspaper, and magazine advertising. Where these avenues are nonexistent, town meetings and community development discussion group programs must be established and used effectively. These programs must not only be aimed at providing solutions to problems, but also encourage and give people the opportunity to contribute to the nation-building program. The primary thrust must be to provide people with the environment in which they can make meaningful and positive contributions to the nationwide attempts being made to facilitate progress in all areas of human life and endeavor freely and fearlessly. The contents of each of these advertising messages and community programs must be aimed at fostering personal integrity, accountability, responsibility, trustworthiness, loyalty, and so on. A well-designed program that is run effectively and efficiently will not only encourage people to contribute their best to the development program, but also see to it that every person performs at his or her best.

Second, revise the existing national educational curricula to include the teaching of issues relating to points just listed. The new HF educational curricula must foster free, open, honest, and extensive nationwide discussions on national issues, pertinent problems prevailing in the country, their main causes, and how to deal with them successfully. The primary object is to lead students to find out for themselves the results of either a well-developed HF or systemwide HF decay. This curriculum must make provisions for the extensive and continued use of case studies, traditional (indigenous) proverbs, riddles, stories, and the like. Students must be given the opportunity to discuss and debate related issues, even to the point of disagreeing with their professors (without any penalties or risks of failing courses) as their critical thinking abilities allow them to. That is, the curriculum must be utilized to help students to build in themselves a generally accepted reference point (i.e., a moral center) against which they can measure their own behavior, actions, attitudes, decisions, and so on.

Third, resist the temptation of using instruments of fear and intimidation to accomplish desired tasks. The utilization of fear and intimidation has been one of the greatest killers of individual voices—especially voices of dissent. Since this is usually the case, the educational program needs to address this issue effectively. The main objective in this case is to help people to develop the ability to tolerate and also learn to respect the views of others, always realizing that their viewpoints are not the best at all times. This kind of education may lead to the development of certain groups (i.e., mass movements or pressure groups) whose sole objective will be to hold leaders both accountable and responsible for their actions and deeds. The groups themselves must serve as national watchdogs, making sure that what needs to be done nationwide is done.

Last, prepare people to develop critical thinking and the ability to evaluate national issues, ideas, suggestions, plans, policies, programs, and projects effectively. People must make informed decisions, choices, or relevant changes and always be ready and willing to listen to and consider the relevance and role of the voices of dissent.

CONCLUSION

Indeed, a way out exists through the difficult and complex tunnels of SEPE problems in every society. Most of the ideas relevant for traveling on this route are known to some leaders in every society. The actual hindrances to pursuing these ideas are personal fear, greed, and dirty human self-indulgence. Few people are willing to put their lives on the line to secure a stable future of hope for the future generations. Many leaders in society today prefer to put on huge, ugly, and heavy masks—pretending not to see the pertinent SEPE problems that surround us all. All they desire is to be called national leaders on whom society confers rights and privileges to be enjoyed all year round. They not only lose touch with reality, but also engage themselves in activities and lifestyles that insulate them against the plight of those who voted them into office. They become leaders without "head." As such, they are usually fully engrossed in the enjoyment of their rights and privileges, since they suffer from the disease of political amnesia regarding why their constituencies voted them to be their representatives in the first place.

We cannot, however, place the whole blame on them, because society itself has failed to help them to acquire the HF in their days of schooling.[8] To successfully deal with this lopsided behavior, the social, economic, political, and educational machinery must assist every citizen to acquire the relevant qualities discussed in this chapter. When societies are able to accomplish these, global development will ensue and become an ongoing process—controlled and directed by people who desire the best for all humanity.

NOTES

1. It must be noted that there is historical evidence to show that leaders who stayed for a long period of time, such as kings, queens, Prime Ministers, Presidents, and so on, and achieved very little failed to focus their attention on HF development. Indeed, any leader

that commits him- or herself to continuing HF development programs will, in the long term, leave a significant legacy of citizens who have either acquired the appropriate HF or are vigorously pursuing it. It is also quite possible that such leaders might have reproduced themselves.

2. In answering this question, each society has to develop its own programs that can be used to achieve its HF development objectives. Indeed, unless society is able to provide a concrete program of activities for HF development, very little will be achieved.

3. It is quite likely that the view that people should be given responsibilities and then held accountable for how they discharge these responsibilities will meet a great deal of resistance. Some might even argue that there is no need to hold people responsible for the behavior of others. Yet a society that pushes for the establishment of rights without responsibilities is heading down the drainpipe. Many countries are experiencing severe difficulties today because of this failure to make people learn both responsibility and accountability. Indeed, in relation to the HF agenda of development, there is no room for problem accommodation. Every person who is placed in a responsible position has to perform his or her tasks as required of him or her. Otherwise, individual duties will not be accomplished as expected.

4. This does not necessarily mean "anything." Whatever is to be done must be in line with the prescriptions of the laws of the land. Indeed, the rule of law must always prevail.

5. The magnitude of fines must be large enough that they will be extremely difficult to pay without going bankrupt. Otherwise, those who are able to pay these fines will usually engage themselves in activities that cause harm to others. When the potency of these fines is strong enough to act as effective deterrence, many professionals will prefer to hold on to their professional ethic and conduct rather than be involved in unethical professional conduct. It must be emphasized here that the human factor model of national and global development does not advocate for the physical torture of fellow human beings.

6. It is reasonable to assign part of the blame to past leadership and everyone who was in positions of trust and yet failed to discharge his or her duties as efficiently as possible.

7. Note that the vehicle metaphor being employed here is not a perfect one, in that while human beings are living things, vehicles are inanimate. As such, the comparison here is more concerned with the principle of consistent vehicle maintenance to keep it running as desired. Even as has always been the case, manufacturers must always continue to update and also develop new models in order to gain and maintain their market share and global competitiveness. Thus, in terms of people, there must be ongoing programs for HF development.

8. The three points presented here prescribe what needs to be done regarding how to prepare people for the HF agenda of development. Note, however, that they do not prescribe any specific activities or program of action. Since every society is unique, the objective here is to provide national leaders with the opportunity to decipher those programs that will work best for their own societies. Where they are not sure about what to do, they may begin by selecting the principles they desire to foster and then determine the best methodologies for accomplishing the intended goals. In addition, they can have consultations with academics whose research interests include the HF and development and seek additional recommendations and advice.

REFERENCES

Abel, A. B., Bernanke, B. S., and Smith, G. W. 1995. *Macroeconomics*. New York: Addison-Wesley.

Abramovitz, M. 1956. Resource and Output Trends in the United States Since 1870. *American Economic Review* 46 (2): 5–23.

Abramovitz, M. 1962. Economic Growth in the United States. *American Economic Review* 52 (4): 762–782.

Adelman, I. 1961. *Theories of Economic Growth and Development*. Stanford, Calif.: Stanford University Press.

Adjibolosoo, S. 1991. Higher Education Must Teach Students to Think. *University Affairs*, June/July, 34.

Adjibolosoo, S. 1993a. The Human Factor in Development. *The Scandinavian Journal of Development Alternatives* 12: 139–149.

Adjibolosoo, S. 1993b. Integrative Education for Productivity and Quality Management: The Role of Business and Engineering Schools. In *Productivity and Quality Management Frontiers-IV*, edited by D. Sumanth, J. A. Edosomwan, R. Poupart, and D. S. Sink. Vol. 2. Norcross, Ga.: Industrial Engineering and Management Press.

Adjibolosoo, S. 1994a. Corruption and Economic Development in Africa: A Comparative Analysis. In *Perspectives on Economic Development in Africa*, edited by F. Ezeala-Harrison and S. Adjibolosoo. New York: Praeger.

Adjibolosoo, S. 1994b. The Human Factor and the Failure of Development Planning and Economic Policy in Africa. In *Perspectives on Economic Development in Africa*, edited by F. Ezeala-Harrison and S. Adjibolosoo. New York: Praeger.

Adjibolosoo, S. 1994c. The Political Economy of Development in Africa: Reflections on Orthodox Thinking and Policy. In *Perspectives on Economic Development in Africa*, edited by F. Ezeala-Harrison and S. Adjibolosoo. New York: Praeger.

Adjibolosoo, S. 1995a. *The Human Factor in Developing Africa*. New York: Praeger.

Adjibolosoo, S. 1995b. Rethinking the Sources of Economic Underdevelopment in Ghana. *Review of Human Factor Studies* 1: 1–35.

Adjibolosoo, S. 1995c. *The Significance of the Human Factor in African Economic Development*. New York: Praeger.

Adjibolosoo, S. 1996a. A Guide to Understanding the Fundamental Principles of Human Factor Theory. *Review of Human Factor Studies* 2: 1–26.

Adjibolosoo, S. 1996b. *Human Factor Engineering and the Political Economy of African Development.* New York: Praeger.

Aghion, P., and Howitt, P. 1992. A Model of Growth through Creative Destruction. *Econometrica* 60 (2): 323–351.

Arndt, H. W. 1978. *The Rise and Fall of Economic Growth: A Study in Contemporary Thought.* Melbourne: Longman Cheshire.

Arrow, K. J. 1962. The Economic Implications of Learning by Doing. *Review of Economic Studies* 9: 155–173.

Barrios de Chungra, D. 1979. Let Me Speak. *Monthly Review* 30 (9): 42–54.

Becker, G. S. 1962. Irrational Behavior and Economic Theory. *Journal of Political Economy* 70: 1–13.

Becker, G. S. 1964. *Human Capital.* New York: Columbia University Press.

Becker, G. S. 1965. A Theory of Allocation of Time. *Economic Journal* 75: 493–517.

Becker, G. S. 1971. *Economic Theory.* New York: Alfred A. Knopf.

Becker, H., and Barnes, H. E. 1952. *Social Thought from Lore to Science: A History and Interpretation of Man's Ideas about Life with His Fellows.* Washington, D.C.: Harren Press.

Becker, H. S. 1963. *Outsiders: Studies in the Sociology of Deviance.* New York: Free Press.

Berger, P. L. 1967. *The Sacred Canopy.* Garden City, N.Y.: Doubleday.

Bernard, V. W., Ottenberg, P., and Redl, F. 1973. Dehumanization and Nuclear War. In *The Solution of Social Problems: Five Perspectives*, edited by M. S. Weinberg and E. Rubington. New York: Oxford University Press.

Blackwell, G. 1990. Northern Lights. *Candian Business*, March, 40–44.

Blake, D. H., and Walters, R. S. 1987. *The Politics of Global Economic Relations.* Englewood Cliffs, N.J.: Prentice-Hall.

Blaug, M. 1965. The Rate of Return on Investment in Education in Great Britain. *The Manchester School* 33 (3): 205–251.

Blumberg, P. 1989. *The Predatory Society: Deception in the American Marketplace.* New York: Oxford University Press.

Borgatta, E., and Meyer, H. J. 1959. *Social Control and the Foundation of Sociology.* Boston: Beacon.

Bottomore, T. 1987. *Sociology: A Guide to Problems and Literature.* London: Allen and Unwin.

Bowman, M. J. 1964. Schultz, Denison and the Contribution of Education to National Income Growth. *Journal of Political Economy*, 72 (5): 450–464.

Braudel, F. 1979. The Wheels of Commerce: Civilization and Capitalism, 15th–18th Century. (Translated by Sian Reynolds.) New York: Harper and Row.

Brennan, D. G. 1968. *Anti-Ballistic Missile: Yes or No?* New York: Hill and Wang.

Buist, M. G. 1974. *At spes non fracta.* New York: Hope and Co.

Business Week, 13 December 1993, 72–85. The Economics of Crime.

Byrne, D. 1969. Attitudes and Attraction. In *Advances in Experimental Social Psychology*, edited by L. Berkowitz. Vol. 4. New York: Academic Press.

Byrne, D. 1971. *The Attraction Paradigm.* New York: Academic Press.

Cameron, R. 1993. *A Concise Economic History of the World: From Paleolithic Times to the Present.* New York: Oxford University Press.

Cantarow, E., Diggs, E., Ellis, K., Marx, J., Robinson, L., and Schein, M. 1973. Women's Liberation. In *The Solution of Social Problems: Five Perspectives*, edited by M. S. Weinberg and E. Rubington. New York: Oxford University Press.

Carmichael, S., and Hamilton, C. V. 1973. Black Power. In *The Solution of Social Problems: Five Perspectives*, edited by M. S. Weinberg and E. Rubington. New York: Oxford University Press.

Champernowne, D. G. 1958. Capital Accumulation and Maintenance of Full Employment. *Economic Journal* 68: 211–224.

Cherif, A. 1996. Ecological Ethic in Academia: A Proposal for a Teaching Survival. *Review of Human Factor Studies* 2 (1): 49–72.

Clark, J. M. 1953. Aims of Economic Life as Seen by Economists. In *Goals of Economic Life*, edited by A. D. Ward. New York: Harper and Brothers.

Clinard, M. B., and Yeager, P. C. 1982. Corporate Organization and Criminal Behavior. In *Corporate and Government Deviance: Problems of Organizational Behavior in Contemporary Society*, edited by M. D. Ermann and R. J. Lundman. New York: Oxford University Press.

Cloward, R. 1973. The Prevention of Delinquent Subcultures. In *The Solution of Social Problems: Five Perspectives*, edited by M. S. Weinberg and E. Rubington. New York: Oxford University Press.

Cloward, R., and Ohlin, L. 1960. *Delinquency and Opportunity*. New York: Free Press.

Coats, S. C. 1993. Personal Connection with Quality. *Executive Excellence* 10: 10.

Cohen, A. 1955. *Delinquent Boys*. New York: Free Press.

Cohen, A. 1966. *Deviance and Control*. Englewood Cliffs, N.J.: Prentice-Hall.

Cohen, Y. A., ed. 1971. *Man in Adaptation: The Institutional Framework*. Chicago: Aldine.

Colander, D. C., and Landreth, H., eds. 1995. *Classic Readings in Economics*. New Haven, Conn.: MaxiPress.

Cooley, C. H. 1918. *The Social Process*. New York: Scribner's.

Corelli, R. 1994. Murder Next Door. *Maclean's*, 18 April, 15–22.

Costello, D. M. 1993. A Cross-Country, Cross-Industry Comparison of Productivity Growth. *Journal of Political Economy*, April, 207–222.

Daly, H. E., and Cobb, J. B. 1989. *For the Common Good: Redirecting the Economy Toward Community, the Environment and a Sustainable Future*. Boston: Beacon Press.

Darwin, C. 1872. *The Origin of Species by Means of Natural Selection*. New York: Modern Library.

Davis, K. 1973. The Population Explosion. In *The Solution of Social Problems: Five Perspectives*, edited by M. S. Weinberg and E. Rubington. New York: Oxford University Press.

Denison, E. F. 1985. *Trends in American Economic Growth, 1929–1982*. Washington, D.C.: The Brookings Institution.

Denny, M., Burnstein, J., Fuss, M., Nakamura, S., and Waverman, L. 1992. "Productivity in Manufacturing Industries, Canada, Japan, and the United States, 1953–1986: Was the Productivity Slowdown" Reversed? *Canadian Journal of Economics*, August, 584–603.

Dicken, P. 1986. *Global Shift: Industrial Change in a Turbulent World*. London: Harper and Row.

Dixit, A. 1973. Models of Dual Economies. In *Models of Economic Growth*, edited by J. A. Mirrlees and N. Stern. Oxford: Macmillan.

Dixit, A. 1976. *The Theory of Equilibrium Growth.* Oxford: Oxford University Press.

Dixit, A. 1990. Growth Theory after Thirty Years. In *Growth/Productivity/Employment,* edited by P. Diamond. Cambridge, Mass.: MIT Press.

Dolman, A. J., ed. 1976. *Rio: Reshaping the International Order* (A Report to the Club of Rome).

Domanick, J. 1989. *Faking It in America: Barry Minkow and the Great ZZZZ Best Scam.* Chicago: Contemporary Books.

Domar, E. D. 1946. Capital Expansion, Rate of Growth and Employment. *Econometrica,* 14 (2): 137–147.

Domar, E. D. 1957. *Essays in the Theory of Economic Growth.* New York: Oxford University Press.

Durant, W. 1939. *The Study of Civilization: The Life of Greece.* New York: Simon and Schuster.

Durkheim, E. 1951. *Suicide.* New York: Free Press.

Dusenberry, J. S. 1958. *Business Cycles and Economic Growth.* New York: McGraw-Hill.

The Economist, 23 April 1994, 25–26. Criminal Ineptitude.

The Economist, 28 May 1994, 15. Brown 40 Years On.

Ekelund, R. B., Jr., and Herbert, R. F. 1990. *A History of Economic Theory and Method.* New York: McGraw-Hill.

Ekman, P. 1989. *Why Kids Lie: How Parents Can Encourage Truthfulness.* New York: Scribner's.

Elliot, M. 1994. Corruption: How Bribes, Payoffs and Crooked Officials Are Blocking Economic Growth. *Newsweek,* 14 November, 40–42.

Ellul, J. 1990. *The Technological Bluff.* Grand Rapids, Mich.: Eerdmans.

Eltis, W. A. 1973. *Growth and Distribution.* New York: Macmillan.

Erikson, E. 1950. *Childhood and Society.* New York: W. W. Norton.

Evangelauf, J. 1990. Business Schools Are Urged to Rethink the Curriculum of MBA Programs. *Chronicle of Higher Education,* 23 May, A30.

Findley, N. 1990a. AT&T Enhanced Fax Offers Major Advance. *Business in Vancouver,* 3–19 November, 23.

Findley, N. 1990b. You Don't Need a Smaller Machine to Enjoy Enhanced Fax. *Business in Vancouver,* 20–26 November, 22.

Forsythe, D. P. 1991. *The Internationalization of Human Rights.* Lexington, Mass.: Lexington Books.

Fortune, 3 October 1994, 30–35. Actual Photo of a Whirlwind.

Fusfeld, D. 1986. *The Age of the Economist.* Glenview, Ill.: Scott, Foresman.

Galbraith, J. K. 1968. *The New Industrial State.* New York: New American Library.

Gerschenkron, A. 1962. *Economic Backwardness in Historical Perspective.* Cambridge: Harvard University Press.

Glyn, A., and Sutcliffe, B. 1971. The Critical Condition of British Capital. *New Left Review* 66 (March–April): 3–33.

Glyn, A., and Sutcliffe, B. 1972. *British Capitalism, Workers and the Profit Squeeze.* London: Penguin Books.

Gordon, B. J. 1975. *Economic Analysis before Adam Smith: Hesiod to Lessius.* New York: Barnes and Noble.

Gordon, M. 1973. Too Many Governments. In *The Solution of Social Problems: Five Perspectives,* edited by M. S. Weinberg and E. Rubington. New York: Oxford University Press.

Gordon, R. J. 1984. *Macroeconomics*. Toronto: Little, Brown.

Goudzwaard, B. 1979. *Capitalism and Progress: A Diagnosis of Western Society*. Toronto: Wedge.

Goyder, G. 1961. *The Responsible Company*. Oxford: Basil Blackwell.

Gray, A. 1959. *The Development of Economic Doctrine*. London: Longmans.

Grinspoon, L. 1973. Marihuana Reconsidered. In *The Solution of Social Problems: Five Perspectives*, edited by M. S. Weinberg and E. Rubington. New York: Oxford University Press.

Grossman, C. M., and Helpman, E. 1991. *Innovation and Growth in the Global Economy*. Cambridge, Mass.: MIT Press.

Guha, A. S. 1981. *An Evolutionary View of Economic Growth*. Oxford: Clarendon Press.

Gurley, J. G. 1979. *Challenges to Capitalism: Marx, Lenin, Stalin, and Mao*. New York: W. W. Norton.

Gurtov, M. 1985. *Global Politics in the Human Interest*. London: Lynne Rienner.

Hagen, E. E. 1962. How Economic Growth Begins: A Theory of Social Change. *Journal of Social Issues* (January): 20–34.

Hahn, F. 1990. Solowian Growth Models. In *Growth, Productivity, Unemployment: Essays to Celebrate Bob Solow's Birthday*, edited by P. Diamond. Cambridge, Mass.: MIT Press.

Hahn, F. 1995. On Growth Theory. In *Economics in a Changing World*, edited by J. Fitoussi. New York: St. Martin's Press.

Hahn, F. H., and Matthews, R. C. O. 1964. The Theory of Economic Growth: A Survey. *Economic Journal*, December.

Hamberg, D. 1971. *Models of Economic Growth*. New York: Harper and Row.

Harrod, R. F. 1939. An Essay in Dynamic Theory. *Economic Journal*, March, 19–33.

Harrod, R. F. 1948. *Towards a Dynamic Economics: Some Recent Developments in Economic Theory and Application to Policy*. London: Macmillan.

Heath, D. H. 1994. *Schools of Hope: Developing Mind and Character in Today's Youth*. San Francisco: Jossey-Bass.

Hecksher, E., and Ohlin, B. 1933. *Interregional and International Trade*. Cambridge, Mass.: Harvard University Press.

Heilbroner, R. L. 1986. *The Worldly Philosophers: The Lives, Times, and Ideas of the Great Economic Thinkers*. New York: Simon and Schuster.

Hicks, J. R. 1966. Growth and Anti-Growth. *Oxford Economic Papers* 18 (3): 257–269.

Hill, M., and Kwen Fee, L. 1995. *The Politics of Nation Building and Citizenship in Singapore*. New York: Routledge.

Hirschi, T., and Stark, R. 1969. Hellfire and Delinquency. *Social Problems* 17: 202–213.

Hobbes, T. 1956. *Leviathan*. 1651. Reprint, Chicago: Henry Regnery.

Hobbs, D., ed. 1995. *Professional Criminals*. Aldershot: Dartmouth.

Holmes, A. F. 1987. *The Idea of a Christian College*. Grand Rapids, Mich.: Eerdmans.

Holmes, A. F. 1991. *Shaping Character*. Grand Rapids, Mich.: Eerdmans.

Huntington, E. 1915. *Civilization and Climate*. New Haven: Yale University Press.

Huntington, E. 1945. *Mainsprings of Civilization*. New York: Wiley.

Ingersoll, D. E., and Matthews, R. K. 1991. *The Philosophic Roots of Modern Ideology: Liberalism, Communism, Fascism*. Englewood Cliffs, N.J.: Prentice-Hall.

James, J., and James, M. 1991. *Passion for Life: Psychology and the Human Spirit*. New York: Dutton.

Janowitz, M. 1978. *The Last Half Century*. Chicago: University of Chicago Press.

Johnson, R. V., and Cressey, D. R. 1973. Drug Addiction and Synanon. In *The Solution of Social Problems: Five Perspectives*, edited by M. S. Weinberg and E. Rubington. New York: Oxford University Press.

Jones, T. B. 1960. *Ancient Civilization*. Chicago: Rand McNally.

Jorgenson, D. 1967. Surplus Agricultural Labor and the Development of the Dual Economy. *Oxford Economic Papers* 19 (3): 288–312.

Jorgenson, D. W. 1961. Development of a Dual Economy. *Economic Journal* 71 (June): 309–334.

Jorgenson, D. W. 1988. Productivity and Postwar U.S. Economic Growth. *Journal of Economic Perspectives* (Fall): 23–41.

Jorgenson, D. W. 1995. *Productivity. Volume 1: Postwar U.S. Economic Growth.* Cambridge: MIT Press.

Kaldor, N. 1957. A Model of Economic Growth. *Economic Journal* 67: 591–624.

Kalecki, M. 1954. *Theory of Economic Dynamics*. London: Allen and Unwin.

Keating, H. R. F. 1991. *Great Crimes*. Stamford, Conn.: Longmeadow Press.

Kerschoff, A. C., and David, K. E. 1962. Value Consensus and Need Complementarity in Mate Selection. *Amercian Sociological Review* 27: 295–303.

Keynes, J. M. 1936. *The General Theory of Employment, Interest and Money*. London: Macmillan.

Knight, D. 1973. The Marshall Program of Delinquency Rehabilitation. In *The Solution of Social Problems: Five Perspectives*, edited by M. S. Weinberg and E. Rubington. New York: Oxford University Press.

Kohn, A. 1986. *False Prophets: Fraud and Error in Science and Medicine*. Oxford: Basil Blackwell.

Krugman, P. R. 1994. *The Age of Diminished Expectations: U.S. Economic Policy in the 1990s*. Cambridge: MIT Press.

Labich, K. 1990. American Takes on the World. *Fortune*, 24 September, 40–48.

Laing, R. D. 1973. A Different Perspective on Schizophrenia. In *The Solution of Social Problems: Five Perspectives*, edited by M. S. Weinberg and E. Rubington. New York: Oxford University Press.

Landreth, H. 1976. *History of Economic Theory: Scope, Method and Content*. Boston: Houghton Mifflin.

Lavine, T. Z. 1989. *From Socrates to Sartre: The Philosophical Quest*. New York: Bantam.

Leibenstein, H. 1957. *Economic Backwardness and Economic Growth: Studies in the Theory of Economic Development*. New York: Wiley.

Leibenstein, H. 1966. Allocative Efficiency Versus X-efficiency. *American Economic Review* 56 (3): 392–415.

Lermet, E. 1951. *Social Pathology: A Systematic Approach to the Theory of Sociopathic Behavior*. New York: McGraw-Hill.

Lesourne, J. F. 1986. *World Perspectives: A European Assessment*. New York: Gordon and Breach.

Levinger, G. K., Senn, D. J., and Jorgenson, B. 1970. Progress toward Permanence in Courtship: A Test of the Kerckhoff–David Hypothesis. *Sociometry* 33: 427–443.

Lewis, W. A. 1954. Economic Development with Unlimited Supplies of Labor. *The Manchester School of Economics and Social Studies* 22 (2): 139–191.

Lewis, W. A. 1955. *The Theory of Economic Growth*. Homewood, Ill.: Richard D. Irwin.

Lindskoog, K. 1993. *Fakes, Frauds, and Other Malarkey: 301 Amazing Stories and How Not to be Fooled*. Grand Rapids, Mich.: Zondervan.

Lineberry, R. 1994. Texan Teen Rapist/Killers Join the Biggest Death Row in the U.S. *The Vancouver Sun*, 26 September 1994, A10.

Lipsey, R. G., Purvis, D., and Steiner, P. O. 1991. *Economics*. New York: Harper Collins.

Lithwick, N. H. 1970. *Economic Growth in Canada: A Quantitative Analysis*. Toronto: University of Toronto Press.

Little, I. M. D. 1957. Classical Growth. *Oxford Economic Papers*, (*N.S.*) 9: 152–177.

Locke, J. 1690. An Essay Concerning the True Original, Extent and End of Civil Government. Reprinted in *The English Philosophers from Bacon to Mill*, edited by E. A. Burtt. New York: The Modern Library, 1967.

Lowry, T. S. 1987. *Pre-Classical Economic Thought*. Boston: Kluwer Academic Publishers.

Lucas, R. E. 1988. On the Mechanics of Economic Development. *Journal of Monetary Economics* 22: 3–42.

MacDonald, G. J. F. 1968. Weather Modifications. *Science Journal*, January, 39.

Maddison, A. 1964. *Economic Growth in the West: Comparative Experience in Europe and North America*. New York: Twentieth Century Fund.

Mankiw, N. G., Romer, D., and Weil, D. 1992. A Contribution to the Empirics of Economic Growth. *Quarterly Journal of Economics* (May): 407–438.

Marx, K. 1904. *A Critique of Political Economy*. Chicago: Kerr.

Marx, K. 1906. *Capital*. 2 vols. Chicago: Kerr.

Marx, K., and Engels, F. 1955. *The Communist Manifesto*. Chicago: Appleton Century Crofts.

Matza, D. 1969. *Becoming Deviant*. Englewood Cliffs, N.J.: Prentice-Hall.

McClelland, D. 1961. *The Achieving Society*. Princeton, N.J.: Van Nostrand.

McCullough, H. B. 1989. *Political Ideologies and Political Philosophies*. Toronto: Thompson Educational Publishing.

McCullough, H. B., ed. 1995. *Political Ideologies and Political Philosophies*. Toronto: Thompson Educational Publishing.

Meyer, J. W. 1977. The Effects of Education as an Institution. *American Journal of Sociology* 83: 55–77.

Mills, C. W. 1943. The Professional Ideology and Social Pathologists. *American Journal of Sociology* 49: 165–180.

Montessori, M. 1912. *The Montessori Method*. New York: Frederick Stokes.

Montessori, M. 1949. *The Absorbent Mind*. Madras, India: Kalakshetra Publications.

Morris, D. 1973. Intimate Behavior. In *The Solution of Social Problems: Five Perspectives*, edited by M. S. Weinberg and E. Rubington. New York: Oxford University Press.

Murdock, G. P. 1949. *Social Structure*. New York: Macmillan.

Myers, K., and Ashkenas, R. 1993. Results-Driven Quality. *Executive Excellence* 10: 17.

Myint, H. 1964. *The Economics of the Developing Countries*. London: Hutchinson.

Naisbitt, J. 1982. *Megatrends: Ten New Directions Transforming Our Lives*. New York: Warner Books.

Niebuhr, R. 1953. The Christian Faith and the Economic Life of Liberal Society. In *Goals of Economic Life*, edited by D. A. Ward. New York: Harper and Brothers.

Nocera, J. 1995. Fatal Litigation. *Fortune*, 16 October, 60–82.

Noel, B., and Watterson, K. 1992. *You Must Be Dreaming*. New York: Poseidon.

Nozick, R. 1974. *Anarchy, State and Utopia*. New York: Basic Books.

Ofori-Amoah, B., and Adjibolosoo, S. 1995. "Crises as Windows of Opportunities for African Development." Paper presented at the Africa 2000 Conference, Hofstra University, Hempstead, New York, October 12–14.

Olson, J. E. 1988. Toward a Global Information Age. In *The Global Market Place*, edited by J. M. Rosow. New York: Facts on File.

Oser, J., and Brue, S. L. 1988. *The Evolution of Economic Thought*. New York: Harcourt Brace Jovanovich.

Ouchi, W. G. 1981. *Theory Z*. New York: Avon Books.

Parenti, M. 1986. *Inventing Reality: The Politics of the Mass Media*. New York: St. Martin's Press.

Park, R., and Burgess, E. W. 1921. *Introduction to the Science of Sociology*. Chicago: University of Chicago Press.

Perelman, M. 1983. *Classical Political Economy: Primitive Accumulation and the Social Division of Labor*. Totowa, N.J.: Rowman and Allanheld.

Peters, T. J., and Austin, N. 1985. *A Passion for Excellence: The Leadership Difference*. New York: Random House.

Peters, T. J., and Waterman, R. H. 1982. *In Search of Excellence: Lessons from America's Best-Run Companies*. New York: Harper and Row.

Piven, F., and Cloward, R. 1973. Disrupting City Services to Change National Priorities. In *The Solution of Social Problems: Five Perspectives*, edited by M. S. Weinberg and E. Rubington. New York: Oxford University Press.

Power, J. H. 1958. The Economic Framework of a Theory of Growth. *Economic Journal* 67: 34–51.

Prescott, E. C. 1988. Robert M. Solow's Neoclassical Growth Model: An Influential Contribution to Economics. *Scandinavian Journal of Economics* 90: 7–12.

Raab, E., and Selznick, G. 1964. *Major Social Problems*. New York: Harper and Row.

Rao, S., and Lempriere, T. 1992. *Canada's Productivity Performance*. Ottawa: Economic Council of Canada.

Reich, C. A. 1973. The Greening of America. In *The Solution of Social Problems: Five Perspectives*, edited by M. S. Weinberg and E. Rubington. New York: Oxford University Press.

Reiffers, J. L., Cartapanis, A., Experton, W., and Fuguet, J. L. 1982. *Transnational Corporations and Endogenous Development*. Paris: UNESCO.

Reiss, I. L. 1980. *Family Systems in America*. New York: Holt, Rinehart and Winston.

Ricardo, D. 1937. *The Principles of Political Economy and Taxation*. London: Dent and Son.

Rider, C. 1995. *An Introduction to Economic History*. Cincinnati: South-Western College Publishing.

Robinson, H. H. 1898. *Loom and Spindle, or Life Among the Early Mill Girls*. Kailua, Hawaii: Pacifica Press.

Robinson, J. 1956. *The Accumulation of Capital*. London: Macmillan.

Robinson, J. 1962. *Essays in the Theory of Economic Growth*. London: Macmillan.

Rogin, L. 1956. *The Meaning and Validity of Economic Theory: A Historical Approach*. Freeport, N.Y.: Books for Libraries.

Roll, E. 1964. *A History of Economic Thought*. Englewood Cliffs, N.J.: Prentice-Hall.

Romer, P. M. 1986. Increasing Returns and Long-Run Growth. *Journal of Political Economy* 94 (5): 1002–1037.

Rosenberg, N. 1979. Adam Smith and Laissez-Faire Revisited. In *Adam Smith and Modern Political Economy: Bicentennial Essays on the Wealth of Nations*, edited by G. P. O'Driscoll, Jr. Ames: Iowa State University Press.

Rosow, J. M., ed. 1988. *The Global Market Place*. New York: Facts on File.

Ross, E. A. 1901. *Social Control: A Survey of the Foundations of Order.* New York: Macmillan.

Ross, R. J. S., and Trachte, K. C. 1990. *Global Capitalism: The New Leviathan.* Albany: State University of New York Press.

Rostow, W. W. 1953. *The Process of Economic Growth.* Oxford: Clarendon Press.

Rostow, W. W. 1960. *The Stages of Economic Growth: Non-Communist Manifesto.* Cambridge: Cambridge University Press.

The Royal Bank of Canada. 1989. *Royal Bank Reporter* (Fall): 15.

Rubington, E. 1973. Rehabilitating the Chronic Drunkenness Offender. In *The Solution of Social Problems: Five Perspectives,* edited by M. S. Weinberg and E. Rubington. New York: Oxford University Press.

Schultz, T. W. 1961. Investment in Human Capital. *American Economic Review* 51: 1–17.

Schumpeter, J. A. 1934. *The Theory of Economic Development.* Cambridge: Harvard University Press.

Schumpeter, J. A. 1943. *Capitalism, Socialism and Democracy.* London: Allen & Unwin.

Schur, E. M. 1973. Abortion Reform. In *The Solution of Social Problems: Five Perspectives,* edited by M. S. Weinberg and E. Rubington. New York: Oxford University Press.

Scull, A. T. 1988. Deviance and Social Control. In *Handbook of Sociology,* edited by N. J. Smelser. Newbury Park, Calif.: Sage.

Sen, A. K. 1970. *Growth Economics.* Harmondsworth, U.K.: Penguin.

Shell, K., ed. 1967. *Essays on the Theory of Optimal Economic Growth.* Cambridge: MIT Press.

Sheshinski, E. 1967. Optimal Accumulation with Learning by Doing. In *Essays on the Theory of Optimal Economic Growth,* edited by K. Shell. Cambridge, Mass.: MIT Press.

Singer, J. L. 1984. *The Human Personality.* New York: Harcourt Brace Jovanovich.

Slater, P. 1973. The Pursuit of Loneliness. In *The Solution of Social Problems: Five Perspectives,* edited by M. S. Weinberg and E. Rubington. New York: Oxford University Press.

Smelser, N. J. 1988. *Handbook of Sociology.* Newbury Park, Calif.: Sage.

Smith, A. 1776. *Wealth of Nations.* Port Washington, N.Y.: Kennikat Press, 1948, 1969.

Sobel, L. A., ed. 1977. *Corruption in Business.* New York: Facts on File.

Solow, R. M. 1956. A Contribution to the Theory of Economic Growth. *Quarterly Journal of Economics* 70: 65–94.

Solow, R. M. 1957. Technical Change and the Aggregate Production Function. *Review of Economics and Statistics* 39: 312–320.

Soule, G. 1963. *Ideas of the Great Economists.* New York: Viking Press.

Spengler, J. J. 1960. Mercantilist and Physiocratic Theory. In *Theories of Economic Growth,* edited by B. F. Hoselitz, J. J. Spengler, J. M. Letiche, E. McKinley, J. Buttrick, and H. J. Brutton. Glencoe, Ill.: Free Press.

Spiro, M. E. 1966. Religion: Problems of Definition and Explanation. In *Anthropological Approaches to the Study of Religion,* edited by M. Banton. New York: Frederick A. Praeger.

Sraffa, P., ed. 1951. *The Works and Correspondence of David Ricardo.* Cambridge: Cambridge University Press.

Staley, E. C. 1989. *A History of Economic Thought: From Aristotle to Arrow.* Oxford: Basil Blackwell.

Stark, R. 1981. Must All Religions Be Supernatural? In *The Social Impact of New Religious Movements*, edited by B. Wilson. New York: Rose of Sharon Press.

Stark, R. 1992. *Sociology*. Belmont, Calif.: Wadsworth.

Stark, R., and Bainbridge, W. S. 1985. *The Future of Religion: Secularization, Revival and Cult Formation*. Berkeley and Los Angeles: University of California Press.

Stark, R., Doyle, D. P., and Rushing, J. L. 1983a. Beyond Durkheim: Religion and Suicide. *Journal for the Scientific Study of Religion* 22: 120–131.

Stark, R., Doyle, D. P., and Rushing, J. L. 1983b. Crime and Delinquency in the Roaring Twenties. *Journal of Crime and Delinquency* 20: 4–23.

Stebbins, G. L. 1971. *Chromosomal Evolution in Higher Plants*. London: Edward Arnold.

Stewart, R. M. 1986. *Readings in Social and Political Philosophy*. New York: Oxford University Press.

Stigler, G. 1947. *Trends in Output and Employment*. New York: National Bureau of Economic Research.

Sundrum, R. M. 1990. *Economic Growth in Theory and Practice*. New York: Macmillan.

Sutherland, E. H. 1982. White Collar Crime is Organized Crime. In *Corporate and Government Deviance: Problems of Organizational Behavior in Contemporary Society*, edited by M. D. Ermann and R. J. Lundman. New York: Oxford University Press.

Swan, T. W. 1956. Economic Growth and Capital Accumulation. *Economic Record* 32: 334–361.

Sweezy, P. 1942. *The Theory of Capitalist Development*. New York: Oxford University Press.

Swindoll, C. R. 1987. *Living Above the Level of Mediocrity: A Commitment to Excellence*. Waco, Tex.: Word Books.

Thirlwall, A. P. 1972. *Growth and Development: With Special Reference to Developing Economies*. London: Macmillan.

Thomas, W. I., and Znaniecki, F. 1927. *The Polish Peasant in Europe and America*. New York: Knopf.

Thurman, L. D. 1978. *How to Think about Evolution and Other Bible–Science Controversies*. Downers Grove, Ill.: Intervarsity Press.

Time Magazine, 13 March 1989, 17–22. The Looting of Greece.

Tinari, F. D. 1986. *Economics: The Options for Dealing with Scarcity*. London: Scott, Foresman.

Tinbergen, J. 1942. Zür Theorie de Langfristigen Wirtschaftsent-Wicklung, *Weltwirtschäftliches Archiv* 55 (1): 511–549. See 1959 English translation in *Jan Tibergen, Selected Papers*, edited by L. H. Klassen, L. M. Koyck, and H. J. Witteven. Amsterdam: North-Holland, 1959.

Tobin, J. 1955. A Dynamic Aggregative Model. *Journal of Political Economy* 63: 103–115.

Toffler, A. 1973. Future Shock. In *The Solution of Social Problems: Five Perspectives*, edited by M. S. Weinberg and E. Rubington. New York: Oxford University Press.

Toffler, A. 1980. *The Third Wave*. New York: William Morrow & Company.

U. S. Department of State. 1977. News Release, March 3.

Walster, E. 1970. The Effect of Self-Esteem on Liking for Dates of Yannis Social Desirabilities. *Journal of Experimental Social Psychology* 6: 240–252.

Walster, E., Aronson, V., Abrahams, D., and Rottman, L. 1966. Importance of Physical Attractiveness in Dating Behavior. *Journal of Personality and Social Psychology* 4: 508–516.

Ward, R. R. 1965. *In the Beginning: A Study of Creation versus Evolution for Young People*. Grand Rapids, Mich.: Baker Book House.

Weber, M. 1930. *The Protestant Ethic and the Spirit of Capitalism*. New York: Charles Scribner's Sons.

Weber, M. 1946. Politics as a Vocation. In *From Max Weber*, edited by H. Gerth and C. W. Mills. New York: Oxford University Press.

Weinberg, M. S., and Rubington, E., eds. 1973. *The Solution of Social Problems: Five Perspectives*. New York: Oxford University Press.

Weinberg, M. S., and Williams, C. J. 1973. Neutralizing the Homosexual Label. In *The Solution of Social Problems: Five Perspectives*, edited by M. S. Weinberg and E. Rubington. New York: Oxford University Press.

Weisberg, B. 1973. The Politics of Ecology. In *The Solution of Social Problems: Five Perspectives*, edited by M. S. Weinberg and E. Rubington. New York: Oxford University Press.

Weisskopf, T. E. 1979. Marxian Crisis Theory and the Rate of Profit in the Postwar Economy. *Cambridge Journal of Economics* 3: 341–378.

Whitehead, A. N. 1926. *Science and the Modern World*. Cambridge: Cambridge University Press.

Wilkins, A. L. 1989. *Developing Corporate Character: How to Successfully Change an Organization without Destroying It*. London: Jossey-Bass.

Wirth, L. 1964. *On Cities and Social Life*. Chicago: University of Chicago Press.

Wolfson, E. 1996. Article in *The Wall Street Journal*, 22 March, A13.

Wootton, B. 1959. *Social Science and Social Pathology*. London: Allen and Unwin.

Wright, E. O. 1978. *Class, Crisis and the State*. London: New Left Books.

Zajonc, R. B. 1968. *Cognitive Theories in Social Psychology*. In *The Handbook of Social Psychology*, edited by G. Lindzey and E. Aronson. Reading, Mass.: Addison-Wesley.

Zuvekas, C., Jr. 1979. *Economic Development: An Introduction*. New York: St. Martin's Press.

INDEX

ABOUT THE AUTHOR

SENYO B-S. K. ADJIBOLOSOO is Professor of Business and Economics at Trinity Western University. He is the Director of the International Institute for Human Factor Development, an institute devoted to researching the human factor and its role in development. His most recent book is *Human Factor Engineering and the Political Economy of African Development* (Praeger, 1996).

ISBN 0-275-95966-X

HARDCOVER BAR CODE